Elizabeth Kolbert was a reporter for the *New York Times* for four-teen years before becoming a staff writer for the *New Yorker*. She is the author of *Field Notes from a Catastrophe: A Frontline Report on Climate Change*. She lives in Williamstown, Massachusetts.

THE ARCTIC

An Anthology

Edited by Elizabeth Kolbert

GRANTA

Granta Publications, 12 Addison Avenue, London W11 4QR
First published in Great Britain by Granta Books, 2007 as
The Ends of the Earth Volume 1: The Arctic
This edition published by Granta Books, 2008
Selection and introduction copyright © Elizabeth Kolbert, 2007

1 3 5 7 9 10 8 6 4 2

ISBN 978-1-84708-027-1

Typeset by M Rules

Printed and bound in Great Britain by
J. H. Haynes & Co. Ltd., Sparkford

CONTENTS

Elizabeth Kolbert

In the spring of 1888, the Norwegian doctor-cum-explorer Fridtjof Nansen set off for Iceland. He boarded a whaling ship in Isafjord and sailed to the east coast of Greenland. Once there, he strapped on a pair of skis and headed out across the ice sheet, a trip of some 500 miles. Save for some problems with the pemmican – the dried meat, which he had ordered from an outfitter in Copenhagen, was too lean, leading 'to a craving for fat which can scarcely be realized by anyone who has not experienced it' – the journey went off without incident. Nevertheless, to get from Christiana – now Oslo – to Gothaab – now Nuuk – and back again took Nansen over a year.

In the spring of 2001, I set off for a research station known as the North Greenland Ice-core Project. I boarded a cargo plane in Schenectady, New York, and disembarked in Kangerlussuaq, on the island's west coast, six hours later. Another two-hour flight – this one on board an LC-130 equipped with skis and, for extra propulsion, little rockets – took me to North GRIP, at the very centre of the ice sheet, at 75° 06′ N. In this way, I completed the first half of Nansen's journey (albeit from the opposite direction) in less than a day. Perhaps if I had spent several weeks at the camp, I would have developed a craving for something; honestly, though, I can't imagine what. The afternoon I arrived, coffee and cake were served in the geodesic dome that doubled as the camp's dining hall. In the evening, there was a cocktail party held in a chamber hollowed out of the ice. Dinner was lamb chops slathered in a tomato cream sauce, accompanied by red wine. As I recall, I skipped dessert that night; I was just too stuffed.

At least twenty scientists were living at North GRIP, and at no point did I wander far enough from the camp to lose sight of the tents. Yet if Arctic travel isn't quite what it used to be, now that the danger, hardship and solitude have been sheared away, it is still an other-worldly experience. The white, the cold, the 3 a.m. sun – the scene was unlike anything I had ever encountered before. Of course, I came home and wrote about it.

This is a book of *writings* about the Arctic, which is not quite the same thing as a book about the Arctic. Almost all the selections are by outsiders to the region – explorers, adventurers, anthropologists, novelists. The predominance of non-natives reflects the fact that Arctic people have, traditionally, transmitted their narratives orally, and also the fact that those who have been drawn to the area have, to an astonishing degree, felt compelled to record their impressions. Even today, the number of people who have travelled to the far north is tiny compared with the number who have travelled to Birmingham, say, or Philadelphia. Yet the literature of the Arctic is immense. Trying to choose the selections for this book, I sometimes felt as if everyone who had ever visited the Arctic had left behind an account of his or her (usually his) experience. In one of his many Klondike tales, 'An Odyssey of the North', Jack London compares the Arctic whiteness to 'a mighty sheet of foolscap' and a dog team racing across the snow to a line drawn in black pencil. For a writer, the image is reversible, so that the blank page – and all its terrors – can also become a metaphor for the ice.

The Arctic is difficult to define. As Barry Lopez notes, 'There is no generally accepted definition for a southern limit' to the region. To use the Arctic Circle as the boundary means including parts of Scandinavia so warmed by the Gulf Stream that they support frog life, while at the same time excluding regions around James Bay, in Canada, that are frequented by polar bears. (The Arctic Circle is designated as 66° 33′ N; however, owing to a slight wobble in the earth's axial tilt, the real circle of polar night shifts by as much as fifty feet a year.) The works collected here touch on travels as far south as Iceland, which, except for the tiny tip of a tiny island, lies entirely below the Arctic Circle, and as far north as the pole itself – if, that is, you accept Robert Peary's claims to have made it there.

Though speculation about a mysterious, frozen island known as Thule dates all the way back to the Greek geographer Pytheas, this collection begins in the early nineteenth century. By that point, the search for the Northwest Passage was already well underway and had already claimed dozens of lives. It is sometimes suggested that this search was motivated by commerce and sometimes by nationalism. But neither force seems quite adequate; as the historian Glyn Williams has observed, the quest 'became almost mystical in nature, beyond reasonable explanation.' I have chosen to focus on the most celebrated – and most disastrous –attempt to find a passage, that led by Sir John Franklin in 1845. Franklin's disappearance prompted a string of rescue missions, many of which also ended badly, and one of which, organized by a Cincinnati businessman named Charles Francis Hall, may have culminated in murder. In the 1960s, Hall's biographer, Chauncey Loomis, travelled to the shore of Thank God Harbor, in northern Greenland, where Hall had been buried, and had his body exhumed. It was in remarkably good shape, demonstrating the cold, hard truth that in the Arctic nothing is ever really lost.

The next generation of explorers was interested in only one direction: due north. I have included accounts of three efforts to reach the pole – those led by Nansen, Peary and Salomon August Andrée. Nansen's attempt involved spending a year in an icebound boat – the *Fram,* or 'Forward' – and two more traversing the ice by dog sled. The farthest Nansen reached was as 86° 14′ N. This was 270 miles short of his goal, but at that point – 1895 – the highest latitude anyone had ever attained. Nansen's Swedish rival, Andrée, came up with the daring if impractical notion of besting him by balloon. With two companions, Andrée set off for the pole from Spitsbergen on July 11 1897. Three days later, after having drifted some 200 miles to the northeast, the balloon – the *Eagle* – crashed and had to be abandoned. The three men spent the next ten weeks trekking across the ice, trying – unsuccessfully – to reach first one and then a second food cache that had been left for them. Their bodies were finally found more than thirty years later on the island of Kvitøya, roughly at the same latitude from which they had departed.

In their writings, explorers like Franklin and Andrée tend to treat the Arctic as a set of problems: unfordable rivers, blinding snow, drifting ice. (Peary's accounts of his adventures barely mentions the cosier sort of adventures that would lead, among other things, to at least two half-Inuit offspring.) But even before the race to the pole was over, a different sort of interest in the Arctic had begun to produce a different sort of literature. Though the Arctic comprises some of the most inhospitable terrain on earth, people have been living there for thousands of years. The fact that native communities flourished in an environment often fatal to non-native travellers challenged conventional notions of progress. Starting in the late nineteenth century, the Arctic became a favoured destination for what might be called explorers of human nature.

Knud Rasmussen is one of the few indigenous authors included in this volume. Born in Ilulissat to a Danish father and Greenlandic mother, Rasmussen was both a prolific writer and a prolific traveller; he participated in eight Arctic expeditions – the so-called Thule expeditions – which studied the region's archaeology, ethnography, geology and botany. *Across Arctic America* is Rasmussen's chronicle of the most famous of these expeditions – the fifth – condensed into a few hundred pages. (The scientific report on the 20,000-mile journey ran to ten volumes.) 'Some archaeologists have made bold to assert that the Eskimos are surviving remnants of the Stone Age we know, and are, therefore, our contemporary ancestors,' Rasmussen writes. 'We don't have to go so far to claim kinship with them, however, for we *recognize* them as brothers.' Rockwell Kent, the American artist, went to live in northern Greenland for a year in the early 1930s; Gontrans De Poncins, a French count, spent fifteen months among the Canadian Inuit in the second half of the decade. Both men were drawn to life in the Arctic because it was remote and dangerous and other. (A similar attraction would later prompt Tété-Michel Kpomassie to make his way from Togo to Greenland's west coast and Gretel Ehrlich to follow Rasmussen's trail.) Their narratives of discovery are just as significantly stories of *self*-discovery.

Several of the works in this collection are explicitly fictional. 'Kasiagsak, the Great Liar' is one of the many native legends collected in the late nineteenth century by Hinrich Rink, a Danish official serving in Greenland. In *The Adventures of Captain Hatteras*, Jules Verne invents a polar explorer easily as obsessed as Peary and Andrée. In *The Voyage of the Narwhal*, Andrea Barrett adds a make-believe ship to the long list of actual ones that went off searching for Franklin and his men. *Independent People*, by the Nobel laureate Halldór Laxness, tells the story of Bjartur of Summerhouses, a sheep-farming, poetry-loving Icelander who endures hardships of an almost comically monstrous variety.

❉

The immediate inspiration for this collection is the 2007-2008 International Polar Year, which, to accommodate researchers in Antarctica, actually lasts until March 2009. This is the fourth International Polar Year – previous ones were held in 1882-3, 1932-3, and 1957-8 – and, like its predecessors, the current IPY is supposed to direct international attention (and resources) towards polar research. The 2007-2008 IPY differs from earlier ones, however, in that its focus is on the disappearance of its subject matter.

The impact of global warming, increasingly evident all over the world, is most apparent in the Arctic, thanks to an effect sometimes known as the Arctic amplification. While average global temperatures have risen by about .6°C (1°F), in the Arctic they have gone up by roughly twice that amount. The change is particularly striking during the coldest months of the year; in Siberia, for example, wintertime temperatures have risen by as much as 4°C (7°F). Since visiting Greenland in 2001, I've made four more trips to the Arctic to report on how the region is changing. Most of those trips were made in the company of scientists, but along the way I also met many native people who spoke eloquently about what is happening. An Inuit hunter named John Keogak, who lives on Banks Island, in the Inuvik Region of Canada's Northwest Territories, told me that he and his fellow-hunters had started to notice that the climate was changing in the mid-1980s. Then a few years ago, people on the island began to see robins, a bird for which the Inuit in his region have no word.

'We just thought, Oh, gee, it's warming up a little bit,' he recalled. 'It was good at the start – warmer winters, you know – but now everything is going so fast. The things that we saw coming in the early 1990s, they've just multiplied.

'Of the people involved in global warming, I think we're on top of the list of who would be most affected,' Keogak went on. 'Our way of life, our traditions, maybe our families. Our children may not have a future. I mean, all young people, put it that way. It's not just happening in the Arctic. It's going to happen all over the world. The whole world is going too fast.'

The warming that has occurred has by now been sufficient to shrink the Arctic ice cap by almost five hundred thousand square miles, to bring millions of acres of permafrost close to the thawing point, and to cause devastating pest outbreaks in the spruce forests of Canada and Alaska. But this is only the beginning. If current trends continue, temperatures in the Arctic will rise by as much as 5°C (9°F) by the end of this century. Sometime before that point, much of the landscape described in these pages will have vanished. For example, current forecasts suggest that a Northwest Passage could be ice-free, at least in summer, by 2025. The North Pole itself could be open water in summer by 2050. Perhaps most ominously of all, the Greenland ice sheet, which at its centre is ten thousand feet thick, could begin to disintegrate. While it might take centuries for the ice sheet to disappear entirely, once the process of disintegration gets underway, it will start to feed on itself, most likely becoming irreversible. (The Greenland ice sheet holds enough water to raise global sea levels by more than twenty feet.) In this way, the claim of the Arctic on our imagination has been inverted. A landscape that once symbolized the sublime indifference of nature will, for future generations, come to symbolize its tragic vulnerability.

CHAPTER 1

'THE EXTREME MISERY OF THE WHOLE PARTY'

from *Narrative of a Journey to the Shores of the Polar Sea* (1823)

John Franklin

*Sir John Franklin, an officer in the British Royal Navy, led three Arctic expeditions in the first half of the nineteenth century. The last of these, which resulted not only in his own death, but in the deaths of all 120-plus members of his crew, is the most famous; it prompted several rescue missions, some of which ended no less disastrously. This excerpt is from the increasingly disjointed diaries Franklin kept during his first Arctic expedition (1819–22), which took him from Hudson Bay to the Coppermine River. Nine of Franklin's men died on the journey – one was shot under mysterious circumstances – and the rest endured desperate privation. Included below is the famous episode in which Franklin and his men dine on their shoes. (*Tripe de roche, *which Franklin refers to several times, is a kind of lichen.)*

In the afternoon we had a heavy fall of snow, which continued all night. A small quantity of *tripe de roche* was gathered; and Crédit, who had been hunting, brought in the antlers and back bone of a deer which had been killed in the summer. The wolves and birds of prey had picked them clean, but there still remained a quantity of the spinal marrow which they had not been able to extract. This, although putrid, was esteemed a valuable prize, and the spine being divided into portions, was distributed equally. After eating the marrow, which was so acrid as to excoriate the lips, we rendered the bones friable by burning, and ate them also.

On the following morning the ground was covered with snow to the depth of a foot and a half, and the weather was very stormy. These circumstances rendered the men again extremely despondent; a settled gloom hung over their countenances, and they refused to pick *tripe de roche*, choosing rather to go entirely without eating, than to make any exertion. The party which went for gum returned early in the morning without having found any; but St. Germain said he could still make the canoe with the willows, covered with canvas, and removed with Adam to a clump of willows for that purpose. Mr. Back accompanied them to stimulate his exertion, as we feared the lowness of his spirits would cause him to be slow in his operations. Augustus went to fish at the rapid, but a large trout having carried away his bait, we had nothing to replace it.

The snow-storm continued all the night, and during the forenoon of the 3rd. Having persuaded the people to gather some *tripe de roche*, I partook of a meal with them; and afterwards set out with the intention of going to St. Germain to hasten his operations, but though he was only three quarters of a mile distant, I spent three hours in a vain attempt to reach him, my strength being unequal to the labour of wading through the deep snow; and I returned quite exhausted, and much shaken by the numerous falls I had got. My associates were all in the same debilitated state, and poor Hood was reduced to a perfect shadow, from the severe bowel complaints which the *tripe de roche* never failed to give him. Back was so feeble as to require the support of a stick in walking; and Dr.

Richardson had lameness superadded to weakness. The voyagers were somewhat stronger than ourselves, but more indisposed to exertion, on account of their despondency. The sensation of hunger was no longer felt by any of us, yet we were scarcely able to converse upon any other subject than the pleasures of eating. We were much indebted to Hepburn at this crisis. The officers were unable from weakness to gather *tripe de roche* themselves, and Samandré, who had acted as our cook on the journey from the coast, sharing in the despair of the rest of the Canadians, refused to make the slightest exertion. Hepburn, on the contrary, animated by a firm reliance on the beneficence of the Supreme Being, tempered with resignation to his will, was indefatigable in his exertions to serve us, and daily collected all the *tripe de roche* that was used in the officers' mess. Mr. Hood could not partake of this miserable fare, and a partridge which had been reserved for him was, I lament to say, this day stolen by one of the men.

October 4. – The canoe being finished, it was brought to the encampment, and the whole party being assembled in anxious expectation on the beach, St. Germain embarked, and amidst our prayers for his success, succeeded in reaching the opposite shore. The canoe was then drawn back again, and another person transported, and in this manner by drawing it backwards and forwards, we were all conveyed over without any serious accident. By these frequent traverses the canoe was materially injured; and latterly it filled each time with water before reaching the shore, so that all our garments and bedding were wet, and there was not a sufficiency of willows upon the side on which we now were, to make a fire to dry them.

It is impossible to imagine a more gratifying change than was produced in our voyagers after we were all safely landed on the southern banks of the river. Their spirits immediately revived, each of them shook the officers cordially by the hand, and declared they now considered the worst of their difficulties over, as they did not doubt of reaching Fort Enterprise in a few days, even in their feeble condition. We had, indeed, every reason to be grateful, and our joy would have been complete had it not been mingled with sincere regret at the separation of our poor Esquimaux, the faithful Junius.

The want of *tripe de roche* caused us to go supperless to bed. Showers of snow fell frequently during the night. The breeze was light next morning, the weather cold and clear. We were all on foot by day-break, but from the frozen state of our tents and bed-clothes, it was long before the bundles could be made, and as usual, the men lingered over a small fire they had kindled, so that it was eight o'clock before we started. Our advance, from the depth of the snow, was slow, and about noon, coming to a spot where there was some *tripe de roche*, we stopped to collect it, and breakfasted. Mr. Hood, who was now very feeble, and Dr. Richardson, who attached himself to him, walked together at a gentle pace in the rear of the party. I kept with the foremost men, to cause them to halt occasionally, until the stragglers came up. Resuming our march after breakfast, we followed the track of Mr. Back's party, and encamped early, as all of us were much fatigued, particularly Crédit, who having to-day carried the men's tent, it being his turn so to do, was so exhausted, that when he reached the encampment he was unable to stand. The *tripe de roche* disagreed with this man and with Vaillant, in consequence of which, they were the first whose strength totally failed. We had a small quantity of this weed in the evening, and the rest of our supper was made up of scraps of roasted leather. The distance walked to-day was six miles. As Crédit was very weak in the morning, his load was reduced to little more than his personal luggage, consisting of his blanket, shoes, and gun. Previous to setting out, the whole party ate the remains of their old shoes, and whatever scraps of leather they had, to strengthen their stomachs for the fatigue of the day's journey. We left the encampment at nine, and pursued our route over a range of black hills. The wind having increased to a strong gale in the course of the morning, became piercingly cold, and the drift rendered it difficult for those in the rear to follow the track over the heights; whilst in the valleys, where it was sufficiently marked, from the depth of the snow, the labour of walking was proportionably great. Those in advance made, as usual, frequent halts, yet being unable from the severity of the weather to remain long still, they were obliged to move on before the rear could come up, and the party, of course, straggled very much.

About noon Samandré coming up, informed us that Crédit and Vaillant could advance no further. Some willows being discovered in a valley near us, I proposed to halt the party there, whilst Dr. Richardson went back to visit them. I hoped too, that when the sufferers received the information of a fire being kindled at so short a distance they would be cheered, and use their utmost efforts to reach it, but this proved a vain hope. The Doctor found Vaillant about a mile and a half in the rear, much exhausted with cold and fatigue. Having encouraged him to advance to the fire, after repeated solicitations he made the attempt, but fell down amongst the deep snow at every step.

CHAPTER 2

'THE RETURN OF LIGHT'

from *Arctic Explorations* (1856)

Elisha Kent Kane

Elisha Kent Kane served as the medical officer on an 1850 American expedition that went in search of John Franklin and his crew. Three years later, he captained a second expedition. Kane was, by all accounts, an ineffectual leader. After spending two winters on their boat, the Advance, *which had frozen into the ice off the west coast of Greenland, he and his men slogged 1,300 miles to the town of Upernavik; amazingly, all but three made it. In this passage from Kane's diaries of 1854, spring has just arrived, and with it a profusion of game. This leads Kane to meditate on the hidden richness of the Arctic and on the possibility that some members of Franklin's crew might still be alive.*

We have more fresh meat than we can eat. For the past three weeks we have been living on ptarmigan, rabbits, two reindeer, and seal.

They are fast curing our scurvy. With all these resources, – coming to our relief so suddenly too, – how can my thoughts turn despairingly to poor Franklin and his crew?

. . . Can they have survived? No man can answer with certainty; but no man without presumption can answer in the negative.

If four months ago, – surrounded by darkness and bowed down

by disease, – I had been asked the question, I would have turned toward the black hills and the frozen sea, and responded in sympathy with them, 'No.' But with the return of light a savage people come down upon us, destitute of any but the rudest appliances of the chase, who were fattening on the most wholesome diet of the region, only forty miles from our anchorage, while I was denouncing its scarcity.

For Franklin, every thing depends upon locality: but, from what I can see of Arctic exploration thus far, it would be hard to find a circle of fifty miles' diameter entirely destitute of animal resources. The most solid winter-ice is open here and there in pools and patches worn by currents and tides. Such were the open spaces that Parry found in Wellington Channel; such are the stream-holes (stromhols) of the Greenland coast, the polynia of the Russians; and such we have ourselves found in the most rigorous cold of all.

To these spots, the seal, walrus, and the early birds crowd in numbers. One which kept open, as we find from the Esquimaux, at Littleton Island, only forty miles from us, sustained three families last winter until the opening of the north water. Now, if we have been entirely supported for the past three weeks by the hunting of a single man, – seal-meat alone being plentiful enough to subsist us till we turn homeward, – certainly a party of tolerably skilful hunters might lay up an abundant stock for the winter. As it is, we are making caches of meat under the snow, to prevent its spoiling on our hands, in the very spot which a few days ago I described as a Sahara. And, indeed, it was so for nine whole months, when this flood of animal life burst upon us like fountains of water and pastures and date-trees in a southern desert.

I have undergone one change in opinion. It is of the ability of Europeans or Americans to inure themselves to an ultra-Arctic climate. God forbid, indeed, that civilized man should be exposed for successive years to this blighting darkness! But around the Arctic circle, even as high as 72°, where cold and cold only is to be encountered, men may be acclimatized, for there is light enough for out-door labor.

Of the one hundred and thirty-six picked men of Sir John Franklin in 1846, Northern Orkney men, Greenland whalers, so many young and hardy constitutions, with so much intelligent experience to guide them, I cannot realize that some may not yet be alive; that some small squad or squads, aided or not aided by the Esquimaux of the expedition, may not have found a hunting-ground, and laid up from summer to summer enough of fuel and food and seal-skins to brave three or even four more winters in succession.

I speak of the miracle of this bountiful fair season. I could hardly have been much more surprised if these black rocks, instead of sending out upon our solitude the late inroad of yelling Esquimaux, had sent us naturalized Saxons. Two of our party at first fancied they were such.

The mysterious compensations by which we adapt ourselves to climate are more striking here than in the tropics. In the Polar zone the assault is immediate and sudden, and, unlike the insidious fatality of hot countries, produces its results rapidly. It requires hardly a single winter to tell who are to be the heat-making and acclimatized men. Petersen, for instance, who has resided for two years at Upernavik, seldom enters a room with a fire. Another of our party, George Riley, with a vigorous constitution, established habits of free exposure, and active cheerful temperament, has so inured himself to the cold, that he sleeps on our sledge-journeys without a blanket or any other covering than his walking-suit, while the outside temperature is 30° below zero. The half-breeds of the coast rival the Esquimaux in their powers of endurance.

There must be many such men with Franklin. The North British sailors of the Greenland seal and whale fisheries I look upon as inferior to none in capacity to resist the Arctic climates.

My mind never realizes the complete catastrophe, the destruction of all Franklin's crews. I picture them to myself broken into detachments, and my mind fixes itself on one little group of some thirty, who have found the open spot of some tidal eddy, and under the teachings of an Esquimaux or perhaps one of their own Greenland whalers, have set bravely to work, and trapped the fox, speared the bear, and killed the seal and walrus and whale. I think of them ever with hope. I sicken not to be able to reach them.

It is a year ago to-day since we left New York. I am not as sanguine as I was then: time and experience have chastened me. There is every thing about me to check enthusiasm and moderate hope. I am here in forced inaction, a broken-down man, oppressed by cares, with many dangers before me, and still under the shadow of a hard wearing winter, which has crushed two of my best associates. Here on the spot, after two unavailing expeditions of search, I hold my opinions unchanged; and I record them as a matter of duty upon a manuscript which may speak the truth when I can do so no longer.

CHAPTER 3

'MURDER IN THE ARCTIC?'

from *Weird and Tragic Shores* (1971)

Chauncey Loomis

In the 1860s, Charles Francis Hall, a Cincinnati businessman-turned-explorer, made two voyages to the Arctic in search of Franklin expedition survivors. Not surprisingly, he found none; nevertheless, his exploits made Hall a popular hero. In 1871, Hall set out on a government-sponsored voyage to the North Pole and within months had died mysteriously. Nearly a hundred years later, his biographer, Chauncey Loomis, travelled to Greenland and exhumed his corpse in the hope of clarifying the circumstances of Hall's death.

For five years after the *Polaris* weighed anchor and steamed through the ice of Thank God Harbor out into Hall Basin, Charles Francis Hall's grave was undisturbed by any human. Eskimos had once hunted the area, but the rings of stone that marked their camp sites were paleolithic; hunting parties had not ventured so far north for hundreds of years. Wind-driven snow and silt blasted the headboard of the grave, but it remained upright, and Hubbard Chester's deep-cut inscription remained sharp and clear. Lemmings burrowed into the mound of the grave, and foxes pawed at its surface, but the coffin beneath was untouched, and the ground willow above remained rooted among the rocks.

In May 1876 Hall's grave had its first human visitors since the departure of the *Polaris*. Members of the British North Polar Expedition led by Captain George Nares arrived with a brass tablet that they had brought from London, knowing they would pass by the gravesite. The tablet was inscribed:

SACRED TO THE MEMORY OF

CAPTAIN C. F. HALL

OF THE U.S. SHIP POLARIS,

WHO SACRIFICED HIS LIFE IN THE ADVANCEMENT OF

SCIENCE

ON NOV^r 8th 1871

—

THIS TABLET HAS BEEN ERECTED

BY THE BRITISH POLAR EXPEDITION OF 1875

WHO FOLLOWING IN HIS FOOTSTEPS HAVE PROFITED BY

HIS EXPERIENCE

While twenty-five members of the expedition stood solemnly by, an American flag was hoisted and the tablet was erected at the foot of the grave. The Nares Expedition, like the Polaris Expedition, was not destined to reach the Pole; not long after the ceremony, two of its men, dead of scurvy, were buried only a few hundred yards away from Hall.

Six years later, the grave was visited again. The Greely Expedition, spending the winter thirty miles across Hall Basin at Lady Franklin Bay, came to check on supplies that the Polaris Expedition had cached and to see what was by then known as Hall's Rest. Sergeant William Cross, while rummaging in the wreckage of Bessels's observatory, which had been crudely dismantled before the *Polaris* left, carved his name on one of the boards that lay scattered about. A year later Cross was dead, the first of nineteen men to die in the terrible ordeal of the Greely Expedition. Between 1898 and 1909 Robert Peary passed Thank God Harbor several times aboard the *Roosevelt*, but, with a singlemindedness Hall himself would have admired, did not take time to go ashore. Knud Rasmussen, on his Thule Expedition, arrived in 1917. He found the original headboard lying face down on the ground, perhaps cuffed by the same bear that had bitten deep into the posts supporting the Nares tablet; Rasmussen could plainly see the marks of the animal's teeth in the wood. After Rasmussen's departure, forty years passed before Hall's grave was visited again. In 1958 an American team led by geologist William Davies and assisted by Danish explorer Count Eigel Knuth landed from the icebreaker *Atka*, the first ship to anchor in Thank God Harbor since the *Polaris*. The purpose of 'Operation Groundhog' was to locate ice-free aircraft-landing sites as emergency alternatives to the bases at Alert and Thule. For a few weeks the sound of a Jeep was heard on Polaris Promontory. Then the area was returned to its accustomed silence. That silence was broken very briefly a few years later when British geologist Peter Dawes spent a few days in the area.

In August 1968 I arrived at Hall's Rest with three companions. Doctor Franklin Paddock, William Barrett, Thomas Gignoux, and I were flown from Resolute, far to the south in the Arctic Archipelago, by one of Canada's finest bush pilots, W. W. Phipps. The day we arrived was clear; as Weldy Phipps flew his Single Otter low across the hills that border the plain of Polaris Promontory, we could see ahead the deep blue of Hall Basin, the shoreline of Thank God Harbor, and, as we lost altitude, the wreckage of Bessels's observatory close to the beach. We circled, looking for the grave. We could not see it, but knew that it was near the observatory, so Weldy landed on a smooth stretch of plain a mile south of the wreckage. After we had unloaded our equipment, Weldy took off immediately, leaving us standing alone on the plain, dazed in sudden awareness of how isolated we were. He was due to return in two weeks, after he fulfilled some other contracts.

In the course of preparing this biography I had read the government's book on the Polaris Expedition, the journals of its men, the ship's log, the official dispatches, the transcript of the Department of the Navy's inquiry, and masses of other material. My conclusion was, not that Hall certainly had been murdered, not even that he *probably* had been murdered, but only that murder was at least possible and plausible. The conclusion of the Board of Inquiry that he had died of 'natural causes, viz, apoplexy,' also was possible and plausible, but it had been reached hastily and only by ignoring much of the evidence that the Board itself had wheedled out of witnesses. Secretary Robeson had been under considerable pressure to end investigation; scandal was in the making. That the government was eager to play down the ugly aspects of the affair is indicated by the official book of the expedition, *Narrative of the North Polar Expedition*, written by Rear Admiral C. H. Davis a year after the inquiry. Davis gave the impression that the expedition had been a Boy Scout Jamboree – a bit rough, of course, but enlivened by good cheer and boyish high jinks. The original source materials that Davis had used and distorted show how false that impression was.

I had applied to Denmark's Ministry for Greenland for a permit to travel to Polaris Promontory; arguing that if the case were recent, a court presented with the evidence would order an autopsy, I requested permission to disinter Hall's body and have Frank Paddock perform an autopsy on it. Given the high latitude of its burial, there was a good chance that the body would be well preserved. Approval of my application came only after many letters and finally a trip to Copenhagen, where I met Count Eigel Knuth. An archeologist and old-time sledge traveler, Knuth was one of the last men to have seen the grave. He also was an adviser to the Ministry on proposed projects in Greenland, and without his agreement I would have no chance of receiving permission. At first it appeared that he would not agree. Hall's grave, he said, was a hallowed place; its remoteness intensified the sense of mystery and beauty associated with any lone grave. The idea of having it disturbed repelled him. After I assured him that I would leave the grave in the condition in which I found it, however, he finally approved.

On the day we arrived at Polaris Promontory we set up camp near the place where Weldy had landed us, about a mile south of the observatory and the grave. We decided not to begin the exhumation until the next day, but after the camp was completed we walked to the gravesite. We could see the Nares tablet first, some distance away across the stony flats. As we approached it, we could see the shape of the mound, covered with large rocks; then a crowbar strangely jutting from the head of the grave; then, finally, Chester's headboard lying face down in the dirt. Change is slow in the cold dry air of the High Arctic; the tablet shone as if it had just been taken from a furnace, and the willow still grew on the mound. Under the benign blue of the sky that day, the place was peaceful — and profoundly still.

We wandered on to the observatory. Here was the litter of man, which is widely strewn throughout the Arctic, all the more noticeable because of the vast inhuman spaces around it. The building no longer stood; its siding lay broken, scattered around its floor as if it had burst from within. Rusted cans, brass nails, iron stoves, a huge davit, an ice saw, shattered glass, and pieces of sailcloth spread out from the observatory like a cancerous growth. Throughout the area were the bowling-ball shapes of ice grenades, packed with black powder that still could explode. While poking through the rubble Tom Gignoux turned over a board, and there was Sergeant Cross's name, carved more than seventy years before when *he* had been doing the poking. Bill Barrett found a broken blue bottle on which the word POISON still could be seen molded into the glass. After momentary, laughing excitement, we realized that it was of little significance: bottles marked POISON could, after all, be contained in a scientific observatory without ominous implications. On the beach I found a Danish shotgun shell, perhaps discharged by Eigel Knuth in 1958. Such sites in the Arctic usually contain layers of history: a hundred yards away were the graves of the two Nares sailors, and not far from them was a paleolithic Eskimo tent-ring.

During the night, under the unsetting sun, the weather changed. When we set out early in the morning to do the job for which we had come, the sky was suitably lowering, the land suitably bleak. The day before had been too bright for such a morbid piece of work.

For a year I had wondered how I would feel when the coffin was opened. Hall might well have become a skeleton – but in the Arctic air, lying on the permanent frost that had prevented his grave diggers from digging deep, he might have been perfectly preserved. It was impossible to know what was in the coffin, and much as I dreaded finding only a skeleton from which nothing could be proved, I also dreaded finding the man himself, just as he had been. Having spent three years violating his mind by reading his private journals, now I was going to violate his body. I had been haunted by a vision of a rather offended face peering out of the coffin, a face asking, 'Is there no limit to what a biographer will do?'

While Frank Paddock, Bill Barrett, and I stood nervously by, Tom Gignoux, not long back from a tour of duty in Vietnam as a

Marine, did most of the digging. All of us wanted to be properly solemn, but our nerves short-circuited our sense of awe, and we found ourselves making absurd jokes. As Tom scraped earth off the long coffin lid, revealing pine that was still pale and fresh, Frank looked down at it and said cheerfully, 'They didn't build it for the short Hall, did they?' We laughed immoderately. We stopped laughing a minute later when we caught a whiff of decay from within the coffin. During the next ten minutes, while Tom pried carefully at the lid, we stood silent. A piece of the lid broke off, and inside we could see a flag – part of the field of stars – and ice.

I removed the lid after Tom had done all the work, and we stood by the edge of the grave looking down. The body was completely shrouded in a flag. From the waist down, it was covered by opaque ice, but at the base of the coffin a pair of stockinged feet stuck abruptly through it. The front of the torso was clear of the ice, but we could see that its back was frozen into the coffin.

Frank carefully peeled the flag back from the face. It was not the face of an individual, but neither was it yet a skull. There were still flesh, a beard, hair on the head, but the eye sockets were empty, the nose was almost gone, and the mouth was pulled into a smile that a few years hence will become the grin of a death's head. The skin, tanned by time and stained by the flag, was tightening on the skull. He was in a strangely beautiful phase in the process of dust returning to dust. The brown skin, mottled by blue stain and textured by the flag that had pressed against it for almost a hundred years, made him somehow abstract – an icon, or a Rouault portrait.

The autopsy took about three hours. We decided not to try to remove the coffin from the grave or the body from the coffin, embedded as they were in ice. Frank Paddock had to straddle the coffin and lean over to do his work, an agonizing posture to hold for that length of time.

It was very discouraging. At first we thought that the body, still well fleshed, was perfectly preserved, but Frank's scalpel revealed that the internal organs were almost entirely gone, melded into the surrounding flesh. Frank persisted in a meticulous search, but found little that held any hope for analysis. A fingernail and some hair, to be tested for arsenic, were the best samples we had. At last, exhausted, Frank gave up. We put the lid back onto the coffin, and Tom Gignoux shoveled earth back into the grave. After we had piled the rocks back onto the mound, I shoved the strange crowbar into the earth where it had been; later I was to be thankful that I remembered to do it. When we left, Hall's Rest appeared the same as it had been, with only one change that disturbed me: the ground willow planted by the men of the *Polaris* was no longer rooted amid the rocks.

We had almost two weeks to wait before Weldy was to return. We whiled away the time roaming Polaris Promontory, realizing only later that most of our roaming was to the south – the grave lay to the north, and we tended to avoid it. The beach made the best walking. Inland, the shale plain stretched out forty miles deep, depressing in its lifelessness, but along the beach there were life, movement, and sound. Sanderlings, sandpipers, and plovers picked at the waterline; fulmars flew offshore. Occasionally we would disturb nesting Arctic terns, to be delighted by their wheeling and darting attacks on us, their excited and exciting screams. One day when a high wind was blowing on the plain, I found a group of clucking ptarmigans strutting down the protected beach, ridiculous birds having a ladies' club meeting. Our rations were meat bars and dried potatoes; the Danes had forbidden us to live off the land, and only great self-discipline prevented mayhem on the beach that day. Every morning we found the tracks of a fox along the edge of the water, challenging us to catch a glimpse of him. Day after day the little creature eluded us; then one evening while I was sitting quietly, hoping to see him on his nightly route, out of the corner of my eye I saw something move behind me. Foolishly, I jumped up to look. The fox had been stalking me while I was waiting for him. He moved away, not running or even trotting, but keeping his dignity in a stately pace, pretending not to be frightened by what must have been the only human being he had ever seen.

The sky and the light constantly change in the Arctic, because weather systems move rapidly there. Leaden clouds would settle, wind would blow, snow would fall; in a few hours the sky would clear to a deep blue and the wind would calm; then there would be a show of mare's tails and mackerel skies, forecasting another storm; and the cycle would begin again. Local fogs inexplicably would blow in, blow out; we would be walking down the beach in clear air, able to see the mountains of Ellesmere Island thirty miles across Hall Basin, when suddenly we would be plunged into clammy murk, able to see only the ghostly shapes of nearby icebergs.

Hall Basin was clear of ice the day we arrived, but two days later a south wind drove ice up from Kennedy Channel – both floe ice and bergs that had been spawned from glaciers to the south, especially the great Humboldt. Looking at and listening to ice was one of our best diversions. If we stood still and stared out across the basin, we could see it move with the currents, very slowly, very steadily. Many of the small bergs along the beach had eroded into fantastic shapes that changed as we saw them from different angles; some were so smooth that they appeared machine-tooled, others rough-textured; some were in strange animal and birdlike forms, others almost geometrically round, square, trapezoidal. As delightful as the sights of the ice were its sounds. Along the beach, we could hear many: the one that the wind makes when it blows uninterrupted by trees or grass, the lapping of the water on the sand, the cry of birds. But the sounds I remember best were of water steadily dripping from thawing icebergs, and the occasional crack and rumble of big ice breaking out in the bay.

Our two weeks of roaming were well spent. They were life-giving, images of the beach helping to purge images of the grave from our minds. After those two weeks, I also better understood the man who lay in the grave, and others like him who have felt impelled to travel to the Arctic, yearning for its cold beauty.

Weldy picked us up on schedule, and a few days later we were back in the United States. After consultation with specialists in pathology and toxicology, Frank Paddock sent the fingernail and the hair to Toronto's Centre of Forensic Sciences, where they were given a neutron-activation test, a highly sophisticated method of analyzing tiny amounts of material. For some reason I was not optimistic about our chances of receiving any significant information from the tests, so it came as a surprise when the Centre reported that they had revealed 'an intake of considerable amounts of arsenic by C. F. Hall in the last two weeks of his life.'

The fingernail had provided the best evidence. Doctor A. K. Perkons of the Centre had sliced it into small segments, working from tip to base, then submitted the segments to the neutron-activation test. The 'read-back' from the neutron bombardment indicated increasing amounts of arsenic in the base segments. At the tip, the fingernail contained 24.6 parts per million of arsenic — at the base it contained 76.7 ppm. Assuming a normal growth rate of 0.7 mm a week, Doctor Perkons concluded that the large jump in Hall's body burden of arsenic occurred in the last two weeks of his life. The fact that his arsenic content was high even before the jump could be explained in several ways. Arsenic was often used medicinally in the nineteenth century, and it also was used in hair-dressings, so many persons then had a relatively high content. The normal content today is only 1.5–6.0 ppm. Also, the soil near the grave contained fairly large amounts of arsenic (22.0 ppm); accord-ing to Perkons, some could have 'migrated' from the soil to the body. 'However,' Perkons went on in the report, 'such migration would not explain the differentially increased arsenic in the sections of both hair and nails toward the root end.'

We checked with other authorities, all of whom accepted the accuracy of the Centre's report and agreed with its conclusion: Charles Francis Hall had received toxic amounts of arsenic during the last two weeks of his life.

What conclusions can be drawn? Excited by the report, after I received it I studied my material on the Polaris Expedition in light of the new information, testing various explanations for the arsenic contained in Hall's body. The trouble, as I soon discovered, was that several explanations were possible.

The following list of symptoms of acute arsenic poisoning is quoted from Gleason, Gosselin, Hodge, and Smith, *Clinical Toxicology of Commercial Products* (Baltimore, 1969):

1. Symptoms usually appear ½ to 1 hour after ingestion.
2. Sweetish metallic taste; garlicky odor of breath and stools.
3. Constriction in the throat and difficulty in swallowing. Burning and colicky pains in esophagus, stomach and bowel.
4. Vomiting and profuse painful diarrhea.
5. Dehydration with intense thirst and muscular cramps.
6. Cyanosis, feeble pulse, and cold extremities.

7. Vertigo, frontal headache. In some cases ('cerebral type') vertigo, stupor, delirium, and even mania develop.
8. Syncope, coma, occasionally convulsions, general paralysis, and death.
9. Various skin eruptions, more often as a late manifestation.

As one looks down the list, one sees many of Hall's symptoms: the initial gastro-intestinal troubles, the difficulty in swallowing, the dehydration, the stupor, delirium, and mania – even the late manifestations of skin eruption noticed by Chester the day before Hall died. Given the results of the neutron-activation test, this should be no surprise. There is no doubt that Hall received a large amount of arsenic during the period that he showed these symptoms. The question is, How did he receive it?

Arsenic would have been available aboard the ship; in the form of arsenious acid, it was commonly used as a medicine in the nineteenth century. 'Arsenious acid,' comments the *Dispensatory of the United States* of 1875 in one of its longest entries, 'has been exhibited in a great variety of diseases.' It was used in the treatment of headaches, ulcers, cancer, gout, chorea, syphilis, even snakebite. In the form of 'Fowler's Solution,' it was a very popular remedy for fever and for various skin diseases. It was a standard part of any sizable medical kit, and obviously the Polaris Expedition had a large medical kit.

Hall may have dosed himself with it. With such a man, suicide is almost inconceivable, but it would not have to have been suicide; he might have died a victim of the capacity for suspicion that had so often erupted in his life. Platt Evens of the percussion-seal-press lawsuit, William Pomeroy, William Parker Snow, Isaac Hayes, Sidney Budington, Patrick Coleman, and nameless others had aroused his fear of jeopardy and his wrathful self-righteousness.

From the beginning, he did not like or trust Emil Bessels. In his sickness, which may indeed have been a stroke, might not he have treated himself rather than put his faith in the 'little German dancing master'? Even during the period when he allowed Bessels to treat him, he may have been taking medicine on his own. Bessels testified that Hall had a personal medical kit, containing among other things 'patent medicines.' Some nineteenth-century patent medicines contained arsenic; although its quantity was not great in any of the medicines that have been tested, Hall might have dosed himself heavily. Or perhaps he gained access to Bessels's kit and took arsenious acid from it. Tookoolito would have helped him do such a thing, and, quiet Eskimo woman that she was, would not have said a word about it later.

But murder also is possible. The coffee that Hall drank when he boarded the ship after his sledge journey could have been poisoned. Although arsenic is usually tasteless, it can leave a 'sweetish metallic taste.' Hall complained to Tookoolito about the coffee. 'He said the coffee made him sick,' she testified. 'Too sweet for him.' About one half hour after he drank it, he felt pains in his stomach and vomited, symptoms that suggest poisoning.

But the pain and the vomiting could have been caused by a stroke, as could many of the other symptoms listed in *Clinical Toxicology*. If Bessels was telling the truth when he said that Hall also suffered partial paralysis, then a stroke is as satisfactory an explanation of many of them as arsenic poisoning. There is also a possibility that Hall suffered both a stroke and arsenic poisoning. The initial attack could have been a stroke, then the arsenic could have been administered later, during the two weeks of his illness. It should be repeated: there is no doubt that the arsenic was administered. The question remains, How was it administered – and by whom?

The persons who had the most access to Hall during his illness were Sidney Budington, Tookoolito, Ebierbing, Hubbard Chester, William Morton, and Emil Bessels. Others could see him, especially those who shared the cabin with him, but these are the persons who were often with him, treating him or feeding him.

Budington, undergoing a psychological ordeal, drinking heavily, apparently afraid of being so far north, is a suspect, but he actually had less access to Hall than the others. Apparently he seldom approached the sick man or did anything for him. Tookoolito, Ebierbing, Chester, and Morton frequently attended, nursed and fed him, but there is no indication of any possible motive for their doing him injury. Like Budington, they cannot be entirely dismissed as suspects, but they are highly unlikely ones.

If Hall was murdered, Emil Bessels is the prime suspect. A trained scientist, he had the knowledge, and, as ship's surgeon, the material needed to administer arsenic. He had access to Hall much of the time – and when Hall refused Bessels access, his condition improved. Joseph Mauch made a note in his journal on November 1, several days after Hall first refused treatment by Bessels: 'Capt. Hall is much better this morning – for the last 2 days he has taken no medicine & today his health is greatly improved, although yet very weak.'

When Bessels treated Hall, he gave him some medicines orally, especially cathartics; arsenic could have been mixed with such medicines. He also gave him injections of what he said was quinine; arsenic also could have been injected, as it sometimes was in the treatment of cancers. When Bryan saw Bessels prepare the injections, the process involved the heating of 'little white crystals,' precisely the way that quinine was usually prepared. But arsenic could be in the form of a white powder, easily mistaken for crystals or mixed with them, and it, too, can be prepared by such heating.

When one considers Bessels as a possible murderer, one notes little things in the transcript of the inquiry that are subject to various interpretations. There is the uncertainty about whether he was in the observatory while Hall was drinking the coffee, as he said he was, or aboard the ship, as Morton and Mauch believed that he might have been. There is his refusal to administer an emetic when Hall was first taken ill; if indeed Hall had suffered a stroke, an emetic would have been dangerous – but an emetic also might have emptied his stomach of poison. There is the persistence of his quinine treatment when Hall's fever had been allayed. And one night, according to Budington's testimony, Bessels came to him complaining that Hall was refusing to take any medicine. Budington volunteered to take the medicine first in front of Hall, like a parent with a child. Bessels refused to let him do so. Small things, straws in the wind.

Bessels had the opportunity, the skill, and probably the material, but why would he do it? He had no apparent rational motive; he would gain nothing concrete by Hall's death. Unlike Budington, for example, he was not afraid of their situation and did not want to retreat south, and therefore Hall's passion to go north was not a threat to him. In fact, Joseph Mauch and Henry Hobby testified that when the *Polaris* was run aground at Etah, Bessels secretively tried to bribe some of the men to return north with him – an ambitious act, and perhaps ambition could be motive enough. With Hall's death, the command actually fell to Budington, but Bessels had more power and independence because Budington was a far weaker man.

But ambition for what? To make major scientific and geographical discoveries and be given full, sole credit for them? This does not seem motive enough for murder. Here we enter the underground streams of mind, the darkness that the Board would not probe. When one of its members asked George Tyson if he thought that 'there was any difficulty between Captain Hall and any of the scientific party that would be an inducement for them to do anything toward injuring him,' Tyson replied firmly, 'No sir.' Then he paused and said, 'Unless a man were a monster, he could not do any such thing as that.' The Board, not wanting to consider the possibility of monstrosity, moved on to other matters, but perhaps the truth lay precisely in monstrosity.

Joseph Henry had warned Hall that Bessels was 'a sensitive man.' He must have been very sensitive to justify Henry's making such a comment in a letter that is remarkable for its dry, official tone, and Bessels's behavior on the Polaris Expedition, his quarrels with both Hall and Budington, indeed suggest that he was at least difficult to deal with. Little is known about his later career, but enough is known to indicate that he remained difficult, perhaps abnormally so. For more than ten years he maintained a connection with the Smithsonian. Part of that time was spent compiling the scientific results of the expedition, and he sometimes received needling letters from Baird suggesting that he hasten his work. There is evidence that the Smithsonian was eager to get rid of him.

One reason was his involvement in a controversy in 1880. An International Polar Year was planned for 1882–3, and in 1880 the scientific community in the United States was much concerned with what the country should do about it. Among those who spoke out was Captain Henry Howgate, who had some rather far-fetched ideas about colonizing the Arctic. On February 16, 1880, an interview on the subject with Emil Bessels appeared in the *New York Herald*, an interview that reveals much about the man. The reporter devoted some time to the difficulty of finding Bessels's office in the Smithsonian: 'To discover this apartment without a guide would be almost as great an act as reaching the North Pole itself.' Then he commented: 'When the portals are entered, passing under the heavy folds of green drapery which nearly hide the entrance, the visitor would suppose he had been suddenly translated into the retreat of Faustus.' As Bessels was interviewed, he indeed acted like Faustus in his worst manifestations – self-assured to the point of arrogance, scornful of others, convinced that all knowledge was his. He laid down for the reporter what the United States should and should not do during the Polar Year. That much of what he said was correct does not mitigate his irritating condescension:

'What do you think of the plan originated by Captain How-gate?'

'Howgate's plan? Why, Captain Howgate did not originate any plan whatever. He merely appropriated the ideas of Dr. Hayes and probably those of Lieutenant Weyprecht. As far as these are concerned Captain Howgate is all right; but with regard to the rest – well, I would prefer to talk about something more rational.'

Bessels read aloud a passage of Howgate's writing about the possibility that a superior Eskimo culture already existed somewhere near the Pole; then he made passing reference to the Polaris Expedition: 'This even beats Dr. Newman, who wrote for the Polaris Expedition a prayer to be read at the North Pole, conse-crating the Pole to liberty, education and religion. I am only astonished that Captain Howgate did not quote him as an Arctic authority.' Bessels was hardly being tactful, as Newman was still Chaplain of the Senate.

When the reporter asked him another question, he said: 'Let me light a fresh cigar before I answer this question.' One can see him, small, natty, his eyes bright with self-assurance, lighting the cigar and leaning back to say, 'It amused me to find that a man writing such bombast [Howgate] should have the insolence to point out what caused other expeditions to fail in reaching the Pole, and in what manner they were mismanaged.'

When Bessels was asked about an Arctic expedition that Howgate had organized not long before, he snapped, 'The sole aim of the thing was to gain cheap reputation and to lay a snare for Congress to appropriate the means for a *real* Arctic expedition.' The interviewer asked Bessels why he thought Howgate's expedition had been a failure. The doctor referred to the scientists who had accompanied the expedition without pay 'for the mere love of science.' Possibly he was thinking of his relationship with Hall when he said, 'They had to submit to the orders of an incompetent, harsh skipper, who most seriously interfered with their duties.' It should be noted that Howgate was not the skipper – by a wild coincidence, the skipper was George Tyson.

Bessels was right to distrust Captain Howgate. Some years later it was proved that he had taken advantage of his position in the Signal Corps to swindle large sums of money. But the intemperance of Bessels's attack might be explained by something other than his belief that Howgate was a fraud. Henry Howgate had been a member of the Board of Inquiry that investigated the Polaris Expedition. There is no indication that he said or did anything during the inquiry to earn Bessels's enmity, but there is at least a possibility that the doctor held a deep-seated grudge against him for his membership on the Board.

Whatever the cause of Bessels's intemperance, it brought the wrath of Spencer Baird down on his head. Baird wrote him an icy letter, castigating him for his loose mouth. Bessels remained at the Smithsonian for a few more years, but apparently under a cloud. Past trouble obviously lies behind the terse note that he received from Baird's secretary in 1883:

Dear Doctor:

We need immediate possession of the room now occupied by you near the north entrance, as we find it necessary to make improved toilet arrangements for visitors. Please therefore remove your property and greatly oblige.

Yours truly,
Wm. J. Rhees

The tone indicates that this was not the first attempt to dislodge him, but it apparently was the last; his Smithsonian salary soon was stopped, and, presumably, the 'retreat of Faustus' became a toilet. Bessels soon after returned to Germany. He died there in 1888 – ironically, of apoplexy.

A difficult man – but a monster? Bessels did not seem a monster in the ordinary course of his life, but perhaps he had monstrosity latent within him. The close atmosphere of a wintered-in ship was a test of anyone's mind. Ambitions, dislikes, abnormalities of any kind could be unbearably magnified and intensified, as the whole history of Arctic exploration reveals. On the Polaris Expedition, Budington and others drank, Tyson brooded, the carpenter went insane, young Joseph Mauch, Noah Hayes, and probably most of the men aboard drifted miserably toward paranoia. Hayes's assertion at the conclusion of his journal rings of hard experience and honest self-awareness: 'I believe that no man can retain the use of his faculties during one long night to such a degree as to be morally responsible.' Bessels scorned Hall, as he apparently scorned many men. Hall was an uneducated boor, but he, Emil Bessels of Heidelberg and Jena, had to serve under him and take his orders. Their relations had been strained at the outset, and Bessels faced at least another year, probably another two years, on that tiny ship, suffering the humiliation of an arrogant man in a subservient position.

Perhaps Bessels murdered Hall. Perhaps. The only certain truth that can be found in this case is a knowledge of the inevitable and final elusiveness of the past. What happened aboard the USS *Polaris* between October 24 and November 8, 1871, can never be entirely known. What went on in the minds of Hall, Bessels, and the others aboard that ship, and what they did furtively on their own, is done, gone, past. The questions that the Board of Inquiry did not ask can be asked today, but many of them cannot be answered.

One way or the other, Charles Francis Hall died, as his friend Penn Clarke said he would, a victim of his own zeal. If a stroke was the primary cause, then he drove himself into it, trying to reach the North Pole at the age of fifty. If Bessels murdered him, then his zeal, which made him strong, also made him an unbearable threat to the doctor's ambitions or a hateful object of the doctor's fears. If he poisoned himself, then it was because the zeal that had made him fiercely independent had also made him fiercely suspicious. The dark side of his independence was his distrust of anyone who seemed in any way to threaten him, his integrity, his desires. Independence is often loneliness, and Hall was a lonely man. Treating himself rather than trusting someone else for treatment would have been a characteristic, almost a symbolic, act.

Will power, energy, and independence are the qualities that made him and perhaps broke him. Nineteenth-century America was filled with the rhetoric of will power, energy, and independence but, as scholars, beginning with Frederick Jackson Turner, have shown, it was an age that increasingly controlled energy and individual will, channeling them into the communal and the cooperative. For better or worse, Hall was the real thing. Pious and patriotic as he was, he had something of the mountain man in him. When he drifted west from New Hampshire, he was looking for wilderness, though he may not have known it. When Cincinnati did not give him what he wanted, then he went north instead of west – not drifting then, but driving with relentless energy and concentrated purpose. In the North, too, he found that full independence was not possible, not among the Eskimos, not aboard the *Polaris*. Hall's voyages to the Arctic were not merely geographical explorations. They were a quest for the kind of independence that was gone from American life – or, closer to the truth, the kind of independence that never existed except in the minds of dreamers like Hall.

Just before we left Polaris Promontory after the exhumation, I returned alone to the grave. I had to fulfill Arctic ritual and bury a cannister there with an account of what we had done. After doing the job, I took a last look at the grave, hoping to feel some of the things that I believed I should feel and had not felt during the day of the autopsy. The biographer and the detective still dominated; in spite of myself, all I did was puzzle about the crowbar at the head of the grave – the crowbar that we had carefully put back in place. After we returned home, while rereading Noah Hayes's journal, I noticed something I had not noticed before; the Indiana farmboy solved at least one mystery and deserves the last word about his hero. The night they buried Hall, he wrote, was too cold, too miserable for them to mount a headboard, so they jammed the crowbar into the mound. 'A fit type of his will,' wrote Hayes, 'an iron monument marks his tomb.'

CHAPTER 4

'SEE THE ESQUIMAUX'

from *The Voyage of the Narwhal* (1998)

Andrea Barrett

The Voyage of the Narwhal is Andrea Barrett's 1998 fictional version of a Franklin rescue expedition. The captain of the Narwhal, *Zechariah 'Zeke' Voorhees, gets separated from his men and is presumed dead; months later he returns home with the Eskimos, Annie and Tom, who have saved him. In this passage, two old friends of Voorhees, Alexandra Copeland and Erasmus Wells, attend his public exhibition of the rescuers.*

Here in the theater's gallery, near the prostitutes scattered like iridescent fish through the shoals of dark-clothed men, Alexandra felt drab in her brown silk dress. Two seats down from her, a woman in a chartreuse gown with lemon-trimmed flounces was striking a deal with a pleasant-looking man. They would meet on the landing, Alexandra heard them agree. Directly after the lecture. The man's voice dropped and the woman shook her head, shivering the egret feathers woven into her hair. 'Twenty dollars,' she said. The man nodded and disappeared, leaving Alexandra to marvel at the transaction.

'There must be a thousand people,' Erasmus said, scanning the crowd. 'Maybe more.'

'It's frightening,' she said. 'How good Zeke is at promoting himself.'

All around the city, on lampposts and tavern doors, in merchants' windows and omnibuses, posters advertised the exhibition. A clumsy woodcut showed Zeke holding a harpoon and Annie a string of fish, Tom peeping out from behind her flared boots. In the background were mountains cut by a fjord, and above those a banner headline: MY LIFE AMONG THE ESQUIMAUX. A caption touted the remarkable discoveries made by Zechariah Voorhees:

Two Fine Specimens of the Native Tribes!
More Exotic than the Sioux and Fox Indians Exhibited by
George Catlin in London and Paris!
See the Esquimaux Demonstrate Their Customs!

Zeke had run a smaller version in the newspaper and mailed invitations to hundreds of his family's friends and business associates – organizing this first exhibition, Alexandra thought, like a military campaign. Ahead of him lay Baltimore, Washington, Richmond, New York, Providence, Albany, Boston.

Erasmus said, 'Can you see Lavinia?' and Alexandra, scouting the boxes on the second tier, finally spotted her dead center, flanked by Linnaeus and Humboldt and Zeke's parents and sisters. She was touching her hair then her cheek then her brooch then her nose, turning her head from side to side as if the mood of the entire audience were expressing itself through her. Everyone, Alexandra thought, made nervous by this month's chain of disasters. Across the ocean, off the coast of Ireland, the telegraph cable being laid with such fanfare had broken. Two trains had crashed south of Philadelphia, killing several passengers; last week a steamship on its way to New York from Cuba had sunk. Each of these seemed to heighten the financial panic set off by a bank failure in Ohio. Banks were closing everywhere; the stock exchange was in an uproar. The papers were full of news about bankrupt merchants and brokers. Alexandra's own family, who had no money to lose, hadn't been touched so far, and the engraving firm seemed stable. But Erasmus, whose income came primarily from his father's investments, had suffered some losses. And Zeke's father's firm was in trouble, which suddenly made Zeke's future – and Lavinia's as well – uncertain. Suddenly it mattered what Zeke charged for the exhibition tickets, and how many tickets were sold. The theater was full of people desperate for distraction.

In the glow of the gaslights Zeke strode out in full Esquimaux regalia, adjusted the position of two large crates, and took his place at the podium. The roar of applause was startling, as was the ease with which he spoke. If he had notes, Alexandra couldn't see them. Swiftly, eloquently, he sketched for the audience an outline of the voyage of the *Narwhal*, making of the confused first months a spare, dramatic narrative.

Their first sights of Melville Bay and Lancaster Sound, their encounters with the Netsilik and their retrieval of the Franklin relics; the discovery of the *Resolute* and their stormy passage up Ellesmere until they were frozen in; their long winter and the visit of Ootuniah and his companions; the first trip to Anoatok. No mention, Alexandra noticed, of Dr. Boerhaave's death, nor of the other men who'd died: nor of Erasmus. It was 'I' all the time, 'I' and 'me' and 'mine'; occasionally 'we' or 'my men.' No names, only him. Beside her, Erasmus fidgeted.

Twenty minutes, she guessed. Twenty minutes for the part of the voyage involving the crew; then another fifteen for Zeke's solo trip north on foot and his return to the empty ship. 'Now,' Zeke was saying, 'now began the most interesting part of my experience in the arctic. I was all alone, and winter was coming. I had to prepare myself.'

From the crates he began to pull things. His hunting rifle, seal-skins, a tin of ship's biscuit, a jar of dried peas. His black notebook, the sight of which made Erasmus groan. Into his talk he wove some stray lines from that, and then read aloud the section about the arrival of Annie and Nessark and Marumah. 'The *angekok* is the tribe's general counselor and advisor,' he explained. 'As well as its wizard. His chief job is to determine the reason for any misfortune visiting the tribe – and the *angekok* of Annie's tribe determined that the cause of their children's sickness was me. So was my life changed by a superstition. From the day these people arrived I entered into a new life.'

He described the journey to Anoatok and his first days there. Then he said, 'But you must meet some of the people among whom I stayed.' He stepped back from the podium and whistled.

There was rattling backstage, and the crack of a whip. Two dogs appeared – not his huge black hunting dogs but beagles, ludicrous in their harnesses, gamely trotting side by side. Apparently Zeke would not subject his own pets to this. Behind them they pulled a small sledge on wheels, with Tom crouched on the crossbars and Annie grasping the uprights and waving a little whip. Both Annie and Tom wore fur jackets with the hoods pulled up and shadowing their faces. When the sledge reached the front of the podium, Zeke gave a sharp command that stopped the beagles. They sat, drool-ing eagerly as Zeke held out bits of biscuit, and then lay down in their traces with their chins on their paws. Their eyes followed Zeke as he moved around the stage, but Annie and Tom stared straight out at the audience, shielding their eyes against the glare.

'These are two of the people who rescued me,' Zeke said. 'The names they use among us are Annie and Tom.'

While they stood still he recited some facts. Annie and Tom belonged to the group of people John Ross had discovered in 1818 and called Arctic Highlanders – there were just a few hundred of them, he said, scattered from Cape York to Etah. Fewer each year; their lives were hard and their children sickened; he feared they were dying out. They moved nomadically throughout the seasons, among clusters of huts a day's journey apart and near good hunting sites. All food was shared among them, as if they were one large family. Because no driftwood reached their isolated shores, they had no bows and arrows, nor kayaks, and in this they differed from the Esquimaux of Boothia and southern Greenland. They'd developed their own ways, substituting bone for wood – bone harpoon shafts and sledge parts and tent poles. 'A true sledge,' Zeke said, 'would have bone crosspieces lashed to the runners with thongs, and ivory strips fastened to the runners.' He went on to explain how they subsisted largely on animals from the sea.

'The term "Esquimaux" is French and means "raw meat eaters",' Zeke said. 'But there's nothing disgusting in this, the body in that violent climate craves blood and the juices of uncooked food.' From the nearest crate he took a paper bundle, which he unwrapped to reveal a Delaware shad. A few strokes of a knife yielded three small squares of flesh. Two he held out to Annie and Tom, keeping the third for himself. The beagles whined. Zeke popped the flesh in his mouth and chewed, while Annie and Tom did the same on either side of him. The audience gasped, and Alexandra could see this pleased Zeke enormously.

'With the help of my two friends,' he said, 'I would like to demonstrate for you some of the elements of daily life among these remarkable people.'

Now Alexandra saw the bulk of what the crates contained. Certainly he hadn't carried all these objects home with him; he must have made some here, with Annie's help and whatever supplies he could find. There was a long-handled net, which Tom seized and carried to the top of one crate. He made darting and swooping motions as Zeke described capturing dovekies. 'These arrive by the million,' Zeke said. 'When the hunter's net is full, he kills each bird by pressing its chest with his fingers, until the heart stops.'

A soapstone lamp – where had this come from? – with a wick made from moss; Zeke filled it with whale oil and had Annie light it with a sliver of wood he first lit with a match, telling the audience they must imagine lumps of blubber slowly melting. In the huts, he said, with these lamps giving off heat and light, with food cooking and wet clothes drying and children frolicking, it had been warm no matter what the outside temperature. He brought out more hides and had Annie demonstrate how the women of her tribe scraped off the inner layers to make the hides pliable. 'This crescent-shaped knife is an *ulo*,' he said, and Annie sat on her knees with her feet tucked beneath her thighs and the skin spread before her, rubbing it with the blade. Beside Alexandra, Erasmus pressed both hands to his ribs.

'Are you all right?' she said. She couldn't take her eyes from the stage.

'That's exactly the way I soften a dried skin before I mount it,' Erasmus said. 'I have a drawshave I use like her *ulo*.'

Zeke said, 'The women chew every inch after it's dried, to make it soft,' and Annie put a bit of the hide in her mouth and ground her teeth. 'I can't show you the threads, which are made from sinews,' he said. 'But the needles are kept in these charming cases.' Annie held up an ivory cylinder, through which passed a bit of hide bristling with needles.

Zeke took Tom's hand and seized a pair of harpoons; then he and Tom lay down and pretended to be inching up on a seal's blowhole, waiting for the seal to surface. As they mimicked the strike Zeke spoke loudly, a flow of vivid words that had the crowd leaning forward. They were seeing what Zeke wanted them to see, Alexandra thought. Not what was really there: not a rickety makeshift sledge, two floppy-eared beagles, a tired woman and a nervous boy moved like mannequins by the force of Zeke's voice. Not them, or a man needing to make a living, but the arctic in all its mystery: unknown landscapes and animals and another race of people.

Her face was wet; was she weeping? As Zeke's antics continued Alexandra found herself thinking of her parents and the last day she'd seen them. Pulling away from the ferry dock, waving goodbye, sure they'd be reunited in a week. Then the noise, the terrible shocking noise. Great plumes of steam and smoke and cinders spinning down to the water – and her parents, everyone, gone. Simply gone.

She turned to Erasmus, who had his face in his hands. Gently she touched him and said, 'You have to look.'

He raised his head for a second but then returned his gaze to his shoes. 'I won't,' he said passionately. 'I hate this. All my life the thing I've hated most is being *looked at*. I can't bear it when people stare at me. I know just how she feels, all of us peering down at her. It's disgusting. It's worse than disgusting. People stared at me like this when I returned from the Exploring Expedition, and again when I came back without Zeke. Now we're doing the same thing to her.'

Had she known this about him? She looked away from him, back at the stage; she felt a shameful pleasure, herself, in regarding Annie and Tom. She longed to draw them.

Annie had pushed her hood back from her sweating face, while Tom had stretched out on the sledge and was pulling at one of the beagle's ears. From his crate Zeke took a wooden figure clothed in a miniature jacket and pants. 'The children play with dolls,' Zeke said. 'Just as ours do.' Tom released the beagle's ear, seizing the doll and pressing it to his chest. Then Zeke was winding string around Annie's fingers, saying, 'Among this tribe, a favorite game with the women and children is called *ajarorpok*, which is much like our child's game of cat's cradle, only more complicated.'

He said something to Annie and stepped away. Annie's hands darted like birds and paused, holding up a shapely web. 'This represents a caribou,' Zeke said.

Alexandra tried to see a creature in the loops and whorls, not knowing that, for Annie, it was as if the stage had suddenly filled with beautiful animals. Not knowing that for Annie this evening moved as if the *angekok* who'd brought Zeke to them had bewitched her, putting her into a trance in which she both was and was not on this stage. The *angekok* had shared with her the secret fire that let him see in the dark, to the heart of things. For her Zeke's bird net wasn't a broomstick and knotted cotton but a narwhal's tusk and plaited sinews; on her fingers she felt the fat she'd scraped from the seal. She was home, and she was also here, doing what she'd been told in a dream to do.

She was to watch these people, ranged in tiers above her, and commit them to memory, so that she could bring a vision of them to her people back home. Their pointed faces and bird-colored garments; the way they gathered in great crowds but didn't touch each other or share their food. Their tools, their cooking implements, their huts that couldn't be moved when the weather changed. In a dream she'd heard her mother's voice, singing the song that had risen from her tribe's first sight of the white men.

Her mother had been a small girl on the summer day when floating islands with white wings had appeared by the narrow edge of ice off Cape York. From the islands hung little boats, which were lowered to the water; these spat out sickly men in blue garments, who couldn't make themselves understood but who offered bits of something that looked like ice, which held the image of human faces; round dry tasteless things to eat; parts of their garments, which weren't made of skins.

'At first,' her mother had said, 'we thought the spirits of the air had come to us.' On the floating island her mother had seen a fat, pink, hairless animal, a man with eyes concealed behind ovals of unmelting ice, bulky objects on which to sit, something like a frozen arm, with which to hit something like a needle. The two men who'd stepped first on the ice had worn hats shaped like cooking pots. Through them, her people had learned they weren't alone in the world.

Much later, when Annie was grown, she'd had her mother's experience to guide her when the other strangers arrived. Kane and his men had taught Annie to understand their ungainly speech, and Annie had learned that the world was larger than she'd understood, though much of it was unfortunate, even cursed. Elsewhere, these visitors said, were lands with no seals, no walrus, no bears; no sheets of colored light singing across the sky. She couldn't understand how these people survived. They'd been like children, dependent on her tribe for clothes, food, sledges, dogs; surrounded by things which were of no use to them and bereft of women. Like children they gave their names to the landscape, pretending to discover places her people had known for generations.

From them she'd gained words for the visions of her mother's childhood: a country called England and another called America; men called officers; ships, sails, mirrors, biscuits, cloth, pig, eyeglasses, chair. Wood, which came from a giant version of the tiny shrubs they knew. Hammer and nails. Later she'd added the words Zeke had taught her while he lived with them; then the names for the vast array of unfamiliar things she'd encountered here. In the dream her mother had given her this task: to look closely at all around her, and to remember everything. To do this while guarding her son.

Her hands darted and formed another shape, which Zeke claimed represented ponds amid hills but in which she saw her home. She felt the warm liver of the freshly killed seal, she tasted sweet blood in her mouth. In the gaslights she saw the moon and the sun, brother and sister who'd quarreled and now chased each other across the sky. At first her mother had thought the strangers must come from these sources of light. Her hands flew in the air.

'Can you see what she's doing?' Alexandra whispered to Erasmus. 'I can't see what she's making.'

'I have to go,' Erasmus said. 'We have to go. Can we go?'

CHAPTER 5

'MOUNT HATTERAS'

from *The Adventures of Captain Hatteras* (1866)

Jules Verne

Jules Verne wrote The Adventures of Captain Hatteras *at the same time that he was working on* Journey to the Centre of the Earth. *Hatteras is an obsessed Arctic explorer who resolves that an Englishman must be the first to reach the North Pole. He sets forth on his boat, the* Forward, *and despite the usual hazards – ice, mutiny, hunger – he reaches his goal, where he finds land or, more specifically, a volcano. The passage below chronicles his decision to touch the pole, even if that means leaping into a flaming crater.*

After [a] substantial conversation, all settled down in the grotto as best they could, and dropped off.

All except for Hatteras. Why did this extraordinary man not sleep? Had the aim of his life not been accomplished? Had he not accomplished the bold project he held dearest? Why did calm not succeed agitation in that burning soul? Was it not natural that, his projects accomplished, Hatteras would fall into a sort of despondency, that his relaxed nerves would need rest? After his success, it would have even been normal to feel that sadness which always follows satisfied desires.

But no. He still appeared over-excited, more so than ever. However, it was not the idea of returning which made him agitated. Did he want to go even further? Did his travel ambition not have any limit, and did he find the world too small because he had been everywhere on it?

Whatever the reason, he could not sleep. And yet, that first night spent at the Pole of the globe was clear and calm. The island was completely uninhabited. Not a single bird in the burning air, not an animal on the cindery ground, not a fish in the boiling waters. Only the dull and distant rumbling of the mountain, with its head producing dishevelled plumes of incandescent smoke.

When Bell, Johnson, Altamont, and the doctor awoke, Hatteras was no longer with them. Worried, they left the grotto, and found the captain standing on a rock. His eyes remained immutably fixed on the summit of the volcano. He had his instruments in his hand; he had clearly just measured the mountain's position.

The doctor went up to him and spoke several times before he could interrupt his contemplation. Finally, the captain seemed to understand.

'Off we go!' said the doctor, examining him attentively. 'Let's explore everywhere on our island; we're ready for our last excursion.'

'The last,' said Hatteras with the intonation of people dreaming out loud, 'yes, the last. But also,' he added very keenly, 'the most wonderful!'

While he spoke, he rubbed his hands over his forehead as if to calm the boiling inside.

Altamont, Johnson, and Bell joined them; Hatteras now seemed to emerge from his hallucinatory state.

'My friends,' he said emotionally, 'thank you for your courage;

thank you for your perseverance; thank you for your superhuman efforts, which have enabled us to set foot on this land!'

'Captain,' said Johnson, 'we only followed orders, and the honour belongs to you.'

'No, no,' replied Hatteras in a violent outpouring; 'to all of you as much as to me! To Altamont and all of us and the doctor as well! Oh, may my heart blow its top in your hands! It can no longer contain its joy and gratitude!'

Hatteras seized the hands of his good companions around him. He came, he went, he was no longer in control of himself.

'We only did our duty as Britons,' said Bell.

'And friends,' added the doctor.

'Yes, but not everyone was able to do his duty. Some failed! However, those who betrayed should be forgiven, like those who let themselves be dragged into betrayal! Poor men! I pardon them, do you hear, doctor?'

'I do,' replied Clawbonny, who was seriously worried at Hatteras's exultation.

'So I don't want them to lose the riches they came so far to earn. No, nothing in my arrangements has changed, and they will be wealthy . . . if ever they get back to Britain!'

It would have been difficult to remain unmoved by the tone Hatteras said these words in.

'But, captain,' said Johnson, trying to joke, 'you'd think you were making your last will and testament.'

'Perhaps I am,' replied Hatteras gravely.

'But you still have a good long life of fame before you,' continued the old sailor.

'Who knows?' said the captain, followed by a long silence.

The doctor did not dare interpret the meaning of these last words.

But Hatteras needed to ensure he was understood, for he added, in a hurried voice he could hardly control:

'My friends, listen to me. We have done a great deal so far, and yet there remains much to do.'

The captain's companions looked at each other with astonishment.

'Remember, we're at the land of the Pole, but not the Pole itself!'

'What do you mean?' said Altamont.

'Could you please explain?' exclaimed the doctor, afraid to guess.

'Yes,' said Hatteras forcefully; 'I said that a Briton would set foot on the Pole of the globe; I said it, and it shall come to pass.'

'What . . . ?' said the doctor.

'We are still forty-five seconds away from that mysterious point,' said Hatteras with growing emotion, 'and to it I shall go!'

'But it's on top of that volcano!' said the doctor.

'I shall go.'

'You can't get there!'

'I shall go.'

'It's a wide open flaming crater!'

'I shall go.'

The energy and conviction with which Hatteras said these last words cannot be conveyed. His friends were stupefied; they looked in terror at the mountain, which was waving its plume of flames in the air.

· The doctor then spoke; he insisted; he pressed Hatteras to renounce his projects; he said everything his heart could conjure up, from humble prayers to friendly threats; but he obtained nothing from the unquiet soul of the captain, caught up in an insanity that could be called 'polar madness'.

There remained only violent means to prevent this madman, who was heading for a fatal fall. But foreseeing that such means would produce serious disorders, the doctor decided to employ them only as a last resort.

In any case, he hoped that physical impossibilities and impenetrable obstacles would prevent Hatteras from executing his project.

'Since such is the case,' he said, 'we will go with you.'

'Good, but only halfway up the mountain! No further! You need to take back to Britain the copy of the affidavit attesting to our discovery if . . .'

'Nevertheless . . .'

'It's decided!' replied Hatteras in an unshakeable tone. Since the prayers of his friends had not changed matters, the captain remained in command.

The doctor did not try to insist further, and a few moments later the little troop had equipped themselves to face difficulties and, led by Duke, had set off.

The sky was shining brightly. The thermometer read fifty-two (11°C). The air was dramatically imbued with the clarity particular to that high latitude. It was eight in the morning.

Hatteras took the lead with his good dog; Bell, Altamont, the doctor, and Johnson followed close behind.

'I'm afraid,' said Johnson.

'There's nothing to fear,' replied the doctor. 'We're right beside you.'

What a remarkable island, and how to depict its special physiognomy, which had the unexpected newness of youth! This volcano did not seem to be very old, and geologists would have concluded that it had been formed at a recent date.

The rocks clung to each other, maintaining themselves only through a miracle of equilibrium. The mountain was, so to speak, merely an agglomeration of stones thrown there. No earth, no moss, not the thinnest lichen, no trace of vegetation. The carbonic acid vomited by the crater had not yet had time to join up with hydrogen from the water or ammonia from the clouds, to form organized matter under the effect of the light.

This island, lost in the open sea, was due only to the accumulation of the successive volcanic ejections; several other mountains of the globe were formed in a similar way; what they threw out from their breast was sufficient to build them, like Etna, which has already vomited a volume of lava larger than its own mass, and Mount Nuovo, near Naples, generated by scoria in the short space of forty-eight hours.

The pile of rocks composing Queen's Island had clearly come out of the entrails of the earth; it was plutonian to the utmost degree. Where it now stood, the endless sea had once stretched, formed in the first days by the condensation of water vapour over the cooling earth; but, as the volcanoes of the old and new worlds went out, or more precisely became dormant, they had to be replaced by new fire-breathing craters.

In effect, the earth can be compared to a vast spherical boiler. Because of the central fire, immense quantities of vapours are generated, stored at a pressure of thousands of atmospheres, and they would blow up the earth if there were no safety valves.

These valves are the volcanoes; when one closes, another opens; and at the Pole, where the terrestrial crust is thinner because of the flattening, it is not surprising that a volcano should have formed, and become visible as its massif rose above the water.

The doctor, while following Hatteras, noticed the strange features; his foot found volcanic tuff, as well as pumiceous slag deposits, ash, and eruptive rocks similar to the syenites and granites of Iceland.

But if he concluded that the islet was of recent formation, this was because the sedimentary terrain had not yet had time to form.

Water was also absent. If Queen's Island had had the advantage of being several centuries old, springs would have been spurting from its breast, as in the neighbourhood of volcanoes. Now, not only was it devoid of liquid molecules, but the steam which rose from the lava streams seemed to be absolutely anhydrous.

This island was thus of recent formation, and just as it had one day appeared, it could easily disappear on another and sink back to the depths of the ocean.

As the men climbed, the going became more and more difficult; the flanks of the mountain were approaching the vertical, and careful precautions had to be taken to avoid landslides. Often tall clouds of ash twisted around the travellers, threatening to suffocate them, and torrents of lava blocked their path. On the few horizontal parts, streams of lava, cooled and solid on the surface, allowed lava to flow bubbling under their hard crusts. Each man therefore had to carefully test the ground in front of him so as not to be suddenly plunged into the rivers of fire.

From time to time the crater vomited out blocks of rock, red hot from the inflamed gases; some of these masses exploded in the air like bombs, and the debris flew enormous distances in all directions.

It can be imagined what countless dangers this ascent of the mountain involved, and how insane one had to be to attempt it.

However, Hatteras climbed with surprising agility and, disdaining the help of his iron-tipped stick, moved up the steepest slopes without hesitation.

Soon he arrived at a circular rock, a sort of plateau about ten feet wide; an incandescent river divided at a ridge of rock higher up, then surrounded it, leaving only a narrow pathway, along which Hatteras boldly moved.

There he stopped, and his companions were able to join him. He seemed to be visually estimating the distance still to be covered;

horizontally, he was less than 600 feet from the crater and the mathematical point of the Pole; but vertically, 1,500 feet still remained to be climbed.

The climb had already lasted three hours; Hatteras did not appear tired; his companions were exhausted.

The summit of the volcano could apparently not be reached. The doctor resolved to prevent Hatteras from climbing any more, at any price. He tried first with gentle means, but the captain's exultation had reached the point of delirium; during the march he had shown every sign of increasing insanity, but anyone who knew him, who had followed him through the various stages of life, could hardly be surprised. As Hatteras rose higher above the ocean, his excitement grew; he no longer lived in the realm of men; he was becoming greater than the mountain itself.

'Hatteras,' the doctor said to him, 'enough! We can't take a single step more.'

'Stay then,' replied the captain in a strange voice. 'I am going higher!'

'No, what you're doing is useless! You're at the Pole of the world!'

'No, no! Higher!'

'My friend, it's me talking to you, Dr Clawbonny. Do you recognize me?'

'Higher, higher!' repeated the madman.

'No! We will not let . . .'

The doctor had not finished before Hatteras made a superhuman effort, jumped across the lava flow, and was out of the reach of his companions.

They uttered a cry; they thought Hatteras had fallen into the torrents of fire; but the captain had landed on the other side, together with his dog Duke, who refused to leave him.

He was hidden behind a curtain of smoke, and his voice could be heard diminishing with the distance.

'Northwards, northwards!' he was crying. 'To the top of Mount Hatteras! Remember Mount Hatteras!'

They could not consider joining the captain; they had only a slim chance of repeating his feat, imbued as he was with the strength and skill particular to madmen; it was impossible to cross that stream of fire, impossible also to go around it. Altamont tried in vain to get over; he nearly perished trying to jump the lava; his companions had to restrain him bodily.

'Hatteras, Hatteras!' the doctor shouted.

But the captain did not reply, and only the barely perceptible barking of Duke echoed over the mountain.

Nevertheless, Hatteras could occasionally be glimpsed through the columns of smoke and ash raining down. Sometimes his arms, sometimes his head emerged from the swirling shapes. Then he would vanish only to reappear higher up, clinging on to rocks. He got smaller at that fantastic speed of objects rising in the air. Half an hour later, he already seemed to be only half his real height.

The air was full of the dull sounds of the volcano; the mountain was vibrating and groaning like an overheated boiler; its flanks could be felt shivering. Hatteras was still climbing. Duke still followed.

Occasionally landslides occurred behind them and enormous boulders, accelerating as they rebounded on the crests, rushed down to drown at the bottom of the polar basin.

Hatteras did not even turn round. He had used his stick as a shaft to hoist the Union Jack. His terrified companions hung on to his every move. He gradually became microscopic, and Duke had shrunk to the size of a large rat.

There came a time when the wind pushed a vast curtain of flame over them. The doctor shouted in anguish; but Hatteras reappeared, still standing, waving his flag.

The vision of this frightening ascent lasted more than an hour. An hour of battle with the loose rocks and the holes full of ash, into which this hero of the impossible often disappeared up to his waist. Sometimes he performed acrobatics, buttressing himself with his knees and back against the projections of the mountain; sometimes he hung by his hands from some ridge, blown in the wind like a dried tuft of dry vegetation.

Finally he reached the top of the volcano, the very mouth of the crater. The hope then came to the doctor that the wretch, having reached his goal, would come back down again, and would only have the dangers of the return to face.

He shouted one last time:

'Hatteras! Hatteras!'

The doctor's appeal was heart-rending and moved the American to the depths of his soul.

'I'll save him!' exclaimed Altamont.

With a single leap across the torrents of fire, almost falling into them, he disappeared amongst the rocks.

Clawbonny had not had time to stop him.

Meanwhile, having reached the peak, Hatteras was advancing over the abyss on an overhanging rock below which there was nothing. Boulders rained down all around. Duke was still with him. The poor animal was apparently already caught up in the vertiginous attraction of the abyss. Hatteras was waving his flag, which was lit up with incandescent reflections, as the red muslin stood out in long folds in the breath from the crater.

Hatteras was shaking the standard with one hand. With the other, he was pointing at the Pole of the celestial globe, directly above him. However, he still seemed to be hesitating. He was still seeking the mathematical point where all the lines of meridian meet, and where, in his sublime obstinacy, he wanted to set foot. All of a sudden, the rock gave way under his feet. He disappeared. A terrible cry from his companions sounded as far as the mountain peak. A second, a century passed! But Altamont was there, and Duke too. The man and the dog had seized the unfortunate creature just as he fell into the chasm.

Hatteras was saved, saved against his will, and half an hour later, the captain of the *Forward* was lying senseless, reposing in the arms of his despairing companions. When he came to again, the doctor examined his eyes in silent distress. But this unconscious regard, like a blind man who looks without seeing, did not respond.

'Good God,' said Johnson, 'he's blind!'

'No, he isn't. My poor friends, we have saved only Hatteras's body. His soul has remained at the summit of the volcano! His reason is dead!'

'Insane!' cried Johnson and Altamont in dismay.

'Insane,' the doctor replied. And large tears ran from his eyes.

CHAPTER 6

'THE WINTER NIGHT'

from *Farthest North* (1897)

Fridtjof Nansen

In 1888, the Norwegian explorer Fridtjof Nansen completed the first ski crossing of the Greenland ice; five years later, he set out for the North Pole. His ship, the Fram, *or* Forward, *had been designed to withstand the crushing pressure of the ice, and the plan was to drift, as opposed to sail, north. The passage below describes the arrival of winter, and a Christmas dinner on board the* Fram. *Nansen eventually reached 86° 14' N, the highest latitude achieved to that point.*

One day differed very little from another on board, and the description of one is, in every particular of any importance, a description of all.

We all turned out at eight, and breakfasted on hard bread (both rye and wheat), cheese (Dutch-clove cheese, Cheddar, Gruyère, and Mysost, or goat's-whey cheese, prepared from dry powder), corned beef or corned mutton, luncheon ham or Chicago tinned tongue or bacon, cod-caviare, anchovy roe; also oatmeal biscuits or English ship-biscuits – with orange marmalade or Frame Food jelly. Three times a week we had fresh-baked bread as well, and often cake of some kind. As for our beverages, we began by having coffee and chocolate day about, but afterwards had coffee only two days a week, tea two, and chocolate three.

After breakfast some men went to attend to the dogs – give them their food, which consisted of half a stock-fish or a couple of dog-biscuits each, let them loose, or do whatever else there was to do for them. The others went all to their different tasks. Each took his turn of a week in the galley – helping the cook to wash up, lay the table, and wait. The cook himself had to arrange his bill of fare for dinner immediately after breakfast, and to set about his preparations at once. Some of us would take a turn on the floe to get some fresh air, and to examine the state of the ice, its pressure, etc. At 1 o'clock all were assembled for dinner, which generally consisted of three courses – soup, meat, and dessert; or, soup, fish, and meat, or, fish, meat, and dessert; or sometimes only fish and meat. With the meat we always had potatoes, and either green vegetables or macaroni. I think we were all agreed that the fare was good; it would hardly have been better at home; for some of us it would perhaps have been worse. And we looked like fatted pigs; one or two even began to cultivate a double chin and a corporation. As a rule, stories and jokes circulated at table along with the bock-beer.

After dinner the smokers of our company would march off, well fed and contented, into the galley, which was smoking-room as well as kitchen, tobacco being tabooed in the cabins except on festive occasions. Out there they had a good smoke and chat; many a story was told, and not seldom some warm dispute arose. Afterwards came, for most of us, a short siesta. Then each went to his work again until we were summoned to supper at 6 o'clock, when the regulation day's work was done. Supper was almost the same as breakfast, except that tea was always the beverage. Afterwards there was again smoking in the galley, while the saloon was transformed into a silent reading-room. Good use was made of the valuable library presented to the expedition by generous publishers and other friends. If the kind donors could have seen us away up there, sitting round the table at night with heads buried in books or collections of illustrations, and could have understood how invaluable these companions were to us, they would have felt rewarded by the knowledge that they had conferred a real boon – that they had materially assisted in making the *Fram* the little oasis that it was in this vast ice desert. About half-past seven or eight cards or other games were brought out, and we played well on into the night, seated in groups round the saloon table. One or other of us might go to the organ, and, with the assistance of the crankhandle, perform some of our beautiful pieces, or Johansen would bring out the accordion and play many a fine tune. His crowning efforts were 'Oh, Susanna!' and 'Napoleon's March Across the Alps in an Open Boat.' About midnight we turned in, and then the night watch was set. Each man went on for an hour. Their most trying work on watch seems to have been writing their diaries and looking out, when the dogs barked, for any signs of bears at hand. Besides this, every two hours or four hours the watch had to go aloft or on to the ice to take the meteorological observations.

I believe I may safely say that on the whole the time passed pleasantly and imperceptibly, and that we throve in virtue of the regular habits imposed upon us.

My notes will give the best idea of our life, in all its monotony. They are not great events that are here recorded, but in their very bareness they give a true picture. Such, and no other, was our life. I shall give some quotations direct from my diary:

Tuesday, September 26th. Beautiful weather. The sun stands much lower now; it was 9° above the horizon at midday. Winter is rapidly approaching; there are 14½° of frost this evening, but we do not feel it cold. To-day's observations unfortunately show no particular drift northward; according to them we are still in 78° 50′ north latitude. I wandered about over the floe towards evening. Nothing more wonderfully beautiful can exist than the Arctic night. It is dreamland, painted in the imagination's most delicate tints; it is color etherealized. One shade melts into the other, so that you cannot tell where one ends and the other begins, and yet they are all there. No forms – it is all faint, dreamy color music, a far-away, long-drawn-out melody on muted strings. Is not all life's beauty high, and delicate, and pure like this night? Give it brighter colors, and it is no longer so beautiful. The sky is like an enormous cupola, blue at the zenith, shading down into green, and then into lilac and violet at the edges. Over the ice-fields there are cold violet-blue shadows, with lighter pink tints where a ridge here and there catches the last reflection of the vanished day. Up in the blue of the cupola shine the stars, speaking peace, as they always do, those unchanging friends. In the south stands a large red-yellow moon, encircled by a yellow ring and light golden clouds floating on the blue background. Presently the aurora borealis shakes over the vault of heaven its veil of glittering silver – changing now to yellow, now to green, now to red. It spreads, it contracts again, in restless change; next it breaks into waving, many-folded bands of shining silver, over which shoot billows of glittering rays, and then the glory vanishes. Presently it shimmers in tongues of flame over the very zenith, and then again it shoots a bright ray right up from the horizon, until the whole melts away in the moonlight, and it is as though one heard the sigh of a departing spirit And all the time this utter stillness, impressive as the symphony of infinitude. I have never been able to grasp the fact that this earth will some day be spent and desolate and empty. To what end, in that case, all this beauty, with not a creature to rejoice in it? Now I begin to divine it. *This* is the coming earth – here are beauty and death. But to what purpose? Ah, what is the purpose of all these spheres? Read the answer, if you can, in the starry blue firmament.

Friday, October 13th. Now we are in the very midst of what the prophets would have had us dread so much. The ice is pressing and packing round us with a noise like thunder. It is piling itself up into long walls, and heaps high enough to reach a good way up the *Fram*'s rigging; in fact, it is trying its very utmost to grind the *Fram* into powder. But here we sit quite tranquil, not even going up to look at all the hurly-burly, but just chatting and laughing as usual. Last night there was tremendous pressure round our old dog-floe. The ice had towered up higher than the highest point of the floe and hustled down upon it. It had quite spoiled a well, where we till now had found good drinking-water, filling it with brine. Furthermore, it had cast itself over our stern ice-anchor and part of the steel cable which held it, burying them so effectually that we had afterwards to cut the cable. Then it covered our planks and sledges, which stood on the ice. Before long the dogs were in danger, and the watch had to turn out all hands to save them. At last the floe split in two. This morning the ice was one scene of melancholy confusion, gleaming in the most glorious sunshine. Piled up all round us were high, steep ice walls. Strangely enough, we had lain on the very verge of the worst confusion, and had escaped with the loss of an ice-anchor, a piece of steel cable, a few planks and other bits of wood, and half of a Samoyede sledge, all of which might have been saved if we had looked after them in time. But the men have grown so indifferent to the pressure now that they do not even go up to look, let it thunder ever so hard. They feel that the ship can stand it, and so long as that is the case there is nothing to hurt except the ice itself.

In the morning the pressure slackened again, and we were soon lying in a large piece of open water, as we did yesterday. To-day, again, this stretched far away towards the northern horizon, where the same dark atmosphere indicated some extent of open water. I now gave the order to put the engine together again; they told me it could be done in a day and a half or at most two days. We must go north and see what there is up there. I think it possible that it may be the boundary between the ice-drift the *Jeannette* was in and the pack we are now drifting south with – or can it be land?

We had kept company quite long enough with the old, now broken-up floe, so worked ourselves a little way astern after dinner, as the ice was beginning to draw together. Towards evening the pressure began again in earnest, and was especially bad round the remains of our old floe, so that I believe we may congratulate ourselves on having left it. It is evident that the pressure here stands in connection with, is perhaps caused by, the tidal wave. It occurs with the greatest regularity. The ice slackens twice and packs twice in 24 hours. The pressure has happened about 4, 5, and 6 o'clock in the morning, and almost at exactly the same hour in the afternoon, and in between we have always lain for some part of the time in open water. The very great pressure just now is probably due to the spring-tide; we had new moon on the 9th, which was the first day of the pressure. Then it was just after midday when we noticed it, but it has been later every day, and now it is at 8 P.M.

The theory of the ice-pressure being caused to a considerable extent by the tidal wave has been advanced repeatedly by Arctic explorers. During the *Fram*'s drifting we had better opportunity than most of them to study this phenomenon, and our experience seems to leave no doubt that over a wide region the tide produces movement and pressure of the ice. It occurs especially at the time of the spring-tides, and more at new moon than at full moon. During the intervening periods there was, as a rule, little or no trace of pressure. But these tidal pressures did not occur during the whole time of our drifting. We noticed them especially the first autumn, while we were in the neighborhood of the open sea north of Siberia, and the last year, when the *Fram* was drawing near the open Atlantic Ocean; they were less noticeable while we were in the polar basin. Pressure occurs here more irregularly, and is mainly caused by the wind driving the ice. When one pictures to one's self these enormous ice-masses, drifting in a certain direction, suddenly meeting hinderances – for example, ice-masses drifting from the opposite direction, owing to a change of wind in some more or less distant quarter – it is easy to understand the tremendous pressure that must result.

Such an ice conflict is undeniably a stupendous spectacle. One feels one's self to be in the presence of titanic forces, and it is easy to understand how timid souls may be overawed and feel as if nothing could stand before it. For when the packing begins in earnest it seems as though there could be no spot on the earth's surface left unshaken. The ice cracks on every side of you, and begins to pile itself up; and all of a sudden you too find yourself in the midst of the struggle. There are howlings and thunderings round you; you feel the ice trembling, and hear it rumbling under your feet; there is no peace anywhere. In the semi-darkness you can see it piling and tossing itself up into high ridges nearer and nearer you – floes 10, 12, 15 feet thick, broken, and flung on the top of each other as if they were feather-weights. They are quite near you now, and you jump away to save your life. But the ice splits in front of you, a black gulf opens, and water streams up. You turn in another direction, but there through the dark you can just see a new ridge of moving ice-blocks coming towards you. You try another direction, but there it is the same. All round there is thundering and roaring, as of some enormous waterfall, with explosions like cannon salvoes. Still nearer you it comes. The floe you are standing on gets smaller and smaller; water pours over it; there can be no escape except by scrambling over the rolling ice-blocks to get to the other side of the pack. But now the disturbance begins to calm down. The noise passes on, and is lost by degrees in the distance.

This is what goes on away there in the north month after month and year after year. The ice is split and piled up into mounds, which extend in every direction. If one could get a bird's-eye view of the ice-fields, they would seem to be cut up into squares or meshes by a network of these packed ridges, or pressure-dikes, as we called them, because they reminded us so much of snow-covered stone dikes at home, such as, in many parts of the country, are used to enclose fields.

Saturday, October 14th. To-day we have got on the rudder; the engine is pretty well in order, and we are clear to start north when the ice opens to-morrow morning. It is still slackening and packing quite regularly twice a day, so that we can calculate on it beforehand. To-day we had the same open channel to the north, and beyond it open sea as far as our view extended. What can this mean? This evening the pressure has been pretty violent. The floes were packed up against the *Fram* on the port side, and were once or twice on the point of toppling over the rail. The ice, however, broke below; they tumbled back again, and had to go under us after all. It is not thick ice, and cannot do much damage; but the force is something enormous. On the masses come incessantly without a pause; they look irresistible; but slowly and surely they are crushed against the *Fram*'s sides. Now (8.30 P.M.) the pressure has at last stopped. Clear evening, sparkling stars, and flaming northern lights.

Sunday, October 15th. To our surprise, the ice did not slacken away much during last night after the violent pressure; and, what was worse, there was no indication of slackening in the morning, now that we were quite ready to go.

Monday, October 16th. Ice quiet and close. Observations on the 12th placed us in 78° 5′ north latitude. Steadily southward. This is almost depressing.

Thursday, October 19th. The ice slackened a little last night. In the morning I attempted a drive with six of the dogs. When I had managed to harness them to the Samoyede sledge, had seated myself on it, and called 'Pr-r-r-r, pr-r-r-r!' they went off in quite good style over the ice. But it was not long before we came to some high pack-ice and had to turn. This was hardly done before they were off back to the ship at lightning speed, and they were not to be got away from it again. Round and round it they went, from refuse-heap to refuse-heap. If I started at the gangway on the starboard side, and tried by thrashing them to drive them out over the ice, round the stern they flew to the gangway on the port side. I tugged, swore, and tried everything I could think of, but all to no purpose. I got out and tried to hold the sledge back, but was pulled off my feet, and dragged merrily over the ice in my smooth sealskin breeches, on back, stomach, side—just as it happened. When I managed to stop them at some pieces of pack-ice or a dust-heap, round they went again to the starboard gangway, with me dangling behind, swearing madly that I would break every bone in their bodies when I got at them. This game went on till they probably tired of it, and thought they might as well go my way for a change. So now they went off beautifully across the flat floe until I stopped for a moment's breathing space. But at the first movement I made in the sledge they were off again, tearing wildly back the way we had come. I held on convulsively, pulled, raged, and used the whip; but the more I lashed the faster they went on their own way. At last I got them stopped by sticking my legs down into the snow between the sledge-shafts, and driving a strong seal-hook into it as well. But while I was off my guard for a moment they gave a tug. I lay with my hinder-part where my legs had been, and we went on at lightning speed – that substantial part of my body leaving a deep track in the snow. This sort of thing went on time after time. I lost the board I should have sat on, then the whip, then my gloves, then my cap – these losses not improving my temper. Once or twice I ran round in front of the dogs, and tried to force them to turn by lashing at them with the whip. They jumped to both sides and only tore on the faster; the reins got twisted round my ankles, and I was thrown flat on the sledge, and they went on more wildly than ever. This was my first experience in dog driving on my own account, and I will not pretend that I was proud of it. I inwardly congratulated myself that my feats had been unobserved.

Saturday, October 21st. I have stayed in to-day because of an affection of the muscles, or rheumatism, which I have had for some days on the right side of my body, and for which the doctor is 'massaging' me, thereby greatly adding to my sufferings. Have I really grown so old and palsied, or is the whole thing imagination? It is all I can do to limp about; but I just wonder if I could not get up and run with the best of them if there happened to be any great occasion for it: I almost believe I could. A nice Arctic hero of 32, lying here in my berth! Have had a good time reading home letters, dreaming myself at home, dreaming of the home-coming – in how many years? Successful or unsuccessful, what does that matter?

I had a sounding taken; it showed over 73 fathoms (135 m.), so we are in deeper water again. The sounding-line indicated that we are drifting southwest. I do not understand this steady drift southward. There has not been much wind either lately; there is certainly a little from the north to-day, but not strong. What can be the reason of it? With all my information, all my reasoning, all my putting of two and two together, I cannot account for any south-going current here — there ought to be a north-going one. If the current runs south here, how is that great open sea we steamed north across to be explained? and the bay we ended in farthest north? These could only be produced by the north-going current which I presupposed.

Sunday, October 22d. Henriksen took soundings this morning, and found 70 fathoms (129 m.) of water. 'If we are drifting at all,' said he, 'it is to the east; but there seems to be almost no movement.' No wind to-day. I am keeping in my den.

Monday, October 23d. Still in the den. To-day, 5 fathoms shallower than yesterday. The line points southwest, which means that we are drifting northeastward. Hansen has reckoned out the observation for the 19th, and finds that we must have got 10 minutes farther north, and must be in 78° 15' N. lat. So at last, now that the wind has gone down, the north-going current is making itself felt. Some channels have opened near us, one along the side of the ship, and one ahead, near the old channel. Only slight signs of pressure in the afternoon.

Tuesday, October 24th. Between 4 and 5 A.M. there was strong pressure, and the *Fram* was lifted up a little. It looks as if the pressure were going to begin again; we have spring-tide with full moon. The ice opened so much this morning that the *Fram* was afloat in her cutting; later on it closed again, and about 11 there was some strong pressure; then came a quiet time; but in the afternoon the pressure began once more, and was violent from 4 to 4.30. The *Fram* was shaken and lifted up; didn't mind a bit.

Wednesday, October 25th. We had a horrible pressure last night. I awoke and felt the *Fram* being lifted, shaken, and tossed about, and heard the loud cracking of the ice breaking against her sides. After listening for a little while I fell asleep again, with a snug feeling that it was good to be on board the *Fram*.

It is quickly getting darker. The sun stands lower and lower every time we see it; soon it will disappear altogether, if it has not done so already. The long, dark winter is upon us, and glad shall we be to see the spring; but nothing matters much if we could only begin to move north. There is now southwesterly wind, and the windmill, which has been ready for several days, has been tried at last and works splendidly. We have beautiful electric light to-day, though the wind has not been especially strong (5–8 m. per second). Electric lamps are a grand institution. What a strong influence light has on one's spirits! There was a noticeable brightening-up at the dinner-table to-day; the light acted on our spirits like a draught of good wine. And how festive the saloon looks! We felt it quite a great occasion – drank Oscar Dickson's health, and voted him the best of good fellows.

To-morrow is the *Fram*'s birthday. How many memories it recalls of the launch-day a year ago!

Thursday, October 26th. 54 fathoms (90 m.) of water when the soundings were taken this morning. We are moving quickly north – due north – says Peter. It does look as if things were going better. Great celebration of the day, beginning with target-shooting. Then we had a splendid dinner of four courses, which put our digestive apparatus to a severe test. The *Fram*'s health was drunk amidst great and stormy applause. The proposer's words were echoed by all hearts when he said that she was such an excellent ship for our purpose that we could not imagine a better (great applause), and we therefore wished her, and ourselves with her, long life (hear, hear!).

Sitting here now alone, my thoughts involuntarily turn to the year that has gone since we stood up there on the platform, and she threw the champagne against the bow, saying: '*Fram* is your name!' and the strong, heavy hull began to glide so gently. I held her hand tight; the tears came into eyes and throat, and one could not get out a word. The sturdy hull dived into the glittering water; a sunny haze lay over the whole picture. Never shall I forget the moment we stood there together, looking out over the scene. And to think of all that has happened these four last months! Separated by sea and land and ice; coming years, too, lying between us – it is all just the continuation of what happened that day. But how long is it to last? I have such difficulty in feeling that I am not to see home again soon. When I begin to reflect, I know that it may be long, but I will not believe it.

To-day, moreover, we took solemn farewell of the sun. Half of its disk showed at noon for the last time above the edge of the ice in the south, a flattened body, with a dull red glow, but no heat. Now we are entering the night of winter. What is it bringing us? Where shall we be when the sun returns? No one can tell.

Friday, October 27th. The soundings this morning showed 52 fathoms (95 m.) of water. According to observations taken yesterday afternoon, we are about 3' farther north and a little farther west than on the 19th. It is disgusting the way we are muddling about here. We must have got into a hole where the ice grinds round and round, and can't get farther. And the time is passing all to no purpose; and goodness only knows how long this sort of thing may go on. If only a good south wind would come and drive us north out of this hobble!

Sunday, October 29th. Peter shot a white fox this morning close in to the ship. For some time lately we have been seeing fox-tracks in the mornings, and one Sunday Mogstad saw the fox itself. It has, no doubt, been coming regularly to feed on the offal of the bears. Shortly after the first one was shot another was seen; it came and smelt its dead comrade, but soon set off again and disappeared. It is remarkable that there should be so many foxes on this drift-ice so far from land.

Monday, October 30th. To-day the temperature has gone down to 18° below zero (–27° C.). I took up the dredge I had put out yesterday. It brought up two pails of mud from the bottom, and I have been busy all day washing this out in the saloon in a large bath, to get the many animals contained in it. They were chiefly starfish, waving starfish, medusæ *(Astrophyton)*, sea-slugs, coral insects *(Alcyonaria)*, worms, sponges, shell-fish, and crustaceans; and were, of course, all carefully preserved in spirits.

Tuesday, October 31st. Forty-nine fathoms (90 m.) of water to-day, and the current driving us hard to the southwest. We have good wind for the mill now, and the electric lamps burn all day. The arc lamp under the skylight makes us quite forget the want of sun. Oh! light is a glorious thing, and life is fair in spite of all privations! This is Sverdrup's birthday, and we had revolver practice in the morning. Of course a magnificent dinner of five courses—chicken soup, boiled mackerel, reindeer ribs with baked cauliflower and potatoes, macaroni pudding, and stewed pears with milk – Ringnes ale to wash it down.

Sunday, November 5th. A great race on the ice was advertised for to-day. The course was measured, marked off, and decorated with flags. The cook had prepared the prizes – cakes, numbered, and properly graduated in size. The expectation was great; but it turned out that, from excessive training during the few last days, the whole crew were so stiff in the legs that they were not able to move. We got our prizes all the same.

So it is Sunday once more. How the days drag past! I work, read, think, and dream; strum a little on the organ; go for a walk on the ice in the dark. Low on the horizon in the southwest there is the flush of the sun – a dark fierce red, as if of blood aglow with all life's smouldering longings – low and far-off, like the dreamland of youth. I can sit and gaze and gaze, my eyes entranced by the dream-glow yonder in the west, where the moon's thin, pale, silver sickle is dipping its point into the blood; and my soul is borne beyond the glow, to the sun, so far off now – and to the home-coming! Our task accomplished, we are making our way up the fjord as fast as sail and steam can carry us. On both sides of us the homeland lies smiling in the sun; and then . . . the sufferings of a thousand days and hours melt into a moment's inexpressible joy. Ugh! that was a bitter gust – I jump up and walk on. What am I dreaming about! so far yet from the goal – hundreds and hundreds of miles between us, ice and land and ice again. And we are drift-ing round and round in a ring, bewildered, attaining nothing, only waiting, always waiting, for what?

Wednesday, November 8th. The storm (which we had had the two previous days) is quite gone down; not even enough breeze for the mill. We tried letting the dogs sleep on the ice last night, instead of bringing them on board in the evening, as we have been doing lately. The result was that another dog was torn to pieces during the night. It was 'Ulabrand,' the old brown, toothless fellow, that went this time. 'Job' and 'Moses' had gone the same way before. Yesterday evening's observations place us in 77° 43' north latitude and 138° 8' east longitude. This is farther south than we have been yet. No help for it; but it is a sorry state of matters; and that we are farther east than ever before is only a poor consolation.

Here I sit in the still winter night on the drifting ice-floe, and see only stars above me. Far off I see the threads of life twisting them-selves into the intricate web which stretches unbroken from life's sweet morning dawn to the eternal death-stillness of the ice. Thought follows thought – you pick the whole to pieces, and it seems so small – but high above all towers one form . . . *Why did you take this voyage?* . . . Could I do otherwise? Can the river arrest its course and run up hill? My plan has come to nothing. That palace of theory which I reared, in pride and self-confidence, high above all silly objections has fallen like a house of cards at the first breath of wind. Build up the most ingenious theories and you may be sure of one thing – that fact will defy them all. Was I so very sure? Yes, at times; but that was self-deception, intoxication. A secret doubt lurked behind all the reasoning. It seemed as though the longer I defended my theory, the nearer I came to doubting it. But *no*, there is no getting over the evidence of that Siberian drift-wood.

But if, after all, we are on the wrong track, what then? Only disappointed human hopes, nothing more. And even if we perish, what will it matter in the endless cycles of eternity?

Monday, December 25th (Christmas-day). Thermometer at 36° Fahr. below zero (−38° C.). I took a walk south in the beautiful light of the full moon. At a newly made crack I went through the fresh ice with one leg and got soaked; but such an accident matters very little in this frost. The water immediately stiffens into ice; it does not make one very cold, and one feels dry again soon.

They will be thinking much of us just now at home and giving many a pitying sigh over all the hardships we are enduring in this cold, cheerless, icy region. But I am afraid their compassion would cool if they could look in upon us, hear the merriment that goes on, and see all our comforts and good cheer. They can hardly be better off at home. I myself have certainly never lived a more sybaritic life, and have never had more reason to fear the consequences it brings in its train. Just listen to to-day's dinner menu:

1. Ox-tail soup;
2. Fish-pudding, with potatoes and melted butter;
3. Roast of reindeer, with pease, French beans, potatoes, and cranberry jam;

4. Cloudberries with cream;
5. Cake and marchpane (a welcome present from the baker to the expedition; we blessed that man).

And along with all this that Ringnes bock-beer which is so famous in our part of the world. Was this the sort of dinner for men who are to be hardened against the horrors of the Arctic night?

Tuesday, December 26th. 36° Fahr. below zero (−38° C.). This (the same as yesterday's) is the greatest cold we have had yet. I went a long way north to-day; found a big lane covered with newly frozen ice, with a quite open piece of water in the middle. The ice rocked up and down under my steps, sending waves out into the open pool. It was strange once more to see the moonlight playing on the coal-black waves, and awakened a remembrance of well-known scenes. I followed this lane far to the north, seemed to see the outlines of high land in the hazy light below the moon, and went on and on; but in the end it turned out to be a bank of clouds behind the moonlit vapor rising from the open water. I saw from a high hummock that this opening stretched north as far as the eye could reach.

The same luxurious living as yesterday; a dinner of four courses. Shooting with darts at a target for cigarettes has been the great excitement of the day. Darts and target are Johansen's Christmas present from Miss Fougner.

Wednesday, December 27th. Wind began to blow this afternoon, 19½ to 26 feet per second; the windmill is going again, and the arc lamp once more brightens our lives. Johansen gave notice of 'a shooting-match by electric light, with free concert,' for the evening. It was a pity for himself that he did, for he and several others were shot into bankruptcy and beggary, and had to retire one after the other, leaving their cigarettes behind them.

Thursday, December 28th. A little forward of the *Fram* there is a broad, newly formed open lane, in which she could lie cross-ways. It was covered with last night's ice, in which slight pressure began to-day. It is strange how indifferent we are to this pressure, which was the cause of such great trouble to many earlier Arctic navigators. We have not so much as made the smallest prepara-tion for possible accident, no provisions on deck, no tent, no clothing in readiness. This may seem like recklessness, but in real-ity there is not the slightest prospect of the pressure harming us; we know now what the *Fram* can bear. Proud of our splendid, strong ship, we stand on her deck watching the ice come hurtling against her sides, being crushed and broken there and having to go down below her, while new ice-masses tumble upon her out of the dark, to meet the same fate. Here and there, amid deafening noise, some great mass rises up and launches itself threateningly upon the bulwarks, only to sink down suddenly, dragged the same way as the others. But at times when one hears the roaring of tremendous pressure in the night, as a rule so deathly still, one cannot but call to mind the disasters that this uncontrollable power has wrought.

I am reading the story of Kane's expedition just now. Unfor-tunate man, his preparations were miserably inadequate; it seems to me to have been a reckless, unjustifiable proceeding to set out with such equipments. Almost all the dogs died of bad food; all the men had scurvy from the same cause, with snow-blindness, frost-bites, and all kinds of miseries. He learned a wholesome awe of the Arctic night, and one can hardly wonder at it.

I am almost ashamed of the life we lead, with none of those darkly painted sufferings of the long winter night which are indis-pensable to a properly exciting Arctic expedition. We shall have nothing to write about when we get home.

CHAPTER 7

'ANDRÉE'S SECOND DIARY'

from *Andrée's Story* (1930)

Salomon August Andrée

Salomon August Andrée was a Swedish engineer who worked in the Stockholm patent office. His plan to reach the North Pole by hydrogen balloon held great appeal for the Swedes, who feared they were losing the polar competition to Fridtjof Nansen and the Norwegians. With two companions, Andrée took off from Spitsbergen on July 11, 1897. There is a good deal of evidence that Andrée knew, but kept secret, the fact that his balloon, the Eagle, was leaking gas and therefore could not make it to the Pole. On July 14 1897, 200 miles from its departure point, the Eagle crashed. Andrée spent the next ten weeks trekking over the ice, finally reaching a tiny island in the Svalbard Archipelago. The excerpt below is all that was decipherable from the final pages of Andrée's diaries, which were discovered thirty years later along with his body and those of his companions.

Page 1   897
        ...... with cutti[ng] ......
        .... beginning of a
        .... the hut hung
        .... the day passed
        ....

...... imp ... ... vation

.... to

.... all too

.... we there as a matter of

...... a not unimportant

...... of the island correctly. But

.... could with

.... the lowland. The question

.... here with everything

.... t ... ...we first

.... to reach

....

.... of

.... should

.... and up

.... on the island.

Page 2 In the evening 5 b ....

Riders or geese ....

5th in the morning ....

the previously mentioned ....

we had ....

lucky that we ....

there and ....

ing it ....

I .... t ...

along the glacier................   ....

from the glacier ....

our hard ... ... not ....

even if late at night............   ....

the day's energetic labour ...   .

middle of the night............ ....
.... for the (flaming) .... outside ...
northern lights neither   ....
warmed ... ...
.... k ....
.... my ....
We christened o[n] [acc]ount   ....
of this the district ....
the place to 'M .... place'.........

Page 3   .... during the day the 6th
.... heavy wind w
.... could not ...... much
.... undertook however a short
.... we at last
.... Swedes
.... to be the
.... icy
.... at once interes-
.... we ... high
.... from the sea found
.... All the ground
.... stone-brash
.... of the gravel was
.... Granite lay partly
.... great walls [ridges?]
.... which however were
.... If ... . could
.... whole
.... (large)
.... in darkness.

.... in the snow-
hut .... transport of the goods
the .... neighbourhood. This was
a heavy .... was done

Page 4 ...... g was busy ... . at ...
feared that... ....
such with ....
which we f. ....
of it. ....
rings ....
cier. ....
had set foot.......... ....
if it possibly ....
to look at tr ....
the glacier ....
ought I think ....
than one ....
the visible ....
the sea but .... k . ...
not since............. ....
to. Our ....
s ... ...
worth ... .
......mon with ... .
and intestine .... envious
now give ... . impression ... innocent
white doves but of .... l carrion
birds ....

Page 5 .... bad weather and we fear ......
.... we keep in the tent the whole day
.... so that we could
.... on the hut.
.... to escape
.... like
.... out on the sea
.... crash ... . grating
.... driftwood
.... to move about a little
.... ermits

CHAPTER 8

'WE REACH THE POLE'

from *The North Pole* (1910)

Robert Peary

The American explorer Robert Peary claimed to have reached the North Pole on 6 April 1909, after having wintered on Ellesmere Island. This claim has been much disputed. Critics have noted that no one who accompanied Peary on the final leg of his journey was trained in navigation, and that the pace the explorer supposedly set after his last support party headed back was several times faster than that set during the rest of the journey. (Disturbed by Peary's lack of corroboration, Congress even held hearings into the matter.) In 1989, National Geographic, *which had been a major backer of Peary's 1909 expedition, concluded that if he did miss the Pole, it was not by more than five miles. This finding, too, has been disputed.*

The last march northward ended at ten o'clock on the forenoon of April 6. I had now made the five marches planned from the point at which Bartlett turned back, and my reckoning showed that we were in the immediate neighborhood of the goal of all our striving. After the usual arrangements for going into camp, at approximate local noon, of the Columbia meridian, I made the first observation at our polar camp. It indicated our position as 89° 57′.

We were now at the end of the last long march of the upward journey. Yet with the Pole actually in sight I was too weary to take the last few steps. The accumulated weariness of all those days and nights of forced marches and insufficient sleep, constant peril and anxiety, seemed to roll across me all at once. I was actually too exhausted to realize at the moment that my life's purpose had been achieved. As soon as our igloos had been completed and we had eaten our dinner and double-rationed the dogs, I turned in for a few hours of absolutely necessary sleep, Henson and the Eskimos having unloaded the sledges and got them in readiness for such repairs as were necessary. But, weary though I was, I could not sleep long. It was, therefore, only a few hours later when I woke. The first thing I did after awaking was to write these words in my diary: 'The Pole at last. The prize of three centuries. My dream and goal for twenty years. Mine at last! I cannot bring myself to realize it. It seems all so simple and commonplace.'

Everything was in readiness for an observation at 6 P.M., Columbia meridian time, in case the sky should be clear, but at that hour it was, unfortunately, still overcast. But as there were indications that it would clear before long, two of the Eskimos and myself made ready a light sledge carrying only the instruments, a tin of pemmican, and one or two skins; and drawn by a double team of dogs, we pushed on an estimated distance of ten miles. While we traveled, the sky cleared, and at the end of the journey, I was able to get a satisfactory series of observations at Columbia meridian midnight. These observations indicated that our position was then beyond the Pole.

Nearly everything in the circumstances which then surrounded us seemed too strange to be thoroughly realized; but one of the strangest of those circumstances seemed to me to be the fact that, in a march of only a few hours, I had passed from the western to the eastern hemisphere and had verified my position at the summit of the world. It was hard to realize that, in the first miles of this brief march, we had been traveling due north, while, on the last few miles of the same march, we had been traveling south, although we had all the time been traveling precisely in the same direction. It would be difficult to imagine a better illustration of the fact that most things are relative. Again, please consider the uncommon circumstance that, in order to return to our camp, it now became necessary to turn and go north again for a few miles and then to go directly south, all the time traveling in the same direction.

As we passed back along that trail which none had ever seen before or would ever see again, certain reflections intruded themselves which, I think, may fairly be called unique. East, west, and north had disappeared for us. Only one direction remained and that was south. Every breeze which could possibly blow upon us, no matter from what point of the horizon, must be a south wind. Where we were, one day and one night constituted a year, a hundred such days and nights constituted a century. Had we stood in that spot during the six months of the arctic winter night, we should have seen every star of the northern hemisphere circling the sky at the same distance from the horizon, with Polaris (the North Star) practically in the zenith.

All during our march back to camp the sun was swinging around in its ever-moving circle. At six o'clock on the morning of April 7, having again arrived at Camp Jesup, I took another series of observations. These indicated our position as being four or five miles from the Pole, towards Bering Strait. Therefore, with a double team of dogs and a light sledge, I traveled directly towards the sun an estimated distance of eight miles. Again I returned to the camp in time for a final and completely satisfactory series of observations on April 7 at noon, Columbia meridian time. These observations gave results essentially the same as those made at the same spot twenty-four hours before.

I had now taken in all thirteen single, or six and one-half double, altitudes of the sun, at two different stations, in three different directions, at four different times. All were under satisfactory conditions, except for the first single altitude on the sixth. The temperature during these observations had been from minus 11° Fahrenheit to minus 30° Fahrenheit, with clear sky and calm weather (except as already noted for the single observation on the sixth).

In traversing the ice in these various directions as I had done, I had allowed approximately ten miles for possible errors in my observations, and at some moment during these marches and countermarches, I had passed over or very near the point* where north and south and east and west blend into one.

---

* Ignorance and misconception of all polar matters seem so widespread and comprehensive that it appears advisable to introduce here a few a b c paragraphs. Anyone interested can supplement these by reading the introductory parts of any good elementary school geography or astronomy.

The North Pole (that is, the geographical pole as distinguished from the magnetic pole, and this appears to be the first and most general stumbling block of the ignorant) is simply the point where that imaginary line known as the earth's axis – that is, the line on which the earth revolves in its daily motion – intersects the earth's surface.

Some of the recent sober discussions as to the size of the North Pole, whether it was as big as a quarter, or a hat, or a township, have been intensely ludicrous.

Precisely speaking, the North Pole is simply a mathematical point, and therefore, in accordance with the mathematical definition of a point, it has neither length, breadth, nor thickness.

If the question is asked, how closely can the Pole be determined (this is the point which has muddled some of the ignorant wiseacres), the answer will be: That depends upon the character of the instruments used, the ability of the observer using them, and the number of observations taken.

Of course there were some more or less informal ceremonies connected with our arrival at our dfficult destination, but they were not of a very elaborate character. We planted five flags at the top of the world. The first one was a silk American flag which Mrs. Peary gave me fifteen years ago. That flag has done more traveling in high latitudes than any other ever made. I carried it wrapped about my body on every one of my expeditions northward after it came into my possession, and I left a fragment of it at each of my successive 'farthest norths': Cape Morris K. Jesup, the northernmost point of land in the known world; Cape Thomas Hubbard, the northernmost known point of Jesup Land, west of Grant Land; Cape Columbia, the northernmost point of North American lands; and my farthest north in 1906, latitude 87° 6' in the ice of the polar sea. By the time it actually reached the Pole, therefore, it was somewhat worn and discolored.

If there were land at the Pole, and powerful instruments of great precision, such as are used in the world's great observatories, were mounted there on suitable foundations and used by practised observers for repeated observations extending over years, then it would be possible to determine the position of the Pole with great precision.

With ordinary field instruments, transit, theodolite, or sextant, an extended series of observations by an expert observer should permit the determination of the Pole within entirely satisfactory limits, but not with the same precision as by the first method.

A single observation at sea with sextant and the natural horizon, as usually taken by the master of a ship, is assumed under ordinary satisfactory conditions to give the observer's position within about a mile.

In regard to the difficulties of taking observations in the arctic regions, I have found a tendency on the part of experts who, however, have not had practical experience in the arctic regions themselves, to overestimate and exaggerate the difficulties and drawbacks of making these observations due to the cold.

My personal experience has been that, to an experienced observer, dressed in furs and taking observations in calm weather, in temperatures not exceeding say

A broad diagonal section of this ensign would now mark the farthest goal of earth – the place where I and my dusky companions stood.

It was also considered appropriate to raise the colors of the Delta Kappa Epsilon fraternity, in which I was initiated a member while an undergraduate student at Bowdoin College, the 'World's Ensign of Liberty and Peace,' with its red, white, and blue in a field of white, the Navy League flag, and the Red Cross flag.

After I had planted the American flag in the ice, I told Henson to time the Eskimos for three rousing cheers, which they gave with the greatest enthusiasm. Thereupon, I shook hands with each member of the party – surely a sufficiently unceremonious affair to meet with the approval of the most democratic. The Eskimos were childishly delighted with our success. While, of course, they did not realize its importance fully, or its world-wide significance, they did understand that it meant the final achievement of a task upon which they had seen me engaged for many years.

40° below zero Fahrenheit, the difficulties of the work resulting from cold alone are not serious. The amount and character of errors due to the effect of cold upon the instrument might perhaps be a subject for discussion, and for distinct differences of opinion.

My personal experience has been that my most serious trouble was with the eyes.

To eyes which have been subjected to brilliant and unremitting daylight for days and weeks, and to the strain of continually setting a course with the compass, and traveling towards a fixed point in such light, the taking of a series of observations is usually a nightmare; and the strain of focusing, of getting precise contact of the sun's images, and of reading the vernier, all in the blinding light of which only those who have taken observations in bright sunlight on an unbroken snow expanse in the arctic regions can form any conception, usually leaves the eyes bloodshot and smarting for hours afterwards.

The continued series of observations in the vicinity of the Pole, noted above, left me with eyes that were, for two or three days, useless for anything requiring

Then, in a space between the ice blocks of a pressure ridge, I deposited a glass bottle containing a diagonal strip of my flag and records of which the following is a copy:

90 N. LAT., NORTH POLE,

April 6, 1909.

Arrived here to-day, 27 marches from C. Columbia.

I have with me 5 men, Matthew Henson, colored, Ootah, Egingwah, Seegloo, and Ookeah, Eskimos; 5 sledges and 38 dogs. My ship, the S. S. *Roosevelt*, is in winter quarters at C. Sheridan, 90 miles east of Columbia.

The expedition under my command which has succeeded in reaching the Pole is under the auspices of the Peary Arctic Club of New York City, and has been fitted out and sent north by the members and friends of the club for the purpose of securing this geographical prize, if possible, for the honor and prestige of the United States of America.

careful vision, and had it been necessary for me to set a course during the first two or three days of our return I should have found it extremely trying.

Snow goggles, as worn by us continually during the march, while helping, do not entirely relieve the eyes from strain, and during a series of observations the eyes become extremely tired and at times uncertain.

Various authorities will give different estimates of the probable error in observations taken at the Pole. I am personally inclined to think that an allowance of five miles is an equitable one.

No one, except those entirely ignorant of such matters, has imagined for a moment that I was able to determine with my instruments the precise position of the Pole, but after having determined its position approximately then, setting an arbitrary allowance of about ten miles for possible errors of the instruments and myself as observer, and then crossing and recrossing that ten mile area in various directions, no one except the most ignorant will have any doubt but what, at some time, I had passed close to the precise point, and had, perhaps, actually passed over it.

The officers of the club are Thomas H. Hubbard, of New York, President; Zenas Crane, of Mass., Vice-president; Herbert L. Bridgman, of New York, Secretary and Treasurer.

I start back for Cape Columbia to-morrow.

ROBERT E. PEARY,

United States Navy.

90 N. LAT., NORTH POLE,

April 6, 1909.

I have to-day hoisted the national ensign of the United States of America at this place, which my observations indicate to be the North Polar axis of the earth, and have formally taken possession of the entire region, and adjacent, for and in the name of the President of the United States of America.

I leave this record and United States flag in possession.

ROBERT E. PEARY,

United States Navy.

If it were possible for a man to arrive at 90° north latitude without being utterly exhausted, body and brain, he would doubtless enjoy a series of unique sensations and reflections. But the attainment of the Pole was the culmination of days and weeks of forced marches, physical discomfort, insufficient sleep, and racking anxiety. It is a wise provision of nature that the human consciousness can grasp only such degree of intense feeling as the brain can endure, and the grim guardians of earth's remotest spot will accept no man as guest until he has been tried and tested by the severest ordeal.

Perhaps it ought not to have been so, but when I knew for a certainty that we had reached the goal, there was not a thing in the world I wanted but sleep. But after I had a few hours of it, there succeeded a condition of mental exaltation which made further rest impossible. For more than a score of years that point on the earth's surface had been the object of my every effort. To its attainment my whole being, physical, mental, and moral, had been dedicated. Many times my own life and the lives of those with me had been risked. My own material and forces and those of my friends had been devoted to this object. This journey was my eighth into the arctic wilderness. In that wilderness I had spent nearly twelve years out of the twenty-three between my thirtieth and my fifty-third year, and the intervening time spent in civilized communities during that period had been mainly occupied with preparations for returning to the wilderness. The determination to reach the Pole had become so much a part of my being that, strange as it may seem, I long ago ceased to think of myself save as an instrument for the attainment of that end. To the layman this may seem strange, but an inventor can understand it, or an artist, or anyone who has devoted himself for years upon years to the service of an idea.

But though my mind was busy at intervals during those thirty hours spent at the Pole with the exhilarating thought that my dream had come true, there was one recollection of other times that, now and then, intruded itself with startling distinctness. It was the recollection of a day three years before, April 21, 1906, when after making a fight with ice, open water, and storms, the expedition which I commanded had been forced to turn back from 87° 6' north latitude because our supply of food would carry us no further. And the contrast between the terrible depression of that day and the exaltation of the present moment was not the least pleasant feature of our brief stay at the Pole. During the dark moments of that return journey in 1906, I had told myself that I was only one in a long list of arctic explorers, dating back through the centuries, all the way from Henry Hudson to the Duke of the Abruzzi, and including Franklin, Kane, and Melville – a long list of valiant men who had striven and failed. I told myself that I had only succeeded, at the price of the best years of my life, in adding a few links to the chain that led from the parallels of civilization towards the polar center, but that, after all, at the end the only word I had to write was failure.

But now, while quartering the ice in various directions from our camp, I tried to realize that, after twenty-three years of struggles and discouragement, I had at last succeeded in placing the flag of my country at the goal of the world's desire. It is not easy to write about such a thing, but I knew that we were going back to civilization with the last of the great adventure stories – a story the world had been waiting to hear for nearly four hundred years, a story which was to be told at last under the folds of the Stars and Stripes, the flag that during a lonely and isolated life had come to be for me the symbol of home and everything I loved – and might never see again.

The thirty hours at the Pole, what with my marchings and countermarchings, together with the observations and records, were pretty well crowded. I found time, however, to write to Mrs. Peary on a United States postal card which I had found on the ship during the winter. It had been my custom at various important stages of the journey northward to write such a note in order that, if anything serious happened to me, these brief communications might ultimately reach her at the hands of survivors. This was the card, which later reached Mrs. Peary at Sydney: –

'90 NORTH LATITUDE, April 7th.

'*My dear Jo,*

'I have won out at last. Have been here a day. I start for home and you in an hour. Love to the "kidsies."

'BERT.'

In the afternoon of the 7th, after flying our flags and taking our photographs, we went into our igloos and tried to sleep a little, before starting south again.

I could not sleep and my two Eskimos, Seegloo and Egingwah, who occupied the igloo with me, seemed equally restless. They turned from side to side, and when they were quiet I could tell from their uneven breathing that they were not asleep. Though they had not been specially excited the day before when I told them that we had reached the goal, yet they also seemed to be under the same exhilarating influence which made sleep impossible for me.

Finally I rose, and telling my men and the three men in the other igloo, who were equally wakeful, that we would try to make our last camp, some thirty miles to the south, before we slept, I gave orders to hitch up the dogs and be off. It seemed unwise to waste such perfect traveling weather in tossing about on the sleeping platforms of our igloos.

Neither Henson nor the Eskimos required any urging to take to the trail again. They were naturally anxious to get back to the land as soon as possible – now that our work was done. And about four o'clock on the afternoon of the 7th of April we turned our backs upon the camp at the North Pole.

Though intensely conscious of what I was leaving, I did not wait for any lingering farewell of my life's goal. The event of human beings standing at the hitherto inaccessible summit of the earth was accomplished, and my work now lay to the south, where four hundred and thirteen nautical miles of ice-floes and possibly open leads still lay between us and the north coast of Grant Land. One backward glance I gave – then turned my face toward the south and toward the future.

CHAPTER 9

'KASIAGSAK, THE GREAT LIAR'

from *Tales and Traditions of the Eskimo* (1875)

Hinrich Rink

Hinrich Rink served as Royal Inspector of South Greenland for the Danish government. During his years on the island, he made many scientific and ethnographic studies of the region. His Tales and Traditions of the Eskimo, *first published in 1875, contains several dozen stories, mostly from Greenland, which Rink transcribed in Danish and then translated into English.*

Kasiagsak, who was living with a great many skilful seal-hunters, always returned in the evening without a catch of his own. When he was out, his wife, named Kitlagsuak, was always restless and fidgety, running out and in looking out for him, in the hope that he might be bringing home something; but he generally returned empty-handed. One day, being out in his kayak, he observed a black spot on a piece of ice, and it soon turned to be a little seal. His first intention was to harpoon it, but he changed his mind, and broke out, saying, 'Poor little thing! it is almost a pity. Perhaps it has already been wounded by somebody else; perhaps it will slide down in the water when I approach it, and then I need only take hold of it with my hands.' So saying he gave a shout, at which the seal was not slow to get down. Presently it appeared close before the point of his kayak; but he called out still louder than before, and the seal went on diving up and down quite close to him. At length he made up his mind to chase and harpoon it; but somehow it always rose at a greater distance, and was soon entirely lost to him. Kasiagsak now put back, merely observing, 'Ye silly thing! ye are not easy to get at; but just wait till next time.'

Another day he went seaward in bright, fine weather. Looking towards land he got sight of the other kayakers, and observed that one of them had just harpooned a seal, and that the others were all hurrying on to his assistance. As to himself, he never stirred, but remained quite unconcerned in his former place. He also noticed that the one who had caught the seal tugged it to the shore, and made it fast to a rock on the beach, intending to return in pursuit of others. He instantly put further out to sea; but when he had got quite out of sight he returned to the beach by a roundabout way, and made straight for the other man's seal, and carried it off. The towing-line was all around ornamented with walrus-teeth, and he was greatly delighted at the prospect of getting home with this prize. Meanwhile his wife had been wandering about in expectation of him, and looking out for the returning kayakers. She at length cried out, 'There is a kayak!' — at which more people came running out; and shading her eyes with her hand, she continued, 'It looks like Kasiagsak, and he moves his arms like one tugging something along with him. Well, I suppose it will now be my turn to give you a share, and ye shall all get a nice piece of blubber.' As soon as he landed she hastened to ask him, 'Where didst thou get that beautiful tugging-line?' He answered, 'This morning at setting out I thought it might come in handy, as I was bent on having a catch, and so I brought it out with me; I have kept it in store this long time.' 'Hast thou, indeed?' she rejoined, and then began the flensing and carving business. She put the head, the back, and the skin aside; all the rest, as well as the blubber, she intended to make a grand feast upon. The other kayakers successively returned, and she took care to inform each of them separately that a seal was already brought home; and when some of the women came back from a ramble on the beach, she repeated the whole thing over to them. But while they were sitting down to supper in the evening, a boy entered, saying, 'I have been sent to ask for the towing-line; as to the seal, that is no matter.' Turning to Kasiagsak, his wife now put in, 'Didst thou tell me an untruth?' He only answered, 'To be sure I did;' whereto his wife remarked, 'What a shame it is that Kasiagsak behaves thus!' but he only made a wry face, saying, 'Bah!' which made her quite frightened; and when they lay down to rest he went on pinching her and whistling until they both fell asleep.

Another day, rowing about in his kayak, he happened to observe a black spot away on a flake of ice. On nearing it he made it out to be only a stone. He glanced round towards the other kayakers, and then suddenly feigned to be rowing hard up to a seal, at the same time lifting the harpoon ready to lance it; but presently went to hide himself behind a projecting point of the ice, from which he managed to climb it and roll the stone into the sea with a splash, making it all froth and foam. Meanwhile he got into his kayak again, making a great roar in order to call the others to his assistance. When they came up to him they observed that he had no bladder, and he said, 'A walrus has just gone down with my bladder; do help me to catch sight of him; meantime I will turn back and tell that I have lanced a walrus.' He hurried landwards, and his wife, who happened to be on the look-out, again shouted, 'A kayaker!' He called out that he had made a lucky hit. 'I almost do believe it is Kasiagsak; do ye hear him in there?' Meantime he had approached the shore, and said, 'In chasing a walrus I lost my bladder; I only came home to tell you this.' His wife now came running into the house, but being in such a hurry she broke the handle of her knife. However, she did not mind this, but merely said, 'Now I can get a handle of walrus-tooth for my knife, and a new hook for my kettle.' In the evening Kasiagsak had chosen a seat on the hindermost part of the ledge, so that only his heels were to be seen. The other kayakers stayed out rather long; but the last of them on entering brought a harpoon-line and a bladder along with him, and turning to Kasiagsak observed, 'I think it is thine; it must have been tied round some stone and have slipped off; here it is.' His wife exclaimed, 'Hast thou been telling us new lies?' at which he only answered her, 'Why, yes; I wanted to play you a trick, you see.'

Another day, when he was kayaking along the coast, he remarked some loose pieces of ice away on a sandy beach at some distance; he rowed up to them and went ashore. Two women, gathering berries, watched his doings all along. They saw him fill his kayak with bits of broken ice; and this done, he waded down into the water till it reached his very neck, and then turned back and got upon the beach, where he set to hammering his kayak all over with stones; and having finally stuffed his coat with ice, he turned towards home. At some distance he commenced shrieking aloud and crying, 'Ah me! a big iceberg went calving (bursting and capsizing) right across my kayak, and came down on the top of me;' and his wife repeated his ejaculations, adding, 'I must go and see about some dry clothes for him.' At last they got him up on shore, and large bits of ice came tumbling out of his clothes, while he went on lamenting and groaning as if with pain, saying, 'I had a very narrow escape.' His wife repeated the tale of his misfortunes to every kayaker on his return home; but at last it so happened that the two women who had seen him likewise returned, and they at once exclaimed, 'Is not that he whom we saw down below the sand-cliffs, stuffing his clothes with ice.' On this, the wife cried out, 'Dear me! has Kasiagsak again been lying to us?' Subsequently Kasiagsak went to pay a visit to his father-in-law. On entering the house he exclaimed, 'Why, what's the matter with you that your lamps are not burning, and ye are boiling dog's flesh?' 'Alas!' answered the master, pointing to his little son, 'he was hungry, poor fellow! and having nothing else to eat we killed the dog.' Kasiagsak boastingly answered him, 'Yesterday we had a hard job at home. One of the women and I had our hands full with the great heaps of seals and walruses that have been caught. I have got both my storehouses chokefull with them; my arms are quite sore with the work.' The father-in-law now rejoined, 'Who would ever have thought that the poor little orphan boy Kasiagsak should turn out such a rich man!' and so saying, he began crying with emotion; and Kasiagsak feigned crying likewise. On parting from them the following day, he proposed that his little brother-in-law should accompany him in order to bring back some victuals, adding, 'I will see thee home again;' and his father said, 'Well, dostn't thou hear what thy brother-in-law is saying? thou hadst better go.' On reaching home, Kasiagsak took hold of a string and brought it into the house, where he busied himself in making a trap, and taking some scraps of frizzled blubber from his wife's lamp, he thrust them out as baits for the ravens. Suddenly he gave a pull at the string, crying out, 'Two! – alas! one made its escape;' and then he ran out and brought back a raven, which his wife skinned and boiled. But his brother-in-law had to look to the other people for some food; and at his departure the next day, he likewise received all his presents from them, and not from Kasiagsak.

Another day he set off in his kayak to visit some people at a neighbouring station. Having entered one of the houses, he soon noticed that some of the inmates were mourning the loss of some one deceased. He questioned the others, and on hearing that they had lost a little daughter named Nepisanguak, he hastened in a loud voice to state, 'We have just got a little daughter at home, whom we have called Nepisanguak;' on which the mourning parents and relations exclaimed, 'Thanks be to thee that ye have called her by that name;' and then they wept, and Kasiagsak also made believe to be weeping; but he peeped through his fingers all the while. Later in the day they treated him richly with plenty of good things to eat. Kasiagsak went on saying, 'Our little daughter cannot speak plainly as yet; she only cries "*apangaja!*"' but the others said, 'She surely means "*sapangaja*"' (sapangat, beads); 'we will give thee some for her;' and at his departure he was loaded with gifts – such as beads, a plate, and some seal-paws. Just as he was going to start, one of the men cried out to him, 'I would fain buy a kayak, and I can pay it back with a good pot; make it known to the people in thy place.' But Kasiagsak said, 'Give it to me; I have got a new kayak, but it is a little too narrow for my size.' At length he started along with his presents, and the pot stuck upon the front part of his kayak. At home he said, 'Such a dreadful accident! a boat must surely have been lost; all these things I bring you here, I have found tossed about on the ice' and his wife hastened into the house to give her cracked old pot a smash, and threw away the shoulder-blades that till now had served her instead of plates, and ornamented her coat with beads, and proudly walked to and fro to make the pearls rattle. The next day a great many kayakers were announced. Kasiagsak instantly kept as far back on the ledge as possible. As soon as the kayakers put in to shore, they called out, 'Tell Kasiagsak to come down and fetch off some victuals we have brought for their little daughter;' but all the reply was, 'Why, they have got no daughter at all.' Another of the men now put in, 'Go and ask Kasiagsak for the new kayak I bought of him;' but the answer was, 'He certainly has no new kayak.' At this information they quickly got up to the house, which they entered, taking their several gifts back, and last of all cutting the flaps ornamented with beads away from the wife's jacket. When the strangers were gone she said as before, 'Kasiagsak has indeed been telling a lie again.' His last invention was this: he one day found a small bit of whale-skin floating on the top of the water, and bringing it home he said, 'I have found the carcass of a whale; follow me and I will show you it:' and the boat was got out, and they started. After a good while they asked him, 'Whereabout is it?' but he merely answered them, 'Away yonder;' and then a little bit further, 'we shall soon get at it.' But when they had gone a long way from home without seeing anything like a floating whale, they got tired of Kasiagsak, and put a stop to all his fibs by killing him then and there.

CHAPTER 10

'SONGS OF THE INUIT'

from *Across Arctic America* (1927)

Knud Rasmussen

Knud Rasmussen, an explorer and anthropologist, was born in 1879 in what is now Ilulissat, Greenland, to a Danish father and an Inuit mother. His knowledge of the Greenlandic language allowed him to communicate with native people across the region. Among the books Rasmussen wrote was Across Arctic America: Narrative of the Fifth Thule Expedition, *which chronicled his three-year, 20,000-mile trek, via dogsled, from Greenland to Siberia. This passage is from a section of the book devoted to a song festival of Inuit living on the shore of a lake in northern Canada. The singing takes place in the tent of Rasmussen's host, Igjugarjuk. (An* angakoq *is a shaman.)*

Women do not as a rule sing their own songs. No woman is expected to sing unless expressly invited by an *angakoq*. As a rule, they sing songs made by the men. Should it happen, however, that a woman feels a spirit impelling her to sing, she may step forth from the chorus and follow her own inspiration. Among the women here, only two were thus favored by the spirits; one was Igjugarjuk's first wife, Kivkarjuk, now dethroned, and the other Akjartoq, the mother of Kinalik.

KIVKARJUK'S SONG

I am but a little woman
Very willing to toil,
Very willing and happy
To work and slave.
And in my eagerness
To be of use,
I pluck the furry buds of willow
Buds like beard of wolf.

I love to go walking far and far away,
And my soles are worn through
As I pluck the buds of willow,
That are furry like the great wolf's beard.

AKJARTOQ'S SONG

I draw a deep breath,
But my breath comes heavily
As I call forth the song.

There are ill rumors abroad,
Of some who starve in the far places,
And can find no meat.

I call forth the song
From above,
Hayaya — haya.

And now I forget
How hard it was to breathe,
Remembering old times,

When I had strength
To cut and flay great beasts.
Three great beasts could I cut up
While the sun slowly went his way
Across the sky.

In addition to ordinary hunting songs and lyrics there are songs of derision, satires with a mercilessly personal address; two men will stand up in turn and accuse each other before the assembled neighbors. These accusations, even when well founded, are received with surprising calmness, whereas 'evil or angry words' may have far more serious effects.

I give here Utahania's impeachment of one Kanaijuaq who had quarrelled with his wife and attempted to desert her, leaving her to her fate out in the wilds; the woman, however, had proved not only able to stand up for herself in a rough-and-tumble, but left her husband of her own accord and went to shift for herself, taking her son with her.

Something was whispered
Of man and wife
Who could not agree.
And what was it all about?
A wife who in rightful anger
Tore her husband's furs across,
Took their canoe
And rowed away with her son.
Ay – ay, all who listen,
What do you think of him,
Poor sort of man?
Is he to be envied,

Who is great in his anger
But faint in strength,
Blubbering helplessly
Properly chastised?
Though it was he who foolishly proud
Started the quarrel with stupid words.

Kanaijuaq retorted with a song accusing Utahania of improper
behavior at home; his hard words however, seemed to make no difference to their friendship. Far more serious was the effect of
malicious words in the case of Utahania's foster-son who was once
upbraided by his foster-father as follows:

'I wish you were dead! You are not worth the food you eat.' And
the young man took the words so deeply to heart that he declared
he would never eat again. To make his sufferings as brief as possible, he lay down the same night stark naked on the bare snow, and
was frozen to death.

Halfway through the festival it was announced that Kinalik, the
woman angakoq, would invoke her helping spirits and clear the way
of all dangers ahead. Sila was to be called in to aid one who could
not help himself. All the singing now ceased, and Kinalik stood
forth alone with her eyes tightly closed. She uttered no incantation,
but stood trembling all over, and her face twitched from time to
time as if in pain. This was her way of 'looking inward,' and pen-
etrating the veil of the future; the great thing was to concentrate all
one's force intently on the one idea, of calling forth good for those
about to set out on their journey.

Igjugarjuk, who never let slip an opportunity of exalting his own
tribe at the expense of the 'salt water Eskimo,' informed me at this
juncture that their angakoqs never danced about doing tricks, nor
did they have recourse to particular forms of speech; the one essen-

tial was truth and earnestness – all the rest was mere trickwork designed to impress the vulgar.

When Kinalik had reached the utmost limit of her concentration, I was requested to go outside the tent and stand on a spot where there were no footmarks, remaining there until I was called in. Here, on the untrodden snow, I was to present myself before Sila, standing silent and humble, and desiring sky and air and all the forces of nature to look upon me and show me goodwill.

It was a peculiar form of worship or devotion, which I now encountered for the first time; it was the first time, also, that I had seen Sila represented as a benign power.

After I had stood thus for a time, I was called in again. Kinalik had now resumed her natural expression, and was beaming all over. She assured me that the Great Spirit had heard her prayer, and that all dangers should be removed from our path; also, that we should have success in our hunting whenever we needed meat.

This prophecy was greeted with applause and general satisfaction; it was plain to see that these good folk, in their simple, innocent fashion, gave us their blessing and had done all they could to render it effective. There was no doubting the sincerity of their goodwill.

On the following night: we were racing at full speed over the wintry surface of Lake Hikoligjuaq. The firm ice was spread with a thin layer of soft, moist snow, acting as a soft carpet to the dogs' paws, and the long rest in complete idleness with plenty of fresh caribou meat had given them a degree of vitality that made it a pleasure to be out once more. We had two lads with us as guides, who had borrowed Igjugarjuk's dogs, but it was not long before they were hopelessly out-distanced, and we had to content ourselves with a guess at our direction.

Early in the morning, before the sun was fairly warm, we reached the southern shore of the lake and camped in a pleasant little valley, fastening the dogs in a thicket of young willow that stood bursting in bud to greet the spring.

In the course of the day we went out to reconnoitre. And it was not long before we came upon a solitary caribou hunter observing us from a little hill. He was just taking to flight when the two lads from the last village, who had now come up, recognized him and called him by name, when he walked up smiling to meet them. He informed us that there was a village of five tents a couple of hours' journey farther inland, and that we could reach the place without difficulty, although the ground was bare. We tried to persuade him to come back with us to the camp, but he preferred to go on ahead and tell his comrades of the strange meeting. And before we had gone far, the whole party came down and overtook us, they had been too impatient to wait for our arrival. It was hard work for the dogs to get the sledge over the numerous hills, and even the level ground was difficult going, sodden as it was with water and broken by tussocks and pools. There were plenty of willing hands, however, and we made our way, albeit slowly, with a great deal of merriment. Miteq and I had to face an endless rain of questions. These inland folk look upon the sea as something wonderful and mysterious, far beyond their ken; and when we explained that we had had to cross many seas in coming from our own land to theirs, they regarded our coming in itself as something of a marvel. And we agreed with them in their surprise at our being able to understand one another's speech.

Suddenly speech and laughter died away; the dogs pricked up their ears, and a strange silence fell upon all. There, full in our way, lay the body of a woman prone on the ground. We stood for a moment at a loss. Then the men went forward, while we held back our dogs. The figure still lay motionless. A loud wailing came from the party ahead, and Miteq and I stood vaguely horrified, not knowing what it meant. Then one of the men came back and explained that we had found the corpse of a woman who had been lost in a blizzard the winter before – and he pointed to one of those bending over her; that was her husband.

It had been a hard winter, and just when the cold was most severe, six of those in the village had died of hunger. A man named Atangagjuaq then determined to set out for a neighboring village in search of aid, and his wife, fearing lest, weak as he was, he might be unable to complete the journey, had followed after him. She herself, however, had been lost in the snow before coming up with him. They had searched for her that winter, and in the following spring, but without result; and now here she lay, discovered by the merest accident right athwart our course.

I walked forward to view the body of this woman who had lost her life in a vain attempt to help her husband. There was nothing repulsive in the sight; she just lay there, with limbs extended, and an expression of unspeakable weariness on her face. It was plain to see that she had walked on and on, struggling against the blizzard till she could go no farther, and sank exhausted, while the snow swiftly covered her, leaving no trace.

The body was left lying as it was; no one touched it. We drove on, and in an hour's time reached the Eskimo camp.

These people are quick to change from one extreme of feeling to another. We had not gone far on our way before the dead woman, to all seeming, was forgotten, and the merriment that had met with so sudden a check broke out afresh. As soon as we had put up our tent, the men got hold of our ski, and went off to try them in a good deep snowdrift that still lay in a gap. They had never seen ski before, and great shouts of laughter greeted the first attempts of those venturesome enough to try them. One of the gayest of the party was Atangagjuaq, who but a few minutes earlier had stood weeping beside the body of his wife.

CHAPTER 11

'THE GARDEN OF EDEN'

from *Salamina* (1935)

Rockwell Kent

In Salamina, *the American artist Rockwell Kent chronicles the year (1932–3) that he spent living and painting on Greenland. This selection describes a five-day stay in an isolated house on the Karrat Fjord. Accompanying Kent is a native Greenlander named Pauline, who has been delivered to him — along with rice, coffee and oatmeal — by his local provisioner, David.*

Sunlight to see by, ice to travel on, and work to do. The work was painting. It was for that that I had come to Greenland; by that, and maybe for that, that I lived and found it *almost* good most anywhere, alone. 'If a man,' said Socrates, 'sees a thing when he is alone, he goes about straightway seeking until he finds someone to whom he may show his discoveries, and who may confirm him in them.' So does the artist then seek solitude that, seeing when he is alone, he shall be constrained to such utterance as may endure to seek and find his friends. They will confirm him.

'Discoveries' – are we discoverers then, we writers, poets, sculptors, picture-painters? It is all anyone at most can be. Leif Ericsson, Magellan, Cook, the architect of the first pyramid, the builder of the first arch, Homer, Shakespeare, Euclid, Newton, Einstein: all are discoverers, revealers, of what was and is, of continents, of natural law, of the human soul. God, let us say, made Adam. It was for Michelangelo to discover, as though for the first time, how beautiful God's Adam was. And it remains for all of us, forever, to discover as though for the first time how beautiful the sunrise is, and the moon, and night, and plain and mountain, land and sea, and man and woman; how *beautiful* life is. And whether we pursue discovery in the environment at home which is familiar to us all, or abroad in the remoter and less-known regions of the earth, we'll find the field still unexplored and rich in undiscovered beauty.

[A]bout five miles from Nugatsiak is the island of Karrat, which, though one of the smaller islands of that archipelago, is an imposing landmark by reason of its comparative isolation and the noble architecture of its mountain mass. With towers and buttressed walls reared high upon a steep escarpment, it has the dignity of a great citadel standing to guard the gateway to the glamorous region of Umiamako. I'd thought of some day camping there, to paint. So that when, having arrived at Nugatsiak on this trip with David, it came to my ears that there stood an untenanted house on the western end of Karrat I had at once but one idea: to look it over with a view to staying there. I promptly called upon the owner, a Nugatsiak man, crawled in to him, bowed low to him and stood with bended head in deference to his ceiling and my head, sat with him and his numerous family in one of the smallest, lowliest, dirtiest, and most friendly houses I'd had cause to enter, and got at once his glad consent to use his Karrat house. 'You'll need the key,' he said. 'It is standing in the lock.'

That I went next day to Karrat with supplies for only overnight was sheer stupidity; for no sooner had I seen the cove where stood the house, and had one glimpse of its stupendous views, than it was settled in my mind to stay my time out there. 'You'll leave me here,' I said to David, 'go straight back to Nugatsiak for the night, bring me more canvases and food tomorrow, and then go hunting where you please; and stay – five days.'

The cove, three sides surrounded by the steep hillsides and ledges of the foreland, lay beautifully sheltered from most winds. Its background was the donjon keep of Karrat; it faced the mountainous environs of the mouth of Kangerdlugsuak. One would breathe deep and fast who lived in such a place.

The house I might not readily have found had I been there alone, so dwarfed were man-sized things. David, who knew the place, drove straight in to the head of the cove, whipped the dogs up the steep and high embankment of a knoll, and stopped. An edge of turf across a mound of snow: that was the house.

It took us but a minute or two to clear away the drifted snow from around the low doorway, to turn the key (the owner had been right, the house was locked), pass through the low turf passageway, and enter. We found ourselves inside a sort of ice cave, dimly and glamorously illuminated by the cold daylight which filtered through the snowbank at the window and through a snowed-up stovepipe hole in the roof. Where, through this hole, and through innumerable leaks in the flat roof, water had trickled there hung great glittering ice stalactites that were at variance with my intentions there. And directly under the stovepipe hole – there was no stove – was an accumulated mound of ice a foot thick at its crest. Walls, ceiling, floor; ice, ice: it wasn't as you'd picture home. No matter; it would do. We brought my things indoors, I set the primus up and lighted it and put on snow to melt; in twenty minutes we were drinking coffee. The sound of dripping water filled the house.

And now, with David waiting to depart, I took pencil and paper and drew up a list of those things of which I'd have need in the days to follow. It was a problem to express my wants in such a way as Pavia would understand: I supplemented pigeon Eskimo by art. Rice, oatmeal, coffee, a Greenland halibut – that's all. Oh, no! a postscript just for fun, to make old Pavia laugh. 'And,' – *'ama,'* I wrote, *'niviassak pinakak.'* And I drew a picture of the thing: a pretty girl. Then, instructing David to bring me from my own supplies a quantity of canvases, I sent him on his way.

Who hasn't, over and over again in the course of his life, fixed up places to live in? Houses out of chairs and shawls, houses in trees, houses of snow, caves, lairs in impenetrable thickets, tents, log houses, lofts, abandoned houses, sheds, boats, homes: the thrill of making them is never lost. I looked my ice cave kindly in the face; it wept encouragement. Enough. And with an ardor worthy of the task I set to knocking the stalactites from its hoary brow, scraping the ice from its incrusted cheeks, digging the ice up from – we'll have to drop our physiognomy – the floor, and melting it, as much as my small pocket primus would, from everywhere. And at bedtime I had the deep satisfaction of having converted a dry cold ice cave into an ice-cold sump. Such, we may say, is progress. I crawled into my sleeping-bag and slept.

Just as a painter doesn't *have* to have a duplex studio, north light, and inside balcony with silk brocades draped over it, so does he not have to have an easel. Outdoors they're such a nuisance that I never use them. A stick to prop the canvas with and stones to hold it down: that's good most any time of year. But in *deep* snow, a couch; I found one in my Karrat house. It was a rather elegant affair, homemade, of course, just wood, but shapely, with a sort of arm or back at one end of it. With this couch planted to its belly in the snow, my canvas propped up at the arm-embellished end, my palette flat in front of it, I sat next morning on the hill and worked.

My theme was mountains, and its foreground, snow, the snow plain of the frozen fiord. So hours passed. It must have been near noon when, looking up, I saw that there had crept into my foreground plane a minute sledge propelled by insect dogs. They *did* look small in that immense environment. I left my work and went to meet them at the house.

David had brought my things, I made that out as he drew near. But what a lot of stuff! My canvases, they bulked up large; but it was hard to see just what he had, against the sun's glare on the snow. The hill now hid both sledge and dogs. I heard the whip's report, the shrill yap of a dog; *'Eu, eu!'* the voice of David. Heads down, tails up, the dogs appear, the dogs, the sledge, the driver – David, and – by God – the girl. My postscript in the flesh.

'So you brought everything,' said I to David as we unpacked.

'Yes,' said he, 'I think so.'

'Then come indoors; we'll all have coffee.'

'Five days. Remember, David, and come back.'

'I will,' said David, and drove off.

Pauline—that was her name—and I watched from the hilltop till he turned the point. We waved good-by.

She was a pleasant, quiet-wayed, mature young woman of twenty. She was dumpy, round-cheeked, good-looking only if one fancied Greenland looks. She was a normal, healthy Greenland Eve. But for the respect that I had formed for Spartan Greenland womanhood I would have felt misgivings about the Eden that I had brought her to. She let me put such thoughts away. And whether, during the days that followed, she was occupied with chipping ice from the ceiling, or with digging out the rotting bones and filth from the frozen bog which was the floor, or shivering in idleness, or wading in the snowdrifts to keep warm, she was absolutely, peacefully, content and happy. Entering that dripping house I'd

shudder and, by way of cheer, ask, *'Ajorpa?'* – 'Are things too bad?'
She'd look up from her work and, smiling, say, *'Ajungulak'* – 'It's
good.' We praise the lark for singing under summer skies; Pauline
would stand there singing by the hour in that cave.

We hadn't much to eat; I hadn't figured on two mouths to feed.
For lunch I cooked a mess of rice and pemmican or fish, for supper,
oatmeal porridge – eaten plain. We had no dishes, so we ate by
turns out of the pot; we had no tableware, so I whittled a wooden
spoon from a piece of board. *'Mamapok,'* said Pauline, tasting the
porridge. That means 'Delicious.'

It never got warm in the house, the primus was too small. And
I couldn't burn it continuously, for I had little petroleum. Within
an hour of putting out the stove the floor and lower walls would
freeze again. Pauline had little on. 'Where are your clothes,
Pauline?' I asked. 'There,' she answered, pointing to a pair of
kamiks and an anorak.

There was no way for us to sleep but in my sleeping-bag. If out
of gallantry I'd given it to her, I would out of misery during the
night have crawled into it beside her. And if I hadn't, no one would
believe it. We both got in the bag. We tried to get in with our
clothes on, and we couldn't. Then we took them off. Two fingers
in one finger of a glove: that tight, we managed it. The nights were
hell. We shared the privilege by turns of working out an arm and
leaving it outside to cool and almost freeze. That was our one relief.
She slept a little, but she didn't sing.

I could have sent Pauline back home the day she came: not for
the world would I have sent her back. I'd written for a girl: well,
here she was. And whether Pavia was to be credited with a rare
sense of humor or with incredible efficiency as a storekeeper is
beside the point. *Sent home!* Pauline could never have lived down
the ignominy. She knew that well; and stayed.

By day she'd clean the house, and wash the pot and spoon, and stroll around and sing. And then at night, following the example of my intentioned shamelessness, she'd strip her pauper's garments off and slither into the warm reindeer bag beside me. Poor little shivering, ice-cold, uncomplaining Eskimo: how almost numb with cold she was! Then warmth would come and with it, sometimes, sleep.

The days were uneventful; they were mild and fair. Over our heads the dark deep vault of blue, before our eyes huge snow-incrusted mountain walls and one restricted vista far across the snow-covered plain of the sea to the distant peaks and ranges of Nugssuak. The peak of Karrat towered over us; its dark-red rocks were gold against the zenith sky. We seldom walked far, for the snow was deep and heavy, but from the summit of the foreland what a view there was! One saw, near by, the marvelously corrugated mountain sides of Kekertarssuak, and then the whole broad tossing panorama of the northern ranges. Pale gold of sun-illumined snow, and blue; with here and there a patch of bare black mountain side to prove the blinding pitch of all the rest. Snow-blind: perhaps our eyes are stricken to preserve our souls.

We rose at earliest daylight, and turned in at dark; almost all day I worked. We had two visitors. The first, a hunter coming out of Kangerdlugsuak, saw me at work and came to pay a call. He was a most unhappy man. He told me that his wife had died, and how his house stood empty now. So good a house, glass in the windows, and a stove. Yes, there it stood in Nugatsiak, no one in it. He sat a long time in silence. 'There were once many houses on Karrat,' he continued. 'One house stood there, another there. Yes, there were many houses here one time. Now, only one. The houses, people—gone.' I thought he'd weep. He used, he said, to catch a lot of seals; now he caught none. Hard days, hard times. And he had nothing now to eat. Would I lend him twenty-five öre? If he got a seal, he would pay me; if he got none, he wouldn't. He told me that his name was Jakob.

Our second visitor was named Abraham. He brought me a letter from Salamina. And he brought me two ptarmigan; of these we made a feast.

Two visitors and a brace of ptarmigan: these were the events of five days in the life of Pauline. The routine of her island days, and those events, might be the type of what her life would be for forty years. A house, a man to do his work, whatever it might be, apart from her, the household chores, long idle hours at the window or outdoors, a little food, a little warmth: these make the pattern of a Greenland woman's life. And children as a by-product. Yes, Pauline in the course of years as she'd stand idly gazing from the window and singing softly to herself would rock her body soothingly to lull her child to sleep. There'd be that difference.

I wonder what it would be like, that island and Pauline, for life. I wonder whether a white man would have sense enough to let things be, just let the days and the relationship run on and not go prying into her exotic soul, nor even thinking that she had a soul, nor caring. The silly fool would doubtless fall in love with her and spoil it all; display, to her astonishment, the strange behavior of romantic love; insist on finding in her placid face some revelation of unfathomed pagan depths; get staring at her disconcertingly, annoying her. If at such antics Pauline didn't get, at last, the poor oaf's measure, size up what he *was* good for in cash expressed in clothes and beads, in *Danish* clothes, in leisure for herself and servants to support it, if she didn't contrive that her fatuous adorer should leave the island and move with her into the great city of Umanak, she'd be a fool – or a philosopher. Pauline, I think, was neither. And if a romantic white man lured by the visionary primitive did fall in love with her, she'd serve him in her own behalf as other 'primitives' have served such men.

Therefore, when on the fifth day David came we packed our household goods and art, and drove away. The people of Nugatsiak crowded around us as we came to land. 'How did you like the pretty girl?' asked Pavia. 'The pretty girl,' I answered him, 'was swell.'

CHAPTER 12

'KABLOONA'

from *Kabloona* (1941)

Gontran De Poncins

In 1938, Gontran De Poncins, a French count, set off to live among the Inuit of King William Island, in the Canadian Arctic. This passage from his book Kabloona — *the title refers to a local term for Europeans — recounts De Poncins' arrival at the camp where he would spend much of the next fifteen months. His host is Utak, who has agreed to assist him in return for trade goods equal to the value of one white fox.*

Night was falling when of a sudden three glimmering points too faint to be called lights pricked the grey scene. The igloos! Through the translucent snow of which these houses are built the feeble gleam of seal-oil lamps was visible, bespeaking the breath of life and the presence of man on this pallid ocean of ice. I crept through a winding tunnel so low that I went on all fours and knocked in the dark against wet and wriggling hairy bodies. These were the dogs. They had taken shelter in the freezing porch against the greater cold outside. Not for an empire would they have stirred out of my path, and over and among them I crawled until I emerged into the igloo.

But was this an igloo? This witch's cave black on one side with the smoke of the lamp and sweating out on the other the damp exudation caused by the warmth of lamp and human bodies! Within, nothing was white save an occasional line that marked the fitting of block to block; and the odor was inconceivable. In the vague light of the lamp shapeless things, men and women, were stirring obscurely. If you wanted a hierarchy of light you might say that before electricity there was the gas-jet, before the gas-jet the lamp, before the lamp the wax taper, before the wax taper the tallow candle, and before the tallow candle the seal-oil vessel. I was in a brown bear's lair, a troglodyte's cave. What would elsewhere be the stone age was here the ice age.

I was too newly come from Outside to see in the igloo anything but filth: the charnel heap of frozen meat piled on the ground behind the lamp; the gnawed fish-heads strewn everywhere; the sordid rags on the lumpish flesh, as if these Eskimos had worn their party clothes to the Post and were here revealing their true selves, the maculate bodies they covered with skin and fur to hide the truth from the White. And to heighten the horror of the scene, one of these Eskimos would fling himself from time to time into the porch — as the tunnel is called through which I had crawled — to drive out the dogs; and a howling would resound as of murder committed in a subterranean chamber.

Even to-day, as I write, it is still difficult for me to explain how it happened that I was able to accustom myself to this life, so that within a month a description like this would seem to me stupid, would seem a recital of non-essentials and a neglect of everything consequent in Eskimo existence.

Fortunately, I was too overcome with weariness to be able to think. Details met my eye and offended it, but they could not reach as far as my brain. My box had been dragged in, and like an automaton I opened it in order to find something to eat, something 'white' that would preserve me from all this. My soup was not there! Had

I forgotten it? Probably; and for the reason that I had thought about it too much not to forget it. What was the Eskimo word for 'soup'? I thumbed through my dictionary without a thought that the Eskimo might never eat soup, and there might be no word for it. Instead, I cursed the dictionary with the curse usual the world over – that a dictionary never contains the words we need. I could not explain to Utak what was missing; but as he saw me hunting, turning my effects over and over, he too – and this was the only comic note of the evening – he too began to hunt, though he knew not what he was hunting. What was I to eat? That frozen fish? That repellent snow-covered thing I could hear grating in their teeth as they chewed?

The household stared at me, and I needed no word of Eskimo to understand what they were thinking: not only had this white man no titbits to offer to them, he had not even brought his own grub. They said nothing, but their disapproval was unmistakable. Sick at heart, I crept into my bag and fell asleep without a morsel of food.

We slept six in a row, squeezed together in an igloo built to hold three, our heads turned towards the porch. The men lay naked in their caribou sleeping-bags. I kept my clothes on, and it was as if I were sleeping in a cage with wild beasts. All night long something dripped from the ceiling upon my face, and though each drop sent a twinge of pain through me, I could not evade it because we were squeezed too tightly together. All night long, too, my neighbor, Utak's brother, made use of the tin that served as chamber-pot, and each time he would hold it out at arm's length without stirring, and empty it under my nose. In a corner an old woman spat the whole night through, and between the one and the other, in a spirit of the deepest gloom of heart, through which the two or three images of warmth and comfort that I summoned were unable to make their way, I fell finally asleep.

When I awoke the igloo was empty except for the old woman: the men had gone fishing.

I crawled out of doors and had a look round. It wanted almost an effort to identify the igloos in this landscape. There were four in all, four molehills made of snow; and had it not been for the harpoons and other accoutrements sticking up like vertical black lines drawn on white paper, I should not have seen them. These strokes were the only signs of the existence of a camp in this white infinity.

The camp was deserted. Nothing stirred. Here and there a puppy lay half buried in the snow. The men had gone with their sleds and their dogs. Every day was for them a day of work and travel: every morning they awoke to the same seasonal chores: ice the runners, harness the dogs, unleash the 40-foot serpentine whip with its 12-inch handle, and go off to the fishing or the hunt.

The camp was built on the flank of a ridge, doubtless because the snow here was more plentiful. Below me I could see a wide flat surface which was a lake. Three out of the five men in the camp had gone ice-fishing on this lake; the other two had preferred to go off to another lake, twenty-five miles distant, on pretext that the fish there were bigger. At this time of year the ice was only two feet thick, and fishing was still easy.

Utak came up from the lake before the rest in order to build me an igloo. It was not to be separated altogether from his own, but would be a sort of lean-to opening into his igloo, and through this opening he and his wife would be able to keep an eye on my tin of biscuits. However, I should at least sleep alone this night.

One hour sufficed Utak for the erection of my spiral shelter, and it was no sooner finished than soiled. The dogs climbed and ran all over it on the outside, as is their habit, and yellowed its dome and sides. Ohudlerk hastened to pay me a visit as soon as I had installed myself. With a great deal of hawking and spitting he explained to me that the igloo was perfect – from which I was to understand how great was my debt to Utak. And Utak himself, by way of creating a fitting atmosphere, came in with the gift of a heap of rotted fish.

An igloo is very pretty when it is new, when it has just been finished and the *iglerk*, the flat couch of snow that rises about fifteen inches from the floor, has been smoothed down. It is so pretty, so white, so pure with its little heaps of powdered snow at the base of the meeting of the blocks, that one is afraid to move in it for fear of soiling it. But the miraculous industry of the Eskimo soon removes this sense of caution and daintiness. In less than a day the igloo is made cosy and homelike: everything is spattered and maculated; the heaps of objects brought inside create great black spots where they lie; the ground is strewn with the debris of fish spat forth in the course of eating; everywhere there are stains of seal blood and droppings of puppies (puppies are allowed indoors).

I am told that there are Eskimos who keep their igloos clean, scraping the floor daily and sprinkling fresh snow over it to cover the stains. This is not the case with the Netsilik of King William Land, who seem to feel the most profound indifference, indeed contempt, for cleanliness. As for my igloo, they invaded it as if in conquered territory; and after all, it was their igloo, I was their guest, they had doubtless the right to treat it as their own. There they sat on my *iglerk*, belching and laughing, picking out a morsel of the fish that lay on the ground – our food and the dogs' as well –

as if they had come each time upon something particularly savory, and spitting the bones out straight in front of them.

I say again that I was too green to have any notion of Eskimo values. Every instinct in me prompted resistance, impelled me to throw these men out, – to do things which would have been stupid since they would have astonished my Eskimos fully as much as they might have angered them. I knew nothing, for example, of the variant of communism they practised, and which I later learned was the explanation of their taking possession of me, their shameless sharing among themselves of my goods, which on this occasion made me think of them as inconceivably impudent, filled with effrontery, and of myself as helpless and in a hopeless situation. They were the masters, I the captive, I said to myself. You wanted to live with the Eskimos, did you? I said. Well, here you are, you silly ass.

Thus, my beginnings went very badly. Worse than the pillage was the fact that two days later my hands froze.

'Una-i-kto!'—It is cold, Utak had said on waking that morning. But we had gone off together on his sled to fish on the great lake whose name I had by now learned. It was called Kakivok-tar-vik, 'the place where we fish with the three-pronged harpoon.'

Half a mile out from shore Utak began by clearing the snow off the surface of the lake with his native shovel in a circle about twelve feet in diameter. Then he knelt down, a hand shading his eyes, his nose to the ice, and tried to judge whether or not the depth of the lake here was what it should be. I did as he did, and could see the bottom of the lake perfectly, the grasses waving and the fish moving past in their tranquil world. As soon as he spied the fish, Utak became feverish. He ran to the sled, which with the dogs had been left a hundred feet off, came back with an ice chisel, and now the ice was flying in an upward rain of chips. He was cutting out a hole, and it was incredible with what speed and precision he worked. I have seen Eskimos go through five feet of ice with one of these chisels in ten minutes. He would stop at every four or five inches, send down a sort of ladle made of bone, and slowly and cautiously bring up the chips.

When the hole had been pierced through, the water flowed in and brought to the surface the odd chips that still remained, which were carefully ladled off. Then, on the far side of the hole, Utak built a wind-screen of three snow blocks, one set straight ahead of him and each of the others serving as wings. This done, he spread a caribou skin, and knelt on it. With his left hand he unrolled a long cord at the end of which hung a small fish made of bone, with two fins. He let the decoy down into the water, and when he jigged, or pulled on the cord, which he did with the regularity of a clock, the fins beat. The little bone fish was like a water-bug swimming. In his right hand, held very near the hole, was the *kakivok*, the great three-pronged harpoon. When the fish, lured by the decoy, came swimming beneath Utak, he would lower his harpoon gently into the hole, and at the proper moment he would strike, and the fish would be speared.

Nothing was more comical than the silhouette of Utak, his bottom in the air, his nose literally scraping the ice, his eyes fixed on the moving water, his whole being as motionless as a deer at the moment when it takes fright and is about to run. At first I had knelt beside him. Then, my hands freezing and my muscles stiff, I stood up to stretch. He became furious, for a man walking round the hole frightens away the fish. But one could hum as much as one pleased without disturbing them, and as Utak peered into the hole he kept up a monotonous humming. I came back to where he crouched, for I was fascinated by what he was doing. This seemed to please him, and undoubtedly it did. The Eskimo is very proud of everything that he does, and to see a white man imitating him is for him the highest flattery.

With what patience that left hand, as regular as a metronome, rose and fell while the hours went by! And what passion the Eskimo put into this form of the chase! What intensity was in his gaze! The tiniest fish that passed drew from him muttered words, and it was clear that the game absorbed him, that time and space had fled leaving him only this hole in the ice over which he would peer for days if necessary. As far as the eye could see in every direction the scene was void of life; and in the midst of this immensity a single man, who might have been alone in the world, was absorbed with a scientist's concentration upon . . . upon what? Upon the art of filling his belly.

Had I not been tortured by the cold, I should have been content to watch for hours this admirable adjustment of primitive man to his element. But, although it could not have been more than fifteen degrees below zero, I was freezing. Doubtless my skin had not yet become adapted to this climate. My fingers burned in my gloves, and I was too vain to speak of it. But while I knelt there, thinking of nothing else, suddenly – a fish! Utak's right hand was closing over the handle of the *kakivok,* and before I could see what had happened, the thing was done, the fish was gasping on the ice, had flung itself twice in the air and then lay still, frozen almost on the spot. And Utak was back in the same posture, absorbed again in his chase.

We had been out several hours, and the pain in my fingers became so unbearable that I could have screamed. The heel of my hands also had begun to harden. When, finally, we stood up, I took off my gloves to have a look and saw that my fingers were waxen. I had frozen my eight fingertips.

Three days later my fingers were still useless: hard as wood, very painful, whenever I touched anything with them they burned, and I could not so much as roll myself a cigarette. Rubbing them with snow did no good. Dipping them in coal-oil merely produced in them a sensation of cold. There was no remedy, and the best I could do was to hope they were not permanently frozen. Meanwhile, I was chained to the igloo like a hospital patient to his bed.

From my *iglerk*, my couch, I watched the life of the women through the opening in the wall between our igloos. Unarnak, Utak's wife, was industriously at work with her *kumak-sheun*, her louse-catcher, a long caribou bone with a tuft of polar-bear hair glued to the end. The hairs must have had an extraordinary attraction for the lice, for this species of hunting was always successful. It was a treat – though I agree, of a special kind – to see Unarnak pull three lice in succession off the hairs and crack them in her teeth.

On the skins that covered their *iglerk* the little boy was naked at play. He strutted, grimaced, chattered, and held behind him a looking-glass while he peered round to see in it the reflection of his bottom.

When the child forgot himself on the caribou skin his mother put out a casual hand and scooped the brine off the couch. The hand of the Eskimo is always busy, and it serves him in a thousand ways: for example, to pick the nose and then carefully place the catch in the mouth – a detail for which I beg to be excused, but nothing is more typically Eskimo than this. It is with her hand that Unarnak trims the wick of the seal-oil lamp; and when she has finished she sucks the oil from her fingers, or else wipes her fingers in her hair – though the latter means a less thorough job. I have never yearned to find myself lord of a harem of native mistresses; but the sight of Unarnak would deprive any white man of the temptation to make her dishonorable proposals.

At the other end of the *iglerk* Utak's mother, Niakognaluk, sat in her habitual seat. Squatting beside the completely shapeless old woman was a yellow bitch with flopping ears, rendered equally shapeless by the fact that she was heavy with a coming litter. The old woman sat all day long scraping skins – a task that never ends in the life of the Eskimo, for weather, snow, and water are constantly soaking and hardening the clothes he wears and the skins he lies on, and it is only by this process of continual scraping that the hides can be softened again and made wearable and usable.

Niakognaluk is the only completely bald woman I have ever seen. She sat in her corner wearing an old woollen bonnet, dressed in hides so worn that all fur and hair was long gone out of them and they were as black and shiny as a blacksmith's leather apron. Bowed over the lamp, working with misshapen hands, her feet folded beneath her, she scraped and scraped; and as she worked tirelessly on she would murmur words which for all I knew might have been addressed to the lamp, to the dog, to herself. When a skin was finished she flung it against the igloo wall with an air of weariness and indifference and got up to get another, holding up her caribou trousers with both hands – the dress of these men and women is much alike – as she staggered across to the pile of skins, bent stiffly down, fumbled in the heap, and reeled back to her corner to squat again over her work.

She had two or three different scrapers to work with, but the real softening was done with her teeth. I have said before, I believe, that the Eskimo's teeth serve him as a third hand, and though I had demonstrations of this again and again, yet each time it was as marvellous in my eyes as a turn at the circus. The miracle was that when Niakognaluk had finished a skin it was really white and as supple as a glove.

Among the Eskimos as with the humble of every land, the Old Woman seemed to express the sum of experience, of hardship, of wisdom. She was symbolic; she was permanence; she was She Who Stays Behind. The others leave or die: she is always there. Each death, each winter, adds its burden to her load of life, bends and bows her a little more, but it does not achieve the breaking of her, and she goes on living. She mutters and seems to grumble, merely because she is old; but because she is old, also, her heart is kind. She makes no demands, and when you make her a little gift she sends forth a worn smile that is warm with friendliness.

Utak's mother was like this. She mumbled constantly over her work. She pretended endlessly that the child, who lived part of the day in the deep hood that hung down her back, would never leave her in peace. Tyrannical as are all Eskimo children, he rode her as if she were a spavined old mare, shook her as if she were a plum-tree; and while she complained her patience was limitless.

Generally the child was out with his mother, and the old woman sat alone with her dog. There was a sort of resemblance between the two. Two slanting slits were all the eyes one saw in the old woman's face, and the same was true of the dog. The bitch's coat and the old woman's covering were of the same color and the same state of decrepitude. Both were worn out by life, neither had any strength left; and when the old woman took up a whip-handle and beat the dog to drive her away, it was feebly and without conviction that she did so. The old dog would moan, but it would not stir. 'You see,' the dog seemed to say; 'you try to beat me, but at bottom you don't even want to. And I don't want to go away. We belong here together.' They would sit motionless, looking at each other, the dog with its flopping ears and bowed legs, the old woman with her rounded back and her misshapen hands. I could imagine their dialogue.

'You ought to be ashamed of yourself!' the old woman seemed to say. 'To go on having puppies at your age! Will you never stop? And I'm sure their father is that Arluk, that useless hound who howls in harness before you've even laid a whip to him. Kigiarna, aren't you ashamed?'

The bitch would flatten herself out, cringing.

'And of course you intend to drop your litter in the warmth of the igloo. Naturally. I'll find the puppies one of these days in my sleeping-bag, and I'll be the one to bring them up. Not for the first time, either. You weren't so concerned about these things when you were younger. Time was when your puppies were born in the porch; out in the snow, even.'

And Kigiarna would approve every word, pitiably.

❀

Among these Netsilik Eskimos, these *Inuit* or 'men, preeminently,' as they boasted themselves, the routine upon waking in the igloo never varied. It went like this.

First, hawk and spit for at least half an hour.

Second, grumble and mutter until your wife, having crawled out of the *krepik,* the deerskin bag, has taken up the circular knife and cut off a great piece of the frozen fish that lies on the ground.

Third, eat the fish, panting and grumbling meanwhile because wife and child are stirring in the *krepik* and getting into the way of your free arm.

Fourth, between each bite, suck your fingers noisily and tell a story or recount your dream, a satisfied appetite having put you in a good humor.

Fifth, with great deal of puffing and snorting, light the Primus

stove. If it refuses to go, fling it across the igloo and slide down
growling into the *krepik*, after which silence is restored in the igloo.

If the Primus should catch with little trouble, sixth, brew tea,
gulp down two or three mugs, and say *'Una-i-kto,'* – 'It is cold,' –
so that the Kabloona (the white man) may be seized with compassion and get up to prepare his grub for you. After each mug of tea,
wipe up the leaves with your fingers and eat them.

Finally, having eaten and drunk and woken the entire household,
come up out of your *krepik*, ready to be off fishing.

The men came in from their jigging and the silent igloo was suddenly filled with stampings, threshings and snortings as of beasts in
a stable. Voices and laughter broke forth; the constant and horrible
coughing and spitting began that seems always to attack the Eskimo
indoors. The tea, which had been boiling all day long above the seal-
oil lamp, was poured into mugs and bowls and its steam rose from
between their hands in an odor of seal while the air of the igloo
became a vapor in which the bodies were seen as shapeless blurs.

Almost immediately an incident took place that gave me a great
fright.

Ohudlerk's son, Kakokto, who had been away fishing on the distant
lake, had come back to visit his father. He and his wife were standing
before me in my igloo, and as it was time to eat and they seemed to be
expecting something, I fed them. Whether it was jealousy or not I do
not know, but while I was talking to the young couple, Unarnak came
in, picked up my sack of flour, and took it into her igloo. There she
proceeded to bake an impressive quantity of *baneks* – a sort of flat
bread – which she distributed to everybody present. I watched her out
of the corner of my eye and observed that she had been lacking in the

first article of courtesy, which was to offer the *baneks* first to me. I waited a moment; then, seeing that the sack was not restored to its place, I told her quietly to put it back where she had found it.

Up to that moment everybody had been in splendid humor – those in my igloo because they had supped handsomely, those in Utak's because they had received an unexpected offering. As soon as I had spoken – in the hearing of every one – silence fell. Unarnak, knowing that I considered her at fault, gathered together all the *baneks* and placed them without a word on my *iglerk*, with an air of complete disinterestedness. But her husband would not take it thus. Like a true Asiatic, this Eskimo conceived his finest vengeance to lie in ridicule. Refusing contemptuously the tea I offered him, he let himself back on his couch and then, the igloo being full of people, smoke, and laughter, lying back, and with an almost casual air, he began to tell them how I had frozen my fingers. It was not hard to guess his story.

'And there was the Kabloona,' he said sarcastically, 'walking in a circle and stamping his feet, blowing on his fingers, making noise enough to frighten away all the fish in the lake, and saying, "*Aiie! Aiie!* My fingers are frozen!" till he looked like an unhappy fish, like the littlest fish in the world.'

All of them roared with laughter, for a game of this sort is always played collectively. Besides, they knew that if they laughed the wonderful story would go on. And it did. I could feel the tone of its rise, could see that Utak had become excited from the very fact of having a tale to tell, and was making it as daring and as cutting as he could.

'Finally we started back,' he went on. 'It was all he could do to drag himself back to his couch, and there he's been lying these three days past, whimpering and showing his fingers and moaning: "*Una-i-kto!*"'

And Utak, with wonderful mimicry, counterfeited not only my gestures but the very timbre of my voice.

'And to-night, finally, for a couple of grains of flour . . .'

The rest found all this very funny, and each time that a burst of laughter greeted one of his sallies Utak would turn towards me to see how I was taking it. Some of the others, indeed, rose from their places and came round to have a good look at me as I sat there, ill and half stupefied with fever, – for it was curious that my frozen fingers had raised my temperature.

I went on talking to Kakokto and his wife as if I had no notion what was towards, but at bottom I was extremely upset by the sudden turn which things had taken. And they did not entirely stop there. For when Utak had finished, he and his wife got up and went triumphantly out to tell their story in the next igloo.

Remembering what Paddy Gibson had said to me about Utak, I slept with one eye open. This fellow is subject to fits of temper, I thought. He killed his stepfather. He had to leave his own family and come to live on this side of the island because of it. I was uneasy. Never before had I heard that word for white man – Kabloona – pronounced with such contempt; and I suspected that this contempt came into an Eskimo's mouth only when he felt positively aggressive. I seemed to myself imprisoned in a disquieting atmosphere and had no notion what might come of this. I knew only one thing – that I could not retreat from the position of indifference and dignity which I had adopted.

I dropped off to sleep, and suddenly I awoke. I had no notion of the time and could hear the child crying. Utak was standing smoking a cigarette, his wife was stirring about, and all three were clothed. Unarnak came into my igloo and, thinking me asleep, picked up swiftly a pile of skins which belonged to them and had been stored with me for want of room in their igloo. They are going to strike camp and desert me, I said to myself, still with my eye on them. They seemed to be consulting each other, to hesitate. Finally they went to bed. Weariness sent me back to sleep – and in the morning it was all over. The first thing I saw on opening my eyes was Utak bending over me, grinning and offering me a mug of tea, a peace token.

CHAPTER 13

'A GREENLAND CHRISTMAS'

from *An African in Greenland* (1981)

Tété-Michel Kpomassie

Tété-Michel Kpomassie was born in Togo in 1941. As a teenager, he opened a book called The Eskimos from Greenland to Alaska *and began, in his words, 'dreaming of eternal cold'. Improbably enough, ten years later he had made his way to Kangerlussuaq. In this passage he is staying in the small village of Rodebay, on the west coast of the island. Hans and Cecilia are his hosts.*

All Greenland adults, both men and women, love cigars, which they smoke in a very curious fashion, not wasting even the ash . . . After taking a few puffs on a lighted cigar, they put it out by spitting on it, and immediately put the burnt end in their mouths and bite off the glowing ash along with a slice of raw tobacco. They turn it rapidly over and over on the tongue – the cigar end is sometimes still red-hot – and chew it, rolling their eyes with ineffable delight as they swallow the hot ash mixed with shreds of tobacco, then spit out black saliva and announce, '*Mam-mâk!*' (It's good!) The rest of the cigar is stowed away in a pocket, to be repeatedly lit, smoked, extinguished, and consumed all over again. According to them, this warms your face and improves your circulation when you're out in a kayak in the cold.

So Hans seemed very happy with my packet of cigars and, wanting to give me a present in return, that evening brought me a seashell he'd picked up on the shore, and a black ballpoint pen, property of the Rodebay school, whose name was engraved on it.

At half-past six I visited Thue, who offered me coffee and a big, hard biscuit. Hendrik and Marianna had moved out with their children and gone to live with Søren Petersen; the house was quieter, but sad and empty. So there was Thue, alone now with his two youngest children and Saqaq, who had not yet left him. Apart from them, he had his kayak – which never brought back any seal and which he wouldn't be able to use for several months while the sea was frozen over – and his sledge, which had several wooden slats missing. And nobody, nobody in the village offered to help him!

Arkaluk no longer had a shirt of his own, and had to wear one of his father's. The shirt was far too big for him, so, to make it fit better, the boy, standing in front of me with the shirt on, started to poke new buttonholes alongside the old ones, using a knife. As he cut the cloth, he bent his head down over his chest and kept sniffing in the snot that dripped from his nostrils.

❋

Friday, December 31. Starting at one in the afternoon, groups of children made the rounds of the houses, though they didn't sing as they had at Christmas. When they came to us, Cecilia doled out cakes and they left with thanks.

That day produced the strangest sight I'd seen since the start of the festivities. Young men disguised as spirits roamed the village in the endless night. They generally gathered by the roadside in front of the unlit house used as a communal workshop for building kayaks and sleds. These 'spirits' looked like great bundles of clothes; they were called *midartut* (*midartôk* in the singular). I was oddly reminded of those grotesque unmasked creatures called *ʒangbéto*, who in the villages of my native land loom up out of the darkness, creep into huts, and by their unexpected and terrifying presence silence little children who cry in the night. But unlike the *ʒangbéto* of Togo, the *midartut* of Greenland play no useful role in society. They spring out and give you a fright, run after passers-by, perform a ponderous dance, sometimes roll on the ground at your feet, and almost never say a word.

We were at Jorgensen and Augustina's, clasping hands and singing carols round the Christmas tree with the children, when a *midartôk* arrived. He was covered in such an array of skins that he must have had trouble breathing; and he had a stick in his hand. As soon as he came in, the terrified children scattered and hid – some under the bed, some behind their father or mother. Hans forgot the pious hymns we'd been singing and broke into a lively, lilting song. The *midartôk* answered with his own wild dance, leaping in the air and banging on the floor with his stick. At the end they gave him a cake, and he left saying, '*kuyanâk*' – the one word he had spoken during the whole performance.

I left Jorgensen's to fetch my tape recorder, so as to record those rousing tunes to which the *midartut* dance. But on my way home I was stopped by a man named Eliassen and his wife. He told me, 'You can see the *midartut* another time. Come and have coffee with us.'

I followed them back to their house, which turned out to be full of people drinking and enjoying themselves. Their pretty little thirteen-year-old daughter was serving the visitors, helped by her sister, Adina, who was six.

The guests were already half stewed. Eliassen, behaving as if his own wife wasn't there, started to take great liberties with one girl: sitting in front of her, he kept teasing her with shouts of '*Tui!*' as he darted his hand up her skirt. Meanwhile his wife sat down opposite me and gave me a long, slow look; then suddenly her face lit up with a sugary smile, exposing her upper gums and three missing teeth, while blue veins pulsed on her neck and flat bosom, where a crucifix gleamed. With the same bedroom eyes, she told me three times, '*Assavakit*' (I love you), in the hearing of her husband, who burst out laughing at the sight of my embarrassment.

I don't know if *assavakit* has some more respectable meaning; apart from the girls, Hans and several other men had often said it to me as a sign of friendship. Probably it also means simply 'I like you.'

We all toasted one another with one glass and then another in quick succession, for, besides cups of coffee, we all had before us three glasses containing different alcoholic drinks, and these were filled as soon as we emptied them. In the living room, women enticed me with come-hither stares and suggestive movements.

In the thick of all this uproar, the door was flung open and in came Thue, quite well dressed. How people detested him! They all blamed him for letting me leave his home. They didn't throw him out, but they wouldn't give him anything to drink. He managed a tight-lipped smile and gave each of the guests a long stare. Then, as if asserting his rights, he suddenly grabbed a glass three-quarters full of *imiak* just as we were shouting '*Skol!*' – but he didn't raise the glass to anyone before he started drinking.

Then the *midartut* arrived, and among them I recognized Maria; some of them had pulled old pink stockings over their heads, weirdly flattening their noses. But soon we heard the church bell ringing: it was midnight, and all these drunken people set off to the church for the service. No *midartôk*, however, took part.

This is when you should see Rodebay – after the New Year's Eve midnight mass. Exhilarated with drink and song, chanting as they roamed through the village, delirious villagers started on another round of visits. I followed the *midartut* into about ten houses, then finally stopped at Knud's, where there was still light in the windows. He was with a little man in a white anorak. As he got up to greet me, Knud signaled to me not to speak too loudly: a woman was curled up asleep on the couch in a dim corner of the living room. I took the glass of beer he handed me to celebrate the New Year, and five minutes later set off home to bed.

As I was crossing the yard, I met a man who kept shining his torch right in my eyes. In my country this is considered rude. Who could it be? I turned my own light on him: it was Johan Dorf. Both of us lowered our torches. Thinking no more of it, I went on my way.

I was right by the door of the outside larder when Dorf attacked me from behind and knocked me to the ground. I got up with grazed fingers, and Dorf, like a vicious mongrel that runs off after creeping up and pouncing on a man, scuttled off to Knud's house. I followed him there to have it out with him at once; as soon as I opened the door he swung around, aimed a kick at my belly, and slammed the door in my face. I heard him screaming inside like a madman, 'Get out of here, you rotten nigger!'

It was the first time I'd ever been called that, though I'd long ago realized that when someone having a dispute with a black man calls him 'rotten nigger' or 'filthy nigger' or some such name, it's always some embittered neurotic trying to work off frustrations that have nothing at all to do with the 'nigger.' In this case Johan Dorf, who was envious by nature, was jealous of my success with the women there.

I managed to get the door open again, but he gave me another kick in the stomach and heaved it shut again. Shouting for Knud, I pulled at the door again, and the bastard gave me a third kick. Trying to dodge it, I slipped and fell on the steps. I was just getting up to open the door yet again when Knud came flying outside.

'Run for it,' he shouted. 'They're fighting inside.'

Winded, and suddenly weak at the knees, feebly I went along.

'Let's go and hide in the school. We're on our own. We're friends, Michel!' Knud panted as we stumbled through the deep snow, floundering into drifts.

We burst into the school building, and Knud double-locked the door. We sat down and he started to cry. Only then did he explain to me that the woman sleeping in his house, so dead drunk that she couldn't walk home, was Johan Dorf's wife.

'But what's that got to do with me?'

All the while, I was trying to control my temper. Knud took my torch to go and see if things had calmed down at his place. He came back very agitated, then went out again. Finally he returned and said we could go back now.

In the yard he had me wait near a shed by the house while he went into the living room. A minute later he came back and called my name.

Two men who had nothing to do with the affair were sitting calmly at the table. The woman in question hadn't stirred: she was still fast asleep. We talked about Dorf's strange behavior, and I informed Knud and his visitors that I intended to report the attack to the police representative; every village has a man with the imposing title of *Usted bestyrer* – literally, 'village administrator' – whose main function is to keep the police informed. Detectives visiting a community where a crime has been committed go and see him first of all. The one in Rodebay was called Knud Jørgensen.

They told me Knud was falling-down drunk, so seeing that the whole village was now unprotected by the law, I decided not to be made a fool of: the next time I saw him, I'd teach Johan Dorf a lesson. I was twenty-four. Johan, strongly built and fat as a pig, was nearly thirty-eight. So he wasn't old – he could put up a fight.

Suddenly the door flew open. Dorf came in and made for his wife. I called his name but he just scowled at me, so I grabbed him by the collar. Trying to hold me back, the others hung onto my coat so hard that it ripped, but I took it off and started fighting. The table overturned. Dorf managed to throw himself on top of me, but I pounded his face with my fists, then felt sick at the sight of the bloody mess I made of him. My *kamiks* slipped in the beer; everybody shouted at once. Finally we stopped, and they pulled Dorf to one side. Knud asked him why he had knocked me down and kicked me in the stomach.

'I don't remember,' he said as he slumped gasping onto the couch.

This idiotic answer made me go for him again. I hit him in the face, and we were at it again, till he sat down, winded once more. Suddenly, in came the little man in the white anorak who had been at Knud's an hour or so earlier; I let this little puppet stand there and wave his arms. Saqaq arrived, learned what was happening, and wanted to give me a hand. Gradually, however, everything calmed down. They showed Dorf the door. He turned back. Knud shouted 'Out!' and gave him a kick in the rear. Some people came to take him and his drunken wife away.

Many of the villagers were afraid of this bully Dorf who, because he ran the Danish shop and handled the trading company's operations in the village (buying seal, fox, and other skins), liked to be feared and to play the top dog. But that evening, his fat face puffed and bleeding, he slunk through the village with lowered

head. They congratulated me on teaching him a lesson, and Knud
suggested a snack.

A group of children came and sang at the window to wish Knud
a happy New Year. He invited them in and handed out cakes. I
calmed down at the sight of these children with their peaceful faces.

But that evening still had surprises in store. When the children
had left, the five of us sat down round the living-room table and
began to pitch into some cold meat. Besides myself and Knud, there
were his houseboy Évat, Saqaq, and the young man Paviâ. A dispute soon broke out among the three young Greenlanders over the
quality of Knud's *imiak*. Saqaq found it too weak, therefore
second-rate. Knud did not reply, but his houseboy Évat couldn't
allow his boss's *imiak* to be slandered like this, so he and his friend
Paviâ saw Saqaq out, but first, to my surprise, they calmly asked
him to apologize and to say thanks by shaking hands with everyone,
beginning with Knud. And so he did, before he left!

Saturday, January 1. We split up at eight in the morning. What
blackness outside! When it was time to leave I couldn't find my
torch; someone had been seen picking it up after the fight, but
nobody remembered who. I went off flanked by Évat and Paviâ,
who saw me all the way to Hans's door.

'It's for your protection,' they told me.

They were afraid of possible reprisals by Dorf's friends.

Our *Usted bestyrer* never asked me anything about the fight.
Recovering from his night on the bottle, he remarked: 'Dorf looks
as if he fell out of a *timissatôq* (helicopter).'

As for Dorf himself, far from making any more trouble, he kept
out of my way. And from that day on, every time he had a row with

someone, they'd say: 'So you think you can push me around because I'm small and weak? I won't fight – you're stronger than me. But try it with Mikilissuak and see what happens!'

In the evening there was a big New Year's dance at the *Forsamlinghus* (the village hall). I went with Hans, who was not sure where Cecilia had got to. We each took a kroner, the admission price.

The village hall, a small clapboard building, was lit inside by an oil lamp. Hendrik stood at the far end of the packed room and played the accordion: he was the only musician, but everyone joined in the singing.

At first, with pride they sang *Nunarput utorkarssuángoravit* (Our Old Country), a fine poem written by Hendrik Lund around 1912, which soon became Greenland's national anthem to a tune by Jonathan Petersen. The poet sings the praises of the *Kalâtdit*, the Greenland man, who survives today and will live on forever, because he can make the most of his country's resources. Then everybody roared the refrain:

> But we must set ourselves new aims,
> And go on growing, that one day we may be
> The respected equals of all other nations.

Hendrik kept squeezing his accordion, but it's not easy dancing to a national anthem! So someone started singing 'Narssaq,' a song that salutes the most fertile region of the south, where cows, ponies, and sheep graze peacefully in the meadows among clapboard houses. Narssaq abounds with forage and food and green fields lying at the foot of the mountains! The song goes on to compare the delights of Narssaq with those of the Biblical lands of Lebanon and Sharon.

During this dance, Søren and his partner Amalia, who had had a few drinks too many, fell flat on the floor. Far from asking if they had hurt themselves, everyone gathered around and held their sides with laughter.

The next song was 'Sunia': When Sunia appears at the far end of the fjord, towing a whale behind his boat, there is great joy in the village. The Inuit happily divide the animal among themselves, and every villager has as much meat and blubber as he wants! But Niels, Lukas, and Markers down so much *mattak* that it sticks in their throats. So they have to be thumped on the back to make all the *mattak* go down! The singers end with the wish that some day Greenlanders will be sailing real whaling ships of their own.

But the liveliest air, started by Hans, was called 'Aanayarak ayag-tugaussok,' Snow White! For the Inuit really have a sung version of this fairy tale.* In this song the wicked stepmother, jealous of Snow White's beauty, throws her out in the snow. But the fox, the crow, the snow goose, and the arctic hare lead her to the turf cottage of the Seven Dwarfs. When Snow White gets there she puts the house to rights, scrubs the floor, trims the wick on the seal-oil lamp, and prepares a tasty meal of dried fish, *mattak*, and reindeer meat. Then the Seven Dwarfs come back from the coal mine. Delighted to find their cottage spick and span, they adopt Snow White; overjoyed, they begin to dance the rhythmic steps of the *sisamak*, the strange dance we ourselves were now dancing. We formed a big circle, and to the music of the accordion took four

* In 1948 the writer Frederik Nielsen published 'Arnajarak,' the Greenland version of 'Snow White and the Seven Dwarfs.' This tale gave birth soon after to a song about the wanderings of the unfortunate princess in the mountains.

steps to the left, four to the right, then swung giddily round with our partners. It was a reel, a cheerful fifteenth-century Scots country dance that the natives had learned from European whalers.

Despite all the liveliness and gaiety, I felt a little disappointed. In their amusements, the inhabitants of this western coast have retained hardly anything of their own cultural heritage, nothing that really belongs to them. The accordion which Hendrik tirelessly played was a foreign instrument. As for the Eskimo drums, made of a circular wooden frame covered with a stretched membrane which is tapped on the edge with a slender stick (strangely enough, never on the membrane itself), nowadays they can be found only at the National Museum in Copenhagen! I rather missed the New Year festivities in my home village, where our dances, not copied from anyone else's, are cadenced to the rhythms of the tom-toms.

To give Hendrik a breather, they brought out records and a small battery-powered record player, and we danced till morning.

On various pretexts, the holiday continued all through the first week of January. On Monday the 3rd, the whole village assembled at the pastor's, where we drank till five in the morning: it was his birthday. The next day was Knud's birthday, and his house never emptied. The following day it was someone else's turn, and so on.

Those who had enough provisions spent only an hour or two a day repairing their outbuildings or kayaks. Only Thue went hunting every day, but only from ten until noon. Today he came back with an eider and a little guillemot. In the dark of their living room, I could dimly see Maria boiling the birds, and Saqaq squatting down. In the other room the oil lamp was burning feebly, and Thue was sitting on the floor drinking. I had a cup of tea with him while he got drunk on 'Patria,' a terrible Danish wine.

January 5. This evening – unusually – we were all home, and everyone was busy with some kind of work. Cecilia sat on the floor with a thimble on her finger, mending the soles of a pair of *kamiks* with a bodkin, some seal sinew thread, and scraps of new skin. She made two patches on each sole, at the heel and toe. Poyo worked on Hans's seal net, while Hans himself concentrated on making a dog whip, which he plaited in a curious way with a single leather thong, so that it resembled a pigtail. The lash was about seven meters long, tapering at the end. Hans started the braiding about fifteen centimeters from the thicker end, that would later be attached to a wooden handle. In the tough leather thong he made a slit through which he passed the other end of the lash, then pulled on it tightly to make a knot. Then he made the next slit, the next knot, and so on. The knots were very tight and close together. It was hard work, but the result was a series of beautiful interlacing patterns, like little superimposed triangles with the apex of one entering the base of the next, while at the same time a number of elegant wavy lines appeared on either side of the leather thong. To pull the knots as tight as possible, Hans used not only his hands and knees but also his teeth, worn down to the gums: he tugged with them and chewed at the leather, with dizzying jerks of his head. He made sixteen knots in all, and then added to the end of the whip a finer lash of very smooth skin that came from a baby narwhal found in its mother's womb. It is this flexible and hard-wearing section which is used to discipline the huskies. After three days' work, the whip was ready. The thick end was attached to the wooden handle by several layers of cord passing over and under the leather. The whip was nine to ten meters long, and very clean and white now. But wait until it had been used for one winter!

Then Hans made an ice chopper. The handle, two meters long, would later be shortened by twenty centimeters. The blade, flat and rather long, was inserted halfway into the handle, which was split at one end; then it was lashed tight with coiled twine, and reinforced lower down by a nailed iron plate, with six nails on each of the handle's four sides. The beveled blade was sharpened with a file.

*

January 6. There were still a few *midartut* to be seen in the village. It all came to an end that evening – it was the last day, the last night, the end of the festivities! Tomorrow the Christmas decorations would be taken down in all the houses . . .

How quiet we all were at home that night! The oil lamp was turned up high, and several candles had been lit at once, as if their combined brightness could drive out our crushing boredom. Hans, who all day long had been alternately sullen and morose, then touchy and surly, slumped in a chair and heaved a loud sigh. He had an Eskimo book in his hand, but he kept nodding off. Cecilia shuttled silently between the living room and the kitchen, where Poyo sat quiet as a mouse. Was it post-Christmas fatigue – here big celebrations are nearly always followed by deep depressions – or was it just the weather? It was piercingly cold now. The Greenland cold, strangely enough, didn't make you shiver or cause your teeth to chatter, for it wasn't just all around you, it was *inside* you. It permeated everything: houses, clothing, people, things. You were reluctant to touch a plate, a pan, a cigarette lighter in your pocket, a watch left at your bedside overnight, and so on.

Yet the arctic cold is less intense and harsh during the months when the ground is still covered by a thick layer of snow than in March and April when that snow is transformed into ice. Today the temperature, which was minus seventeen degrees in the morning, dropped to minus nineteen. The weather had been mild up to now, considering it was the middle of the arctic winter. But by January I already felt as if I were living in a refrigerator.

Well now . . . A few days before, old Sophia and her husband Knud had introduced me to one of their daughters, Else, who had recently arrived for the holidays from Jakobshavn, where she worked as a nurse. I spent that night in their house, in bed with Else. The coal stove went out as soon as everyone was in bed, and the inside temperature plummeted. At two in the morning, I still couldn't get to sleep. How cold it was, my God, how cold! A woman's warmth doesn't protect you completely from that sort of cold! Yet we had two blankets and an eiderdown over us, and I was wearing a pull-over, too! Else wore nothing!

The next day, January 7, when school started again, the temperature dropped to minus twenty-two degrees. I looked on as poor little children emerged from houses whose faintly glowing windows were curtained with frost, and watched them trudge to school mutely through the frigid whiteness. A great silence reigned in the village. That return to school after the holidays was one of the saddest sights I have ever seen: not one voice, not one sound, not a single dog barking.

The local men, who also seemed to have taken a long Christmas holiday, returned to their hunting that same day. Clad in animal skins, with their ice picks on their shoulders, they headed for the bay, which gave off a grayish haze.

The men had started work again, but not for long, you can be sure. On Thursday, January 13, towards one o'clock in the afternoon, the villagers climbed a mountain behind the village to witness, so they told me, the first appearance of the sun: we did in fact see a faint yellow glow on the horizon, but the sun itself would remain invisible for another few months.

This 'return' of the sun, which seemed to me completely imaginary, gave rise that night to the most curious of the Greenland celebrations, a dance in the town hall that only adult males and their wives may attend – young people are not admitted.

Before going to this affair, Jørgensen and his wife Augustina looked in at our house. Hans, who was getting dressed, appeared in his underclothes and called to his friend's wife. Augustina got up at once and joined him in the bedroom, while her husband stayed with Cecilia in the living room, and never lost his smile. The couple reappeared soon afterward. This time Hans was dressed and wearing boots – of different colors. Apparently this was done on purpose, because he looked at his feet, clicked his tongue, and gave a sly smile. I couldn't account for this freak of fancy, but Jørgensen and some other men going to the dance had apparently had the same odd notion and were also wearing boots that didn't match.

Hans and Jørgensen took a quick drink and set off with their wives. I followed the two couples as far as the village hall, where a man standing guard at the door refused to admit me. 'You're not married,' he said. But the pastor spotted me from inside and asked that I be let in.

For the first time, I saw coffee being served in the village hall during a dance. The women were no longer separated from the men, as they usually were, but sitting with them. I felt out of place, with everybody paired off from the start. After midnight, with great uproar and loud singing, and faces pouring with sweat, people began to exchange wives. I had read that those present at these public wife-swappings practiced what was referred to as 'dowsing the lamps,' but that didn't happen on this occasion. You just saw a man get up and go sit beside another couple. He talked for a few moments, then simply left the hall with the other man's wife. Sometimes this happened while the other partner was dancing. The husband thus relieved of his wife looked around him, spotted another woman who might or might not be sitting with her husband, and went up to her. Soon after that, he too went off with a woman who was not his wife. Though the husbands relieved of their mates in this way gave the impression of not being too upset, it looked to me as if most of the women, if you watched closely, were only half willing. Still, like the co-wives in my native land, they seemed resigned to an age-old tradition.

Cecilia went off on Jørgensen's arm! I ran into Hans, who was heading towards a small group at the other end of the hall. Seeing his friend lead his wife away, he told me jokingly: 'You should have got cracking with her, but now she's gone – so hard luck!'

Around one in the morning I left the hall, which was now three-quarters empty. At home I was getting ready for bed when the door opened: it was Hans, coming home with Augustina.

She didn't leave until nine o'clock the next morning. Cecilia didn't get home until eleven.

Hans simply asked her: 'Were you cold there in the night?'

'*Namik!*'

'That's good.'

And that was all! Life resumed or just continued as if nothing had happened between the two of them, who had just openly swapped partners.

So Cecilia was Jørgensen's standby wife, while his wife Augustina was Hans's. Jørgensen was Hans's best friend. Apparently this exchange of wives took place only among friends, obeyed precise rules, and united the two men by an unbreakable tie. Though this practice brought them fresh pleasure, it also involved strict duties, and was not to be compared with the brief exchanges of girlfriends by the young unmarried men. Neither the Jørgensen family nor Hans's would ever go short of food if one of the two men returned empty-handed from hunting, or fell ill, so long as the other had killed a seal.

Motives of survival, then, have given rise to the strange custom of wife-swapping in the Far North. In this light, certain details of behavior which had made no sense to me a few weeks earlier now appeared in a different perspective. For instance, I remembered Cecilia protesting sharply when Jørgensen told me that his wife Augustina and I should become close friends. A third man – particularly a foreigner – admitted into this union of two couples could endanger, and even destroy, the alliance that would protect one of the two wives in the event (since women don't hunt) that her husband got killed. In the same way, Thue, practically a widower, couldn't enter into the firm and sacred friendship to be formed between two men only by means of their wives, and which laid the basis of unfailing mutual help between the two families.

But if the exchange of wives was a matter only for the couples concerned, why make a public exhibition of it by organizing a dance before the exchange takes place? Probably so as to have no secrets from the village. Hans packed away his boots of different colors, whose significance may be found in the exchange itself, and said to me: 'They fit me like a pair of gloves, but they're sometimes hard to wear!'

For my part, I had grasped the meaning of exchanging wives in the Arctic. All the same, I couldn't help wondering what my father and uncles, my brothers, and above all my grandfather would have to say about it, when I told the tale back home. Perhaps they'd simply think I'd been living among madmen.

'But you're a strange lot, too,' Hans shot back, 'with your eight wives and more under one roof, when it's hard enough living with just one!'

CHAPTER 14

'IN A FAR COUNTRY' (1899)

Jack London

In 1897, Jack London joined the Klondike gold rush. While in the Yukon, he developed scurvy and, as a result, eventually lost his four front teeth. 'In a Far Country' is one of the first stories London published. He sold it to Overland Monthly *in 1899, reportedly for $7.50.*

When a man journeys into a far country, he must be prepared to forget many of the things he has learned, and to acquire such customs as are inherent with existence in the new land; he must abandon the old ideals and the old gods, and oftentimes he must reverse the very codes by which his conduct has hitherto been shaped. To those who have the protean faculty of adaptability, the novelty of such change may even be a source of pleasure; but to those who happen to be hardened to the ruts in which they were created, the pressure of the altered environment is unbearable, and they chafe in body and in spirit under the new restrictions which they do not understand. This chafing is bound to act and react, producing divers evils and leading to various misfortunes. It were better for the man who cannot fit himself to the new groove to return to his own country; if he delay too long, he will surely die.

The man who turns his back upon the comforts of an elder civilization, to face the savage youth, the primordial simplicity of the North, may estimate success at an inverse ratio to the quantity and quality of his hopelessly fixed habits. He will soon discover, if he be a fit candidate, that the material habits are the less important. The exchange of such things as a dainty menu for rough fare, of the stiff leather shoe for the soft, shapeless moccasin, of the feather bed for a couch in the snow, is after all a very easy matter. But his pinch will come in learning properly to shape his mind's attitude toward all things, and especially toward his fellow man. For the courtesies of ordinary life, he must substitute unselfishness, forbearance, and tolerance. Thus, and thus only, can he gain that pearl of great price, – true comradeship. He must not say 'Thank you'; he must mean it without opening his mouth, and prove it by responding in kind. In short, he must substitute the deed for the word, the spirit for the letter.

When the world rang with the tale of Arctic gold, and the lure of the North gripped the heartstrings of men, Carter Weatherbee threw up his snug clerkship, turned the half of his savings over to his wife, and with the remainder bought an outfit. There was no romance in his nature, – the bondage of commerce had crushed all that; he was simply tired of the ceaseless grind, and wished to risk great hazards in view of corresponding returns. Like many another fool, disdaining the old trails used by the Northland pioneers for a score of years, he hurried to Edmonton in the spring of the year; and there, unluckily for his soul's welfare, he allied himself with a party of men.

There was nothing unusual about this party, except its plans. Even its goal, like that of all other parties, was the Klondike. But the route it had mapped out to attain that goal took away the breath of the hardiest native, born and bred to the vicissitudes of the

Northwest. Even Jacques Baptiste, born of a Chippewa woman and a renegade *voyageur* (having raised his first whimpers in a deerskin lodge north of the sixty-fifth parallel, and had the same hushed by blissful sucks of raw tallow), was surprised. Though he sold his services to them and agreed to travel even to the never-opening ice, he shook his head ominously whenever his advice was asked.

Percy Cuthfert's evil star must have been in the ascendant, for he, too, joined this company of argonauts. He was an ordinary man, with a bank account as deep as his culture, which is saying a good deal. He had no reason to embark on such a venture, – no reason in the world, save that he suffered from an abnormal development of sentimentality. He mistook this for the true spirit of romance and adventure. Many another man has done the like, and made as fatal a mistake.

The first break-up of spring found the party following the ice-run of Elk River. It was an imposing fleet, for the outfit was large, and they were accompanied by a disreputable contingent of half-breed *voyageurs* with their women and children. Day in and day out, they labored with the bateaux and canoes, fought mosquitoes and other kindred pests, or sweated and swore at the portages. Severe toil like this lays a man naked to the very roots of his soul, and ere Lake Athabasca was lost in the south, each member of the party had hoisted his true colors.

The two shirks and chronic grumblers were Carter Weatherbee and Percy Cuthfert. The whole party complained less of its aches and pains than did either of them. Not once did they volunteer for the thousand and one petty duties of the camp. A bucket of water to be brought, an extra armful of wood to be chopped, the dishes to be washed and wiped, a search to be made through the outfit for some suddenly indispensable article, – and these two effete scions of civilization discovered sprains or blisters requiring instant attention. They were the first to turn in at night, with a score of tasks yet undone; the last to turn out in the morning, when the start should be in readiness before the breakfast was begun. They were the first to fall to at meal-time, the last to have a hand in the cooking; the first to dive for a slim delicacy, the last to discover they had added to their own another man's share. If they toiled at the oars, they slyly cut the water at each stroke and allowed the boat's momentum to float up the blade. They thought nobody noticed; but their comrades swore under their breaths and grew to hate them, while Jacques Baptiste sneered openly and damned them from morning till night. But Jacques Baptiste was no gentleman.

At the Great Slave, Hudson Bay dogs were purchased, and the fleet sank to the guards with its added burden of dried fish and pemmican. Then canoe and bateau answered to the swift current of the Mackenzie, and they plunged into the Great Barren Ground. Every likely-looking 'feeder' was prospected, but the elusive 'pay-dirt' danced ever to the north. At the Great Bear, overcome by the common dread of the Unknown Lands, their *voyageurs* began to desert, and Fort of Good Hope saw the last and bravest bending to the tow-lines as they bucked the current down which they had so treacherously glided. Jacques Baptiste alone remained. Had he not sworn to travel even to the never-opening ice?

The lying charts, compiled in main from hearsay, were now constantly consulted. And they felt the need of hurry, for the sun had already passed its northern solstice and was leading the winter south again. Skirting the shores of the bay, where the Mackenzie disembogues into the Arctic Ocean, they entered the mouth of the Little Peel River. Then began the arduous up-stream toil, and the two Incapables fared worse than ever. Tow-line and pole, paddle and tump-line, rapids and portages, – such tortures served to give the one a deep disgust for great hazards, and printed for the other a fiery text on the true romance of adventure. One day they waxed mutinous, and being vilely cursed by Jacques Baptiste, turned, as worms sometimes will. But the half-breed thrashed the twain, and sent them, bruised and bleeding, about their work. It was the first time either had been man-handled.

Abandoning their river craft at the headwaters of the Little Peel, they consumed the rest of the summer in the great portage over the Mackenzie watershed to the West Rat. This little stream fed the Porcupine, which in turn joined the Yukon where that mighty highway of the North countermarches on the Arctic Circle. But they had lost in the race with winter, and one day they tied their rafts to the thick eddy-ice and hurried their goods ashore. That night the river jammed and broke several times; the following morning it had fallen asleep for good.

'We can't be more'n four hundred miles from the Yukon,' concluded Sloper, multiplying his thumb nails by the scale of the map. The council, in which the two Incapables had whined to excellent disadvantage, was drawing to a close.

'Hudson Bay Post, long time ago. No use um now.' Jacques Baptiste's father had made the trip for the Fur Company in the old days, incidentally marking the trail with a couple of frozen toes.

'Sufferin' cracky!' cried another of the party. 'No whites?'

'Nary white,' Sloper sententiously affirmed; 'but it's only five hundred more up the Yukon to Dawson. Call it a rough thousand from here.'

Weatherbee and Cuthfert groaned in chorus.

'How long I'll that take, Baptiste?'

The half-breed figured for a moment. 'Workum like hell, no man play out, ten – twenty – forty – fifty days. Um babies come' (designating the Incapables), 'no can tell. Mebbe when hell freeze over; mebbe not then.'

The manufacture of snowshoes and moccasins ceased. Somebody called the name of an absent member, who came out of an ancient cabin at the edge of the camp-fire and joined them. The cabin was one of the many mysteries which lurk in the vast recesses of the North. Built when and by whom, no man could tell. Two graves in the open, piled high with stones, perhaps contained the secret of those early wanderers. But whose hand had piled the stones?

The moment had come. Jacques Baptiste paused in the fitting of a harness and pinned the struggling dog in the snow. The cook made mute protest for delay, threw a handful of bacon into a noisy pot of beans, then came to attention. Sloper rose to his feet. His body was a ludicrous contrast to the healthy physiques of the Incapables. Yellow and weak, fleeing from a South American fever-hole, he had not broken his flight across the zones, and was still able to toil with men. His weight was probably ninety pounds, with the heavy hunting-knife thrown in, and his grizzled hair told of a prime which had ceased to be. The fresh young muscles of either Weatherbee or Cuthfert were equal to ten times the endeavor of his; yet he could walk them into the earth in a day's journey. And all this day he had whipped his stronger comrades into venturing a thousand miles of the stiffest hardship man can conceive. He was the incarnation of the unrest of his race, and the old Teutonic stubbornness, dashed with the quick grasp and action of the Yankee, held the flesh in the bondage of the spirit.

'All those in favor of going on with the dogs as soon as the ice sets, say ay.'

'Ay!' rang out eight voices, – voices destined to string a trail of oaths along many a hundred miles of pain.

'Contrary minded?'

'No!' For the first time the Incapables were united without some compromise of personal interests.

'And what are you going to do about it?' Weatherbee added belligerently.

'Majority rule! Majority rule!' clamored the rest of the party.

'I know the expedition is liable to fall through if you don't come,' Sloper replied sweetly; 'but I guess, if we try real hard, we can manage to do without you. What do you say, boys?'

The sentiment was cheered to the echo.

'But I say, you know,' Cuthfert ventured apprehensively; 'what's a chap like me to do?'

'Ain't you coming with us?'

'No-o.'

'Then do as you damn well please. We won't have nothing to say.'

'Kind o' calkilate yuh might settle it with that canoodlin' pardner of yourn,' suggested a heavy-going Westerner from the Dakotas, at the same time pointing out Weatherbee. 'He'll be shore to ask yuh what yur a-goin' to do when it comes to cookin' an' gatherin' the wood.'

'Then we'll consider it all arranged,' concluded Sloper. 'We'll pull out tomorrow, if we camp within five miles, – just to get everything in running order and remember if we've forgotten anything.'

❈

The sleds groaned by on their steel-shod runners, and the dogs strained low in the harnesses in which they were born to die. Jacques Baptiste paused by the side of Sloper to get a last glimpse of the cabin. The smoke curled up pathetically from the Yukon stove-pipe. The two Incapables were watching them from the door-way.

Sloper laid his hand on the other's shoulder.

'Jacques Baptiste, did you ever hear of the Kilkenny cats?'

The half-breed shook his head.

'Well, my friend and good comrade, the Kilkenny cats fought till neither hide, nor hair, nor yowl, was left. You understand? – till nothing was left. Very good. Now, these two men don't like work. They won't work. We know that. They'll be all alone in that cabin all winter, – a mighty long, dark winter. Kilkenny cats, – well?'

The Frenchman in Baptiste shrugged his shoulders, but the Indian in him was silent. Nevertheless, it was an eloquent shrug, pregnant with prophecy.

Things prospered in the little cabin at first. The rough badinage of their comrades had made Weatherbee and Cuthfert conscious of the mutual responsibility which had devolved upon them; besides, there was not so much work after all for two healthy men. And the removal of the cruel whip-hand, or in other words the bulldozing half-breed, had brought with it a joyous reaction. At first, each strove to outdo the other, and they performed petty tasks with an unction which would have opened the eyes of their comrades who were now wearing out bodies and souls on the Long Trail.

All care was banished. The forest, which shouldered in upon them from three sides, was an inexhaustible woodyard. A few yards from their door slept the Porcupine, and a hole through its winter robe formed a bubbling spring of water, crystal clear and painfully cold. But they soon grew to find fault with even that. The hole would persist in freezing up, and thus gave them many a miserable hour of ice-chopping. The unknown builders of the cabin had extended the side-logs so as to support a cache at the rear. In this was stored the bulk of the party's provisions. Food there was, without stint, for three times the men who were fated to live upon it. But the most of it was of the kind which built up brawn and sinew, but did not tickle the palate. True, there was sugar in plenty for two ordinary men; but these two were little else than children. They early discovered the virtues of hot water judiciously saturated with sugar, and they prodigally swam their flapjacks and soaked their crusts in the rich, white syrup. Then coffee and tea, and especially the dried fruits, made disastrous inroads upon it. The first words they had were over the sugar question. And it is a really serious thing when two men, wholly dependent upon each other for company, begin to quarrel.

Weatherbee loved to discourse blatantly on politics, while Cuthfert, who had been prone to clip his coupons and let the commonwealth jog on as best it might, either ignored the subject or delivered himself of startling epigrams. But the clerk was too obtuse to appreciate the clever shaping of thought, and this waste of ammunition irritated Cuthfert. He had been used to blinding people by his brilliancy, and it worked him quite a hardship, this loss of an audience. He felt personally aggrieved and unconsciously held his mutton-head companion responsible for it.

Save existence, they had nothing in common, – came in touch on no single point. Weatherbee was a clerk who had known naught but clerking all his life; Cuthfert was a master of arts, a dabbler in oils, and had written not a little. The one was a lower-class man who considered himself a gentleman, and the other was a gentleman who knew himself to be such. From this it may be remarked that a man can be a gentleman without possessing the first instinct of true comradeship. The clerk was as sensuous as the other was æsthetic, and his love adventures, told at great length and chiefly coined from his imagination, affected the supersensitive master of arts in the same way as so many whiffs of sewer gas. He deemed the clerk a filthy, uncultured brute, whose place was in the muck with the swine, and told him so; and he was reciprocally informed that he was a milk-and-water sissy and a cad. Weatherbee could not have defined 'cad' for his life; but it satisfied its purpose, which after all seems the main point in life.

Weatherbee flatted every third note and sang such songs as 'The Boston Burglar' and 'The Handsome Cabin Boy,' for hours at a time, while Cuthfert wept with rage, till he could stand it no longer and fled into the outer cold. But there was no escape. The intense frost could not be endured for long at a time, and the little cabin crowded them – beds, stove, table, and all – into a space of ten by twelve. The very presence of either became a personal affront to the other, and they lapsed into sullen silences which increased in length and strength as the days went by. Occasionally, the flash of an eye or the curl of a lip got the better of them, though they strove to wholly ignore each other during these mute periods. And a great wonder sprang up in the breast of each, as to how God had ever come to create the other.

With little to do, time became an intolerable burden to them. This naturally made them still lazier. They sank into a physical lethargy which there was no escaping, and which made them rebel at the performance of the smallest chore. One morning when it was his turn to cook the common breakfast, Weatherbee rolled out of his blankets, and to the snoring of his companion, lighted first the slush-lamp and then the fire. The kettles were frozen hard, and there was no water in the cabin with which to wash. But he did not mind that. Waiting for it to thaw, he sliced the bacon and plunged into the hateful task of bread-making. Cuthfert had been slyly watching through his half-closed lids. Consequently there was a scene, in which they fervently blessed each other, and agreed, thenceforth, that each do his own cooking. A week later, Cuthfert neglected his morning ablutions, but none the less complacently ate the meal which he had cooked. Weatherbee grinned. After that the foolish custom of washing passed out of their lives.

As the sugar-pile and other little luxuries dwindled, they began to be afraid they were not getting their proper shares, and in order that they might not be robbed, they fell to gorging themselves. The luxuries suffered in this gluttonous contest, as did also the men. In the absence of fresh vegetables and exercise, their blood became impoverished, and a loathsome, purplish rash crept over their bodies. Yet they refused to heed the warning. Next, their muscles and joints began to swell, the flesh turning black, while their mouths, gums, and lips took on the color of rich cream. Instead of being drawn together by their misery, each gloated over the other's symptoms as the scurvy took its course.

They lost all regard for personal appearance, and for that matter, common decency. The cabin became a pigpen, and never once were the beds made or fresh pine boughs laid underneath. Yet they could not keep to their blankets, as they would have wished; for the frost was inexorable, and the fire box consumed much fuel. The hair of their heads and faces grew long and shaggy, while their garments would have disgusted a ragpicker. But they did not care. They were sick, and there was no one to see; besides, it was very painful to move about.

To all this was added a new trouble, – the Fear of the North. This Fear was the joint child of the Great Cold and the Great Silence, and was born in the darkness of December, when the sun dipped below the southern horizon for good. It affected them according to their natures. Weatherbee fell prey to the grosser superstitions, and did his best to resurrect the spirits which slept in the forgotten graves. It was a fascinating thing, and in his dreams they came to him from out of the cold, and snuggled into his blankets, and told him of their toils and troubles ere they died. He shrank away from the clammy contact as they drew closer and twined their frozen limbs about him, and when they whispered in his ear of things to come, the cabin rang with his frightened shrieks. Cuthfert did not understand, – for they no longer spoke, – and when thus awakened he invariably grabbed for his revolver. Then he would sit up in bed, shivering nervously, with the weapon trained on the unconscious dreamer. Cuthfert deemed the man going mad, and so came to fear for his life.

His own malady assumed a less concrete form. The mysterious artisan who had laid the cabin, log by log, had pegged a wind-vane to the ridge-pole. Cuthfert noticed it always pointed south, and one day, irritated by its steadfastness of purpose, he turned it toward the east. He watched eagerly, but never a breath came by to disturb it. Then he turned the vane to the north, swearing never again to touch it till the wind did blow. But the air frightened him with its unearthly calm, and he often rose in the middle of the night to see if the vane had veered, – ten degrees would have satisfied him. But no, it poised above him as unchangeable as fate. His imagination ran riot, till it became to him a fetich. Sometimes he followed the path it pointed across the dismal dominions, and allowed his soul to become saturated with the Fear. He dwelt upon the unseen and the unknown till the burden of eternity appeared to be crushing him. Everything in the Northland had that crushing effect, – the absence of life and motion; the darkness; the infinite peace of the brooding land; the ghastly silence, which made the echo of each heart-beat a sacrilege; the solemn forest which seemed to guard an awful, inexpressible something, which neither word nor thought could compass.

The world he had so recently left, with its busy nations and great enterprises, seemed very far away. Recollections occasionally obtruded, – recollections of marts and galleries and crowded thoroughfares, of evening dress and social functions, of good men and dear women he had known, – but they were dim memories of a life he had lived long centuries agone, on some other planet. This phantasm was the Reality. Standing beneath the wind-vane, his eyes fixed on the polar skies, he could not bring himself to realize that the Southland really existed, that at that very moment it was a-roar with life and action. There was no Southland, no men being born of women, no giving and taking in marriage. Beyond his bleak sky-line there stretched vast solitudes, and beyond these still vaster solitudes. There were no lands of sunshine, heavy with the perfume of flowers. Such things were only old dreams of paradise. The sun-lands of the West and the spicelands of the East, the smiling Arcadias and blissful Islands of the Blest, – ha! ha! His laughter split the void and shocked him with its unwonted sound. There was no sun. This was the Universe, dead and cold and dark, and he its only citizen. Weatherbee? At such moments Weatherbee did not count. He was a Caliban, a monstrous phantom, fettered to him for untold ages, the penalty of some forgotten crime.

He lived with Death among the dead, emasculated by the sense of his own insignificance, crushed by the passive mastery of the slumbering ages. The magnitude of all things appalled him. Everything partook of the superlative save himself – the perfect cessation of wind and motion, the immensity of the snow-covered wilderness, the height of the sky and the depth of the silence. That wind-vane, – if it would only move. If a thunderbolt would fall, or the forest flare up in flame. The rolling up of the heavens as a scroll, the crash of Doom – anything, anything! But no, nothing moved; the Silence crowded in, and the Fear of the North laid icy fingers on his heart.

Once, like another Crusoe, by the edge of the river he came upon a track, – the faint tracery of a snowshoe rabbit on the delicate snow-crust. It was a revelation. There was life in the Northland. He would follow it, look upon it, gloat over it. He forgot his swollen muscles, plunging through the deep snow in an ecstasy of anticipation. The forest swallowed him up, and the brief midday twilight vanished; but he pursued his quest till exhausted nature asserted itself and laid him helpless in the snow. There he groaned and cursed his folly, and knew the track to be the fancy of his brain; and late that night he dragged himself into the cabin on hands and knees, his cheeks frozen and a strange numbness about his feet. Weatherbee grinned malevolently, but made no offer to help him. He thrust needles into his toes and thawed them out by the stove. A week later mortification set in.

But the clerk had his own troubles. The dead men came out of their graves more frequently now, and rarely left him, waking or sleeping. He grew to wait and dread their coming, never passing the twin cairns without a shudder. One night they came to him in his sleep and led him forth to an appointed task. Frightened into inarticulate horror, he awoke between the heaps of stones and fled wildly to the cabin. But he had lain there for some time, for his feet and cheeks were also frozen.

Sometimes he became frantic at their insistent presence, and danced about the cabin, cutting the empty air with an axe, and smashing everything within reach. During these ghostly encounters, Cuthfert huddled into his blankets and followed the madman about with a cocked revolver, ready to shoot him if he came too near. But, recovering from one of these spells, the clerk noticed the weapon trained upon him. His suspicions were aroused, and thenceforth he, too, lived in fear of his life. They watched each other closely after that, and faced about in startled fright whenever either passed behind the other's back. This apprehensiveness became a mania which controlled them even in their sleep. Through mutual fear they tacitly let the slush-lamp burn all night, and saw to a plentiful supply of bacon-grease before retiring. The slightest movement on the part of one was sufficient to arouse the other, and many a still watch their gazes countered as they shook beneath their blankets with fingers on the trigger-guards.

What with the Fear of the North, the mental strain, and the ravages of the disease, they lost all semblance of humanity, taking on the appearance of wild beasts, hunted and desperate. Their cheeks and noses, as an aftermath of the freezing, had turned black. Their frozen toes had begun to drop away at the first and second joints. Every movement brought pain, but the fire box was insatiable, wringing a ransom of torture from their miserable bodies. Day in, day out, it demanded its food, – a veritable pound of flesh, – and they dragged themselves into the forest to chop wood on their knees. Once, crawling thus in search of dry sticks, unknown to each other they entered a thicket from opposite sides. Suddenly, without warning, two peering death's-heads confronted each other. Suffering had so transformed them that recognition was impossible. They sprang to their feet, shrieking with terror, and dashed away on their mangled stumps; and falling at the cabin door, they clawed and scratched like demons till they discovered their mistake.

❀

Occasionally they lapsed normal, and during one of these sane intervals, the chief bone of contention, the sugar, had been divided equally between them. They guarded their separate sacks, stored up in the cache, with jealous eyes; for there were but a few cupfuls left, and they were totally devoid of faith in each other. But one day

Cuthfert made a mistake. Hardly able to move, sick with pain, with his head swimming and eyes blinded, he crept into the cache, sugar canister in hand, and mistook Weatherbee's sack for his own.

January had been born but a few days when this occurred. The sun had some time since passed its lowest southern declination, and at meridian now threw flaunting streaks of yellow light upon the northern sky. On the day following his mistake with the sugar-bag, Cuthfert found himself feeling better, both in body and in spirit. As noontime drew near and the day brightened, he dragged himself outside to feast on the evanescent glow, which was to him an earnest of the sun's future intentions. Weatherbee was also feeling somewhat better, and crawled out beside him. They propped themselves in the snow beneath the moveless wind-vane, and waited.

The stillness of death was about them. In other climes, when nature falls into such moods, there is a subdued air of expectancy, a waiting for some small voice to take up the broken strain. Not so in the North. The two men had lived seeming æons in this ghostly peace. They could remember no song of the past; they could conjure no song of the future. This unearthly calm had always been, — the tranquil silence of eternity.

Their eyes were fixed upon the north. Unseen, behind their backs, behind the towering mountains to the south, the sun swept toward the zenith of another sky than theirs. Sole spectators of the mighty canvas, they watched the false dawn slowly grow. A faint flame began to glow and smoulder. It deepened in intensity, ringing the changes of reddish-yellow, purple, and saffron. So bright did it become that Cuthfert thought the sun must surely be behind it, — a miracle, the sun rising in the north! Suddenly, without warning and without fading, the canvas was swept clean. There was no color in the sky. The light had gone out of the day. They caught their breaths in half-sobs. But lo! the air was a-glint with particles of scintillating frost, and there, to the north, the wind-vane lay in vague outline on the snow. A shadow! A shadow! It was exactly midday. They jerked their heads hurriedly to the south. A golden rim peeped over the mountain's snowy shoulder, smiled upon them an instant, then dipped from sight again.

There were tears in their eyes as they sought each other. A strange softening came over them. They felt irresistibly drawn toward each other. The sun was coming back again. It would be with them to-morrow, and the next day, and the next. And it would stay longer every visit, and a time would come when it would ride their heaven day and night, never once dropping below the sky-line. There would be no night. The ice-locked winter would be broken; the winds would blow and the forests answer; the land would bathe in the blessed sunshine, and life renew. Hand in hand, they would quit this horrid dream and journey back to the Southland. They lurched blindly forward, and their hands met, – their poor maimed hands, swollen and distorted beneath their mittens.

But the promise was destined to remain unfulfilled. The Northland is the Northland, and men work out their souls by strange rules, which other men, who have not journeyed into far countries, cannot come to understand.

An hour later, Cuthfert put a pan of bread into the oven, and fell to speculating on what the surgeons could do with his feet when he got back. Home did not seem so very far away now. Weatherbee was rummaging in the cache. Of a sudden, he raised a whirlwind of blasphemy, which in turn ceased with startling abruptness. The other man had robbed his sugar-sack. Still, things might have happened differently, had not the two dead men come out from under the stones and hushed the hot words in his throat. They led him quite gently from the cache, which he forgot to close. That consummation was reached; that something they had whispered to him in his dreams was about to happen. They guided him gently, very gently, to the woodpile, where they put the axe in his hands. Then they helped him shove open the cabin door, and he felt sure they shut it after him, – at least he heard it slam and the latch fall sharply into place. And he knew they were waiting just without, waiting for him to do his task.

'Carter! I say, Carter!'

Percy Cuthfert was frightened at the look on the clerk's face, and he made haste to put the table between them.

Carter Weatherbee followed, without haste and without enthusiasm. There was neither pity nor passion in his face, but rather the patient, stolid look of one who has certain work to do and goes about it methodically.

'I say, what's the matter?'

The clerk dodged back, cutting off his retreat to the door, but never opening his mouth.

'I say, Carter, I say; let's talk. There's a good chap.'

The master of arts was thinking rapidly, now, shaping a skillful flank movement on the bed where his Smith & Wesson lay. Keeping his eyes on the madman, he rolled backward on the bunk, at the same time clutching the pistol.

'Carter!'

The powder flashed full in Weatherbee's face, but he swung his weapon and leaped forward. The axe bit deeply at the base of the spine, and Percy Cuthfert felt all consciousness of his lower limbs leave him. Then the clerk fell heavily upon him, clutching him by the throat with feeble fingers. The sharp bite of the axe had caused

Cuthfert to drop the pistol, and as his lungs panted for release, he fumbled aimlessly for it among the blankets. Then he remembered. He slid a hand up the clerk's belt to the sheath-knife; and they drew very close to each other in that last clinch.

Percy Cuthfert felt his strength leave him. The lower portion of his body was useless. The inert weight of Weatherbee crushed him, – crushed him and pinned him there like a bear under a trap. The cabin became filled with a familiar odor, and he knew the bread to be burning. Yet what did it matter? He would never need it. And there were all of six cupfuls of sugar in the cache, – if he had foreseen this he would not have been so saving the last several days. Would the wind-vane ever move? It might even be veering now. Why not? Had he not seen the sun to-day? He would go and see. No; it was impossible to move. He had not thought the clerk so heavy a man.

How quickly the cabin cooled! The fire must be out. The cold was forcing in. It must be below zero already, and the ice creeping up the inside of the door. He could not see it, but his past experience enabled him to gauge its progress by the cabin's temperature. The lower hinge must be white ere now. Would the tale of this ever reach the world? How would his friends take it? They would read it over their coffee, most likely, and talk it over at the clubs. He could see them very clearly. 'Poor Old Cuthfert,' they murmured; 'not such a bad sort of a chap, after all.' He smiled at their eulogies, and passed on in search of a Turkish bath. It was the same old crowd upon the streets. Strange, they did not notice his moosehide moccasins and tattered German socks! He would take a cab. And after the bath a shave would not be bad. No; he would eat first. Steak, and potatoes, and green things, – how fresh it all was! And what was that? Squares of honey, streaming liquid amber! But why did they bring so much? Ha! ha! he could never eat it all. Shine!

Why certainly. He put his foot on the box. The bootblack looked curiously up at him, and he remembered his moosehide moccasins and went away hastily.

Hark! The wind-vane must be surely spinning. No; a mere singing in his ears. That was all, – a mere singing. The ice must have passed the latch by now. More likely the upper hinge was covered. Between the moss-chinked roof-poles, little points of frost began to appear. How slowly they grew! No; not so slowly. There was a new one, and there another. Two – three – four; they were coming too fast to count. There were two growing together. And there, a third had joined them. Why, there were no more spots. They had run together and formed a sheet.

Well, he would have company. If Gabriel ever broke the silence of the North, they would stand together, hand in hand, before the great White Throne. And God would judge them, God would judge them!

Then Percy Cuthfert closed his eyes and dropped off to sleep.

CHAPTER 15

'LAND HO!'

from *In the Land of White Death* (1917)

Valerian Albanov

In 1912, Valerian Albanov, a Russian navigator, signed on to an expedition to search out new hunting grounds. Two hundred miles east of Novaya Zemlya, the expedition's ship, the Santa Anna, *became frozen in. It drifted for a year and a half, carried nearly 2,500 miles by the moving ice. Finally, Albanov and thirteen other crew members left the* Santa Anna, *and set off on foot for Franz Josef Land. Only he and one other man completed the journey. In the excerpts below, Albanov recounts his departure from the ship, in January 1914, and his first sighting of land, six months later.*

Late in the evening the lieutenant called me once more into his cabin to give me a list of items we would be taking with us and which I must, if possible, return to him at a later date. Here is that list as it was entered into the ship's record: 2 Remington rifles, 1 Norwegian hunting rifle, 1 double-barreled shotgun, 2 repeating rifles, 1 ship's log transformed into a pedometer for measuring distances covered, 2 harpoons, 2 axes, 1 saw, 2 compasses, 14 pairs of skis, 1 first-quality malitsa, 12 second-quality malitsi, 1 sleeping bag, 1 chronometer, 1 sextant, 14 rucksacks, and 1 small pair of binoculars.[*]

Brusilov asked me if he had forgotten to list anything. His pettiness astounded me. It was as if he thought there were horses waiting at the gangway to take those of us who would be leaving to the nearest railway station or steamship terminal. Had the lieutenant forgotten that we were about to set off on foot on a daunting trek across drifting ice, in order to search for an unknown landmass, and this under worse conditions than any men who had gone before us? Did he have no greater concerns on this last evening than toting up rucksacks, axes, a defective ship's log, a saw, and harpoons? If truth be told, even as he read the list to me, I felt myself succumbing to a familiar rage. I experienced the sensation of strangling as my throat constricted in anger. But I controlled myself and reminded Brusilov that he had forgotten to list the tent, the kayaks, the sledges, a mug, cups, and a galvanized bucket. He immediately wrote down the tent, but decided not to mention the dishes. 'I will not list the kayaks or sledges, either,' he offered. 'In all probability they will be badly damaged by the end of your trip, and the freight to ship them from Svalbard would cost more than they are worth. But if you succeed in getting them to Alexandrovsk, deliver them to the local police for safekeeping.' I told Brusilov I was in agreement with this.

I left the lieutenant's cabin very upset, and went below. On the way to my cabin, Denisov stopped me to ask where I would open the packet of ship's mail and post the letters – in Norway or Russia?

---

[*] Malitsi are heavy, sacklike, Samoyed garments sewn from reindeer hide, with the fur on the inside. Slipped over the head, they have crude openings to accommodate the arms and the face. Thirteen of the men in Albanov's party used malitsi in lieu of sleeping bags at night.

That was the last straw, and I could not contain my emotions any longer. I exploded and threatened to dump not only the mail, but also the rucksacks, the cups, and the mugs into the first open lead we came to, because I had serious doubts that we would ever reach a mail train in Norway, Russia, or anywhere else. But then I quickly regained my composure and promised Denisov that, wherever we landed, I would make every effort to see that the ship's mail reached its destination.

Denisov went on his way, reassured. The ship was dark. Everyone had gone to bed. I was dismayed and depressed. It was as if I were already wandering across the endless, icy wastes, without any hope of returning to the ship, and with only the unknown lying ahead.

On that gloomy, decisive night prior to my departure from the *Saint Anna*, filled with anxiety, I wondered about each of the men who would be accompanying me. I already possessed grave doubts about their health and stamina. One was fifty-six years old and all of them complained of sore feet; not one of them was really fit. One man had open sores on his legs, another had a hernia, a third had been suffering from pains in his chest for a long time, and all, without exception, had asthma and palpitations.

In short, these were the dark thoughts that assailed and disheartened me that evening. Was this a premonition of some great misfortune that I was heading for, with no hope of escape?

June 9. The wind swings back and forth between the northwest and the west-northwest. Despite the overcast skies, I was able to determine that with no effort on our part we had reached 80° 52′ north and 40° 20′ east of Greenwich. But I cannot guarantee the exactness of the longitude.

As I have often done, at around nine in the evening I climbed onto a high ice formation to study the horizon. Ordinarily I saw what looked like islands in every direction, but which on closer examination turned out to be either icebergs or clouds. This time, I sighted something quite different on the shimmering horizon. I was so staggered that I sat down on the ice to clean the lenses of my binoculars and rub my eyes. My pulse was racing in great anticipation, and when I fixed my apprehensive gaze once more on the vision that held such promise, I could discern a pale, silver strip with sinuous contours running along the horizon and then disappearing to the left. The right-hand side of this phenomenon was outlined with unusual clarity against the azure of the sky. This whole formation, including its gradations of color, reminded me of a phase of the moon. The left edge seemed to grow slowly paler while the right stood out even more distinctly, like a yellowish line traced along the blue horizon. Four days earlier I had observed a similar phenomenon; but the bad light led me to think that it was a cloud. During the night I returned five times to check on my strange discovery, and each time my original impression was more or less clearly confirmed; the main features of shape and color had certainly not changed. So far, nobody else had noticed this wonderful sight. I had to restrain myself severely from dashing back to the tent and shouting with excitement: 'Wake up, everyone, come and see that our prayers have been answered at last and we are about to reach land!' I was then convinced that it was land that I could see, but I wanted to keep my discovery secret, so I contented myself with thinking: 'If you others want to see this miracle, you will have to open your eyes.' But my companions were as oblivious as ever, and had not even noticed my ill-concealed excitement. Instead of going out and inspecting the horizon, the only way of evaluating our immediate prospects, they either went back to sleep or started to hunt for 'game' – as we have named the lice that are regular guests in our malitsi. That seems to be more important to them!

June 10. The morning was beautiful. My hypothetical land stood out even more clearly, its yellowish hue increasingly extraordinary. Its shape was totally different from what I had been expecting as I scanned the horizon over the past two months. Now I could also see, to my left, a few isolated headlands, set quite far back, however, and between them seemed to be glaciers. I wondered idly how far away we were, for my eyes were not at all used to judging such distances. I estimated that there must be fifty or sixty nautical miles to the most distant peaks; how far we might be from the shore could not even be roughly determined: twenty to thirty-five nautical miles, perhaps more, perhaps less. The only certainty was that we were now closer to being rescued than we had been for the last two years. I silently offered up my thanks; but how on earth could we get there?

At around noon I managed to fix our position from the sun. We were crossing latitude 80° 52′. Wind from the south. We ate quickly, packed up our belongings, and decided to head for land. By nine o'clock we had covered between two and three miles and made the decision not to pitch the tent until we reached land. Could we do it? The ice floes were in perpetual motion; it was almost impossible to advance without resorting to the kayaks. We spotted quite a few bear tracks; we also succeeded in shooting a seal.

Evening has arrived. We sit together in the tent with mixed feelings, for not only have we failed to reach the island, we are now even farther away from it than this morning. The weather is very gloomy;

it is snowing and raining, with wind from the south. The surface of the ice was dreadful; my companions call it 'glutinous.' It was impossible to make any sort of progress today, either on foot or by kayak. Exhausted, soaked through, and famished, we decided to stop and pitch the tent. South wind still blowing. Major efforts have brought us no more than two miles at the most. But we managed to kill a seal, which we are cooking; we have brewed up a very nourishing broth with the seal's blood. Once we really start cooking we do not skimp on the size of the portions. Today we had a good, solid breakfast; at midday a bucketful of soup and just as much tea; in the evening, a pound of meat each, washed down with more tea. Our food supply is ample, for in addition to what I have just mentioned, each man receives a pound of ship's biscuits per day. Our appetites are wolfish! In gloomy moments we are struck by the thought that such voraciousness normally occurs in cases of severe starvation. God protect us from that!

Yesterday I noticed that seven pounds of biscuit had disappeared. This unfortunate discovery forced me to call my companions together and inform them that if it happened again, I would hold all of them responsible and reduce their rations; and if I managed to catch the ignominious thief red-handed, I would shoot him on the spot. However bitter it seems, I must admit there are three or four men in the group with whom I have nothing in common.

Only someone who has experienced such an ordeal can fully understand how impatient I was to reach the island where our two-year odyssey through the Arctic wastes would finally end. Once we reached our landfall, our situation would improve dramatically. We would be able to capture hosts of birds and walruses and we would also be able to take a bath. We have not washed now for two months. Catching a chance glimpse of my face in the sextant's mirror the other day gave me a terrible fright. I am so disfigured that I am unrecognizable, covered as I am with a thick layer of filth. And we all look like this. We have tried to rub off some of this dirt, but without much success. As a result we look even more frightening, almost as if we were tattooed! Our underclothes and outer garments are unspeakable. And since these rags are swarming with 'game,' I am sure that if we put one of our infested jerseys on the ground, it would crawl away all by itself!

Here is a glimpse of life inside the tent: Everyone is squatting in a circle on the ground; with grim expressions, they are silently absorbed in some serious-looking task. What can these men be doing? Hunting lice! This 'pastime' is always reserved for the evening. It is the only possible form of hygiene, since we have neither soap nor water for proper ablutions. And even if we had some water, the fearful cold would prevent us from washing. All too often we have not even had enough water to quench our thirst.

Some of us had originally taken a vow not to wash until we reached land. Who would have suspected that it would be two months before we sighted land? No wonder we all felt the need to indulge in our nightly 'hunt.' This communal activity united us in a remarkable fashion, and all the squabbles usually ceased during those hours.

In the afternoon I went out with three men on a reconnaissance. Beyond the four leads we will have to cross tomorrow morning, we shall find better going. The ice blocks are unusually dark and dirty, with algae, sand, and even rocks sticking to them. We took a couple of small stones, seaweed, and two small pieces of wood with us, as our first gift from the land — an olive branch, so to speak.

We found a lot of bear tracks. The weather, as usual, is damp and foggy. There is wet snow falling, almost rain. Wind from the south.

June 11. A satisfactory day's march. We covered four miles. Toward evening, we pitched camp on a little ice floe surrounded by pools and brash ice. The morning's northeasterly had by evening become a chilly northerly. The current has pushed us away toward the east, and now our island of salvation appears to be farther south. Good hunting: one seal and a duck. Our eyes are very painful again.

June 12. The wind is still blowing from the north, but the weather is warm and clear. Only the kayak crossings were difficult: We covered scarcely more than a mile. Seven of the men, including myself, are suffering from serious eye inflammation. While crossing one of the open leads we had the serious misfortune of dropping one of our two remaining Remingtons into the sea. It was Lunayev who dropped it, with Smirennikov's assistance. Such negligence made me so angry that I lost my temper and struck out at anybody who crossed my path. This is the second rifle we have lost because of heedless behavior, and anyone who can picture himself in my shoes would surely understand my frustration with such unforgivable carelessness. Now we have just one rifle for which there is abundant ammunition. The smaller repeating rifle is hardly of any use, since there are only eighty cartridges left for it. We still have shells for the shotgun, but it is almost useless against bears, which may be lurking behind every block of ice.

I would have liked to take a sun shot with the sextant, but my eyes were not up to it. The sun seemed to be misty and indistinct and I could not see the horizon at all. According to my companions who can still see clearly, our island is particularly visible today: One can even make out a few details. We saw many eiders in flight that must have come from the island. As our supply of seal meat has run out, for lunch we cooked the bear meat we dried the other day, and in the evening we prepared a soup from the same meat. There is no more sugar, and the tea will last only a few more days.

We are still making little headway trekking over the ice. But we have thought up a new strategy: We work out our course from the top of a rise – that is, we identify the places ahead of time where our kayaks or skis are most likely to get through. Often we are forced to skirt along the edge of a channel on our skis, dragging the sledge-laden kayak behind us on the water. But chunks of disintegrating icebergs, called growlers, often obstruct the boats, and it is not a simple affair to get them moving again. From time to time during our backbreaking toil, one of us sinks through the ice, and that is when we see who can move the fastest. It is imperative to leap out of the icy water, remove one's boots that are rapidly filling up, empty them, and get back to work, all in a matter of seconds!

June 13. The wind has shifted, coming now from the south-south-west. We set off at eight o'clock and traveled, with only an hour's break, until six-thirty in the evening. The end result: about five miles. We had to cross more extensive pack ice that had been eroded by the wave action and covered in deep snow. Crossing a channel we were startled when a bearded seal suddenly bounded out of the water. We also saw a great many ordinary seals but were unable to shoot one.

When the horizon grew lighter, those of us who were not suffering from snow blindness were able to see the island to the southeast. From now on, the tides will probably swirl growlers and brash ice continually along the shores, and we shall be confronted with this repulsive stuff, this ice porridge, all the way to our landfall. Toward evening, the wind from the south-southwest picked up, bringing with it fine hail.

June 14. The same wind persists, with cold, dark weather. We did two and a half miles this morning. On very thin ice, Konrad suddenly broke through a seal's breathing hole that had been drifted over. Totally submerged, he became tangled in his hauling line while the sledge slid forward and covered the hole. We all rushed to his rescue, cut the hauling line, dragged the sledge aside, and pulled Konrad out. He was soaked to the skin and had swallowed some water. We had to pitch the tent right away and light a fire to warm him up.

Our supplies are dwindling. We have only 120 pounds of biscuits left, and our reserves of meat are finished; for lunch we had nothing but biscuit soup, to which we added our last can of condensed milk. The dire state of our supplies forced us to take some quick action, and we decided on some long-term plans that included abandoning the tent and continuing in our nearly empty kayaks. We would be sorry to leave behind nearly all our belongings: axes, harpoons, ski poles, spare skis, warm clothing, footgear, and empty cans. These represent a considerable load, but at the same time how indispensable all such things will be if we have to winter over on these islands. And in all probability, we will not be spared a wintering.

No sooner had we set off again than we came upon some seals and shot two of them. Fortune had smiled upon us once again during our hour of need. This lucky event restored our courage to such a degree that we went back for the tent. The route was dreadful and required great caution; we barely covered one mile.

CHAPTER 16

'ICELANDIC PIONEER'

from *Independent People* (1934)

Halldór Laxness

The Nobel Prize-winning author Halldór Laxness was born in Iceland in 1902. Over his long career — he died at the age of 95 — he wrote fifty-one novels. Independent People, *Laxness's most celebrated work, was published in Icelandic in 1934. It tells the story of Bjartur of Summerhouses, a stiff-necked sheep farmer who recites traditional bal-lads while enduring unspeakable miseries. In the passage below, Bjartur has gone looking for a lost sheep from his flock.*

It is one of the peculiarities of life that the most unlikely accident, rather than the best-laid plan, may on occasion determine the place of a man's lodging; and thus it fared for Bjartur of Summerhouses now. Just as he was about to cross one of the many gullies that cleave the sides of the valley all the way down to the river, he saw some animals leap lightly down a watercourse not far ahead of him and come to a halt well out on the river bank. He saw immediately that they were reindeer, one bull and three cows. They tripped about on the bank for a little while, the bull next the river and the cows seeking shelter in his lee, all with their antlers in the weather and their hindquarters facing the man, for the wind was blowing from across the river.

Halting in the gulley, Bjartur eyed the animals for some moments. They kept up a continual shifting about, but always so that they were turned away from him. They were fine beasts, probably just in their prime, so it was no wonder that it occurred to Bjartur that he was in luck's way tonight, for it would be no mean catch if he could trap only one of them even. The bull especially looked as if it would make an excellent carcass, judging by its size, and he had not forgotten that reindeer venison is one of the tastiest dishes that ever graced a nobleman's table. Bjartur felt that even if he did not find the ewe, the trip would have proved well worth while if he managed now to capture a reindeer. But supposing that he caught the bull, how was he to kill it so that its blood did not run to waste? — for from reindeer blood may be made really first-class sandwich meat. The best plan, if he could only manage it, would be to take it back home alive, and with this intention in his mind he searched his pockets for those two articles which are most indispensable to a man on a journey, a knife and some string, and found both, a nice hank of string and his pocket-knife. He thought: 'I'll make a rush at him now and get him down. Then I'll stick the point of my knife through his nose, thread the string through the hole, and make a lead of it. In that way I ought to be able to lead him most of the way over the moors, or at least till I come to some easily remembered spot where I can tether him and keep him till I go down to the farms and fetch men and materials.' Summerhouses was, of course, easily a day's journey for a man travelling on foot. When Bjartur had completed his plan of attack he stole half-bent down the gully till he was opposite the reindeer, where they stood with their horns in the wind on the strip between the gully and the river. He stole cautiously over the runnels, crept silently up the bank, and, peeping over the edge, saw that he was no more than twelve feet from the buck. His muscles began to taughten with the

thrill of the hunt and he felt a certain amount of palpitation. Inch
by inch he pulled himself higher over the brink, until he was standing on the bank; slowly, very slowly he stole up to the bull, half a
pace alongside – and the next instant had leaped at him and gripped
him by one of the antlers, low down near the head. At the man's
unexpected attack, the animals gave a sudden bound, flung up their
heads, and pricked their ears, and the cows were off immediately,
running lightly down the river through the drizzling snow. At first
the bull had intended making off with Bjartur holding on to its head
as if he made no difference at all, but Bjartur hung on and the bull
could not get free, and though it tossed its head repeatedly, it was
none the freer for it. But Bjartur soon found that his hold on the
antler was uncertain, there being something on it like smooth bark
that kept on slipping in his grip, and the creature too lively to allow
a secure purchase anywhere else. He saw too, when it came to the
point, that he would have to abandon his hope of getting under the
animal's neck and gripping it with a wrestling hold, for its horns
were of the sharpest and the prospect of having them plunged into
his bowels not particularly attractive. For a while they continued
their tug of war, the reindeer gradually gaining ground, till it had
reached a tolerable speed and had dragged Bjartur quite a distance
down the river. Then involuntarily there flashed across Bjartur's
mind the trick he had been taught from childhood to use with wild
horses: try to get alongside them, then jump on their backs. It succeeded. Next instant he was sitting astride the reindeer's back
holding on to its antlers – and said later that though this animal
species seemed light enough on its feet, a bull reindeer was as rough
a ride as he had ever come across, and, indeed, it took him all his
time to hang on. But the jaunt was not to be a long one. For when
the bull had hopped a few lengths with this undesirable burden on
his back without managing to shake it off, he saw quickly that

desperate measures would have to be taken and, making a sudden leap at right angles to his previous course, shot straight into Glacier River and was immediately churning the water out of his depth.

Well, well. Bjartur had set out on a trip after sheep right enough, but this was becoming something more in the nature of a voyage. Here he was sitting neither more nor less than up to the waist in Glacier River, and that on no ordinary steed, but on the only steed that is considered suitable for the most renowned of adventures. But was Bjartur really proud of this romantic progress? No, far from it. He had at the moment no leisure to study either the distinctive features of his exploit or the rarity of its occurrence, for he had as much as he could do to hold his balance on the reindeer's back. Desperately he hung on to its horns, his legs glued to its flanks, gasping for breath, a black mist before his eyes. The rush of the water swept the animal downstream for a while, and for a long time it seemed as if it intended making no effort to land. Across the river the banks, which rose high and steep out of the water, showed intermittently through the snow, but in spite of the nearness of land Bjartur felt himself as unhappily situated as a man out in mid-ocean in an oarless boat. Sometimes the cross-currents caught the bull, forcing it under, and then the water, so unbearably cold that it made his head reel, came up to the man's neck and he was not sure which would happen first, whether he would lose consciousness or the deer would take a dive that would be the end of him. In this fashion they were carried down Glacier River for some time.

At long last it began to look as if the bull was thinking of landing. Bjartur suddenly realized that they had neared the eastern bank of the river and were now not more than a yard or two from the jagged fringe of ice that formed the only shore. They were carried downstream along by the ice for a while longer, but as the banks rose everywhere with equal steepness from the ice edge, the matter of effecting a landing remained a most unattractive project. Bjartur nevertheless felt that his best course, if the bull neared the land sufficiently, would be to seize the opportunity and throw himself overboard, then try to haul himself up on the ice, for this stay in cold water was becoming more than he could stand. He realized, of course, that it would be a death-jump that could only end in one of two ways. Finally there came a time when the bull swam for a few yards not more than half an arm's length from the ice, and the man watched his chance, let go of the antlers, heaved himself out of the water, and swung the upper part of his body on to the ice; and there Bjartur parted from the bull, never to set eyes on it again, and with a permanent dislike for the whole of that animal species.

There occurred moments, both then and later, when it struck Bjartur that the bull reindeer was no other than the devil Kolumkilli in person.

The ice was thin and broke immediately under the man's weight, so that he was near to being carried away with the fragments; but as his days were not yet numbered he managed somehow to hang on to the unbroken ice, and succeeded finally in wriggling his lower limbs also out of the water. He was shaking from head to foot with the cold, his teeth chattering, not a single dry stitch in all his clothes. But he did not feel particularly safe on this narrow fringe of ice and began now to tackle the ascent of the river bank. This in itself was a sufficiently hazardous undertaking, for the bank was not only precipitous, but also covered with icicles formed by the rising of the river, and there could only be one end to a fall if hand or foot should lose its grip. As he was fatigued after his exploit in the water, it took him longer to work his way up to the top than it would otherwise have done, but finally the moment arrived when he was standing safe and sound on the eastern bank of Glacier River – on the far pastures of another county. He took off his jacket and wrung it out, then rolled about in the snow to dry himself, and considered the snow warm in comparison with the glacier water. At intervals he stood up and swung his arms vigorously to rid himself of his shivering. It was, of course, not long before he realized to the full what a trick the bull had played on him by ferrying him over Glacier River. In the first place he had cheated him of the quarters he had proposed to use for the night, the shepherds' hut on the western side of the river. But that actually was only a trifle. Altogether more serious was to find himself suddenly switched to the eastern bank of Glacier River, for the river flowed north-east, whereas Bjartur's direction home lay a trifle west of north-west. To cross the river he would therefore be forced to make a detour in an opposite direction to Summerhouses, all the way down to the aerial ferry in the farming districts, and this was not less than a twenty hours' walk, even at a good speed, for the nearest farm in Glacierdale was at least fifteen hours away. Though he were to travel day and night this adventure of his would thus delay him almost forty-eight hours — and that in weather like this, and his lambs still out.

He was pretty well worn out, though loath to admit it to himself, and his wet clothes would be a poor protection if he decided to bury himself in the snow in this hardening frost. The snowflakes grew smaller and keener; no sooner had they fallen than the wind lifted them again and chased them along the ground in a spuming, knee-deep smother. His underclothes remained unaffected by the frost as long as he was on the move, but his outer clothes were frozen hard and his eyelashes and beard stiff with ice. In his knapsack there remained one whole blood pudding, frozen hard as a stone, and half of another; he had lost his stick. The night was as black as pitch, and the darkness seemed solid enough to be cut with a knife. The wind blew from the east, sweeping the blizzard straight into the man's face. Time and time again be tumbled from another and yet another brink into another and yet another hollow where the powdery snow took him up to the groin and flew about him like ash. One consolation only there was: happen what might, he could not lose his way, for on his left he had Glacier River with its heavy, sullen roar.

He swore repeatedly, ever the more violently the unsteadier his legs became, but to steel his senses he kept his mind fixed persistently on the world-famous battles of the rhymes. He recited the most powerful passages one after another over and over again, dwelling especially on the description of the devilish heroes, Grimur Ægir and Andri. It was Grimur he was fighting now, he thought; Grimur, that least attractive of all fiends, that foul-mouthed demon in the form of a troll, who had been his antagonist all along; but now an end would be put to the deadly feud, for now the stage was set for the final struggle. In mental vision he pursued Grimur the length of his monstrous career, right from the moment when Groa the Sibyl found him on the foreshore, yellow and stuffed with treachery; and again and again he depicted the monster in the poet's words, bellowing, wading in the earth up to the thighs, filled with devilish hate and sorcery, fire spouting from his grinning mouth, by human strength more than invincible:

> *The monster lived on moor or fen;*
> *The sea was in his power.*
> *He'd shamelessly drink the blood of men,*
> *The steaming flesh devour.*

> *The crags before him split apart,*
> *The rivers ran in spate;*
> *He cleft the rocks by magic art,*
> *His cunning was so great.*

For this fiend there was not a shred of mercy in Bjartur. No matter how often he sprawled headlong down the gullies, he was up again undaunted and with redoubled fury making yet another attack, grinding his teeth and hurling curses at the demon's gnashing jaws, determined not to call a halt before Grimur's evil spirit had been hounded to the remotest corners of hell and the naked brand had pierced him through and his death-throes had begun in a ring-dance of land and sea.

Again and again he imagined that he had made an end of Grimur and sent him howling to hell in the poet's immortal words, but still the blizzard assailed him with undiminished fury when he reached the top of the next ridge, clawed at his eyes and the roots of his beard, howled vindictively in his ears, and tried to hurl him to the ground – the struggle was by no means over, he was still fighting at close quarters with the poison-spewing thanes of hell, who came storming over the earth in raging malice till the vault of heaven shook to the echo of their rush.

His loathsome head aloft he reared,
With hellish hate he roared.
His slavering lips with froth were smeared,
Vilely his curses poured.

And so on, over and over again.

Never, never did these thanes of hell escape their just deserts. No one ever heard of Harekur or Gongu-Hrolfur or Bernotus being worsted in the final struggle. In the same way no one will be able to say that Bjartur of Summerhouses ever got the worst of it in his world war with the country's spectres, no matter how often he might tumble over a precipice or roll head over heels down a gully – 'while there's a breath left in my nostrils, it will never keep me down, however hard it blows.' Finally he stood still, leaning against the blizzard as against a wall; and neither could push the other back. He then resolved to house himself in the snow and began looking for a sheltered spot in a deep gully. With his hands he scooped out a cave in a snowdrift, trying to arrange it so that he could sit inside on his haunches to pile up the snow at the mouth, but the snow, loose and airy, refused to stick together, and as the man was without implements, the cave simply fell in again. He had not rested long in the snowdrift before the cold began to penetrate him; a stiffness and a torpor crept up his limbs, all the way to his groin, but what was worse was the drowsiness that was threatening him, the seductive sleep of the snow, which makes it so pleasant to die in a blizzard; nothing is so important as to be able to strike aside this tempting hand which beckons so voluptuously into realms of warmth and rest. To keep the oblivion of the snow at bay it was his custom to recite or, preferably, sing at the top of his voice all the obscene verse he had picked up since childhood, but such sur- roundings were never very conducive to song and on this occasion his voice persisted in breaking; and the drowsiness continued to envelop his consciousness in its mists, till now there swam before his inner eye pictures of men and events, both from life and from the Ballads – horse-meat steaming on a great platter, flocks of sheep bleating in the fold, Bernotus Borneyarkappi in disguise, clergy- men's wanton daughters wearing real silk stockings; and finally, by unsensed degrees, he assumed another personality and discovered himself in the character of Grimur the Noble, brother of Ulfar the Strong, when the visit was paid to his bedchamber. Matters stood thus, that the King, father of the brothers, had taken in marriage a young woman, who, since the King was well advanced in years, found a sad lack of entertainment in the marriage bed and became a prey to melancholy. But eventually her eyes fell on the King's son,

Grimur the Noble, who far outshone all other men in that kingdom, and the young Queen fell so deeply in love with this princely figure that she could neither eat nor sleep and resolved finally to go to him at night in his chamber. Of the aged King, his father, she spoke in the most derisive of terms:

> *Of what use to red-blood maid*
> *Sap of such a withered blade?*
> *Or to one so sore in need,*
> *Spine of such a broken reed?*

Grimur, however, found this visit displeasing and relished even less such shameless talk, but for some time he retreated in courtly evasion of the issue. But

> *No refusals ought availed,*
> *Words of reason here had failed.*
> *All intent on lustful play*
> *Softly on the bed she lay.*

And before Grimur the Noble had time to marshal his defences, there occurred the following:

> *In her arms she clasped him tight,*
> *Warm with promise of delight;*
> *Honey-seeming was her kiss,*
> *All her movements soft with bliss.*

But at this moment there dawned upon Grimur the Noble the full iniquity of what was taking place, and springing to his feet in a fury, he turned upon the shameless wanton:

Up the hero rose apace,
Smote her sharply on the face;
Scornful of such shameful deed,
Thrust her to the floor with speed.

Angrily the hero cried,
Whilst she lay, bereft of pride:
'Lustful art thou as a swine,
Little honour can be thine.'

'To hell with me, then,' cried Bjartur, who was now standing in the snow after repulsing the seductive bed-blandishments of the lecherous Queen. Did the heroes of the rhymes ever allow themselves to be beguiled into a life of adultery, debauchery, and that cowardice in battle which characterizes those who are the greatest heroes in a woman's embrace? Never should it be said of Bjartur of Summerhouses that on the field of battle he turned his back on his foes to go and lie with a trollopy slut of a queen. He was in a passion now. He floundered madly about in the snow, thumping himself with all his might, and did not sit down again till he had overcome all those feelings of the body that cry for rest and comfort, everything that argues for surrender and hearkens to the persuasion of faint-hearted gods. When he had fought thus for some time, he stuck the frozen sausages inside his trousers and warmed them on his flesh, then gnawed them from his fist in the darkness of this relentless winter night and ate the driving snow as savoury.

This was rather a long night. Seldom had he recited so much poetry in any one night; he had recited all his father's poetry, all the ballads he could remember, all his own palindromes backwards and forwards in forty-eight different ways, whole processions of dirty poems, one hymn that he had learned from his mother, and all the lampoons that had been known in the Fourthing from time imme-morial about bailiffs, merchants, and sheriffs. At intervals he struggled up out of the snow and thumped himself from top to toe till he was out of breath.

Finally his fear of frost-bite became so great that he felt it would be courting disaster to remain quietly in this spot any longer, and as it must also be wearing on towards morning and he did not relish the idea of spending a whole day without food in a snowdrift miles from any habitation, he now decided to forsake his shelter and leave the consequences to take care of themselves. He forced his way at first with lowered head against the storm, but when he reached the ridge above the gully, he could no longer make any headway in this fashion, so he slumped forward on to his hands and knees and made his way through the blizzard on all fours, crawling over stony slopes and ridges like an animal, rolling down the gullies like a peg; bare-handed, without feeling.

On the following night, long after the people of Brun, the nearest farm of Glacierdale, had retired to bed – the storm had raged relentlessly now for a full twenty-four hours – it came to pass that the housewife was wakened from her sleep by a hubbub at the window, a groaning, even a hammering. She woke her husband, and they came to the conclusion that some creature gifted with the power of reasoning must surely be afoot and about the house, though on this lonely croft visitors were the last thing to be expected in such a storm – was it man or devil? They huddled on their most necessary garments and went to the door with a light. And when they had opened the door, there toppled in through the drift outside a creature resembling only in some ways a human being; he rolled in through the doorway armoured from head to foot in ice, nose and mouth encrusted, and came to rest in a squatting position with his back against the wall and his head sunk on his chest, as if the monstrous spectre, despairing of maltreating him further, had finally slung him through the door and up against the wall; the light of the house shone on this visitor. He panted heavily, his chest heaving and groaning, and made an effort to clear his throat and spit, and when the crofter asked him who he was and where he came from, he tried to get to his feet, like an animal trying to stand up on its hind legs, and gave his name – 'Bjartur of Summerhouses.'

The crofter's son had now risen also, and together he and his father made an attempt to help their visitor into the room, but he refused any such assistance. 'I'll walk by myself,' he said, 'I'll follow the woman with the lamp.' He laid himself across the son's bed and for a while made no answer to their questions, but mumbled like a drunkard, rumbled like a bull about to bellow. At last he said:

'I am thirsty.'

The woman brought him a three-pint basin of milk, and he set it to his mouth and drank it off, and said as he passed her the basin: 'Thanks for the drink, mother.' With her warm hands she helped to thaw the clots of ice in his beard and eyebrows, then drew off his frozen clothes and felt with experienced fingers for frost-bite. Fingers and toes were without feeling, his skin smarting with frost, but otherwise he appeared to have taken no hurt. When the crust of ice had been thawed off, he stretched himself out naked in the son's warm bed and had seldom felt so comfortable in all his life. After the housewife had gone to prepare him some food, father and son sat down beside him, their eyes bewildered, as if they did not really believe this phenomenon and did not know quite what to say.

In the end it was he who spoke, as he asked in a hoarse voice from under the coverlet:

'Were your lambs in?'

They replied that they were, and asked in turn how it had come about that he had landed here, on the eastern bank of Glacier River, in murderous weather that would kill any man.

'Any man?' he repeated querulously. 'What do the men matter? I always thought it was the animals that came first.'

They continued to question him.

'Oh, as a matter of fact I was just taking a little walk by myself,' he vouchsafed. 'I missed a ewe, you see, and took a stroll along the heights there just to soothe my mind.'

For a while he was silent, then he added:

'It's been a trifle rough today.'

'It wasn't any pleasanter last night either,' they said, 'a regular hurricane.'

'Yes,' agreed Bjartur, 'it was just a trifle rough last night, too.'

They wanted to know where he had put in the night, and he replied: 'In the snow.' They were particularly curious about how he had managed to cross Glacier River, but he would give no details. 'It's a nice thing to have one's lambs out in this,' he said mournfully.

They said that in his shoes they wouldn't trouble themselves about lambs tonight, but think themselves lucky to be where they were.

'It's easy to see,' he replied, 'that you people have found your feet. But I am fighting for my independence. I have worked eighteen years for the little livestock I have, and if they're under snow, it would be better for me to be under snow too.'

But when the woman had brought him a meal in bed and he had eaten his fill, he lay down without further discourse and was asleep and snoring loudly.

CHAPTER 17

'THE LAND, BREATHING'

from *Arctic Dreams* (1985)

Barry Lopez

Barry Lopez's Arctic Dreams *is a far-ranging study of the northern landscape and the creatures — muskoxen, polar bears, narwhals — who inhabit it. It won the National Book Award for Nonfiction. The passage below is from the chapter on migration.*

It was still dark, and I thought it might be raining lightly.

I pushed back the tent flap. A storm-driven sky moving swiftly across the face of a gibbous moon. Perhaps it would clear by dawn. The ticking sound was not rain, only the wind. A storm, bound for somewhere else.

Half awake, I was again aware of the voices. A high-pitched cacophonous barking, like terriers, or the complaint of shoats. The single outcries became a rising cheer, as if in a far-off stadium, that rose and fell away.

Snow geese, their night voices. I saw them flying down the north coast of Alaska once in September, at the end of a working day. The steady intent of their westward passage, that unwavering line, was uplifting. The following year I saw them over Banks Island, migrating north in small flocks of twenty and thirty. And that fall

I went to northern California to spend a few days with them on their early wintering ground at Tule Lake in Klamath Basin.

Tule Lake is not widely known in America, but the ducks and geese gather in huge aggregations on this refuge every fall, creating an impression of land in a state of health, of boundless life. On any given day a visitor might look upon a million birds here – pintail, lesser scaup, Barrow's goldeneye, cinnamon teal, mallard, northern shoveler, redhead, and canvasback ducks; Great Basin and cackling varieties of Canada geese, white-fronted geese, Ross's geese, lesser snow geese; and tundra swans. In open fields between the lakes and marshes where these waterfowl feed and rest are redwinged blackbirds and Savannah sparrows, Brewer's sparrows, tree swallows, and meadowlarks. And lone avian hunters – marsh hawks, red-tailed hawks, bald eagles, the diminutive kestrel.

The Klamath Basin, containing four other national wildlife refuges in addition to Tule Lake, is one of the richest habitats for migratory waterfowl in North America. To the west of Tule Lake is another large, shallow lake called Lower Klamath Lake. To the east, out past the tule marshes, is a low escarpment where barn owls nest and the counting marks of a long-gone aboriginal people are still visible, incised in the rock. To the southwest, the incongruous remains of a Japanese internment camp from World War II. In agricultural fields to the north, east, and south, farmers grow malt barley and winter potatoes in dark volcanic soils.

The night I thought I heard rain and fell asleep again to the cries of snow geese, I also heard the sound of their night flying, a great hammering of the air overhead, a wild creaking of wings. These primitive sounds made the Klamath Basin seem oddly untenanted, the ancestral ground of animals, reclaimed by them each year. In a few days at the periphery of the flocks of geese, however, I did not feel like an interloper. I felt a calmness birds can bring to people;

and, quieted, I sensed here the outlines of the oldest mysteries: the nature and extent of space, the fall of light from the heavens, the pooling of time in the present, as if it were water.

There were 250,000 lesser snow geese at Tule Lake. At dawn I would find them floating on the water, close together in a raft three-quarters of a mile long and perhaps 500 yards wide. When a flock begins to rise from the surface of the water, the sound is like a storm squall arriving, a great racket of shaken sheets of corrugated tin. (If you try to separate the individual sounds in your head, they are like dry cotton towels snapping on a windblown clothesline.) Once airborne, they are dazzling on the wing. Flying against broken sunlight, the opaque whiteness of their bodies, a whiteness of water-polished shells, contrasts with grayer whites in their translucent wings and tail feathers. Up close they show the dense, impeccable whites of arctic fox. Against the bluish grays of a storm-laden sky, their whiteness has a surreal glow, a brilliance without shadow.

When they are feeding in the grain fields around Tule Lake, the geese come and go in flocks of five or ten thousand. Sometimes there are forty or fifty thousand in the air at once. They rise from the fields like smoke in great, swirling currents, rising higher and spreading wider in the sky than one's field of vision can encompass. One fluid, recurved sweep of ten thousand of them passes through the spaces within another, counterflying flock; while beyond them lattice after lattice passes, like sliding Japanese walls, until in the whole sky you lose your depth of field and feel as though you are looking up from the floor of the ocean through shoals of fish.

What absorbs me in these birds, beyond their beautiful white-ness, their astounding numbers, the great vigor of their lives, is how adroitly each bird joins the larger flock or departs from it. And how each bird while it is a part of the flock seems part of something larger than itself. Another animal. Never did I see a single goose move to accommodate one that was landing, nor geese on the water ever disturbed by another taking off, no matter how closely bunched they seemed to be. I never saw two birds so much as brush wingtips in the air, though surely they must. They roll up into a headwind together in a seamless movement that brings thousands of them gently to the ground like falling leaves in but a few seconds. Their movements are endlessly attractive to the eye because of a tension they create between the extended parabolic lines of their flight and their abrupt but adroit movements, all of it in three dimensions.

And there is something else that draws you in. They come from the ends of the earth and find this small lake every year with unfailing accuracy. They arrive from breeding grounds on the northern edge of the continent in Canada, and from the river valleys of Wrangel Island in the Russian Arctic. Their ancient corridors of migration, across Bering Strait and down the Pacific coast, down the east flank of the Rockies, are older than the nations they fly from. The lives of many animals are constrained by the schemes of men, but the determination in these lives, their traditional pattern of movement, are a calming reminder of a more fundamental order. The company of these birds in the field is guileless. It is easy to feel transcendent when camped among them.

Birds tug at the mind and heart with a strange intensity. Their ability to flock elegantly as the snow goose does, where individual birds turn into something larger, and their ability to navigate over great stretches of what is for us featureless space, are mysterious, sophisticated skills. Their flight, even a burst of sparrows across a city plaza, pleases us. In the Arctic, one can see birds in enormous numbers, and these feelings of awe and elation are enhanced. In spring in the Gulf of Anadyr, off the Russian coast, the surface of the water flashes silver with schools of Pacific herring, and flocks of puffins fly straight into the water after them, like a hail of gravel. They return with the herring to steep cliffs, where the broken shells of their offspring fall on gusts of wind into the sea by the thousands, like snow. On August 6, 1973, the ornithologist David Nettleship rounded Skruis Point on the north coast of Devon Island and came face to face with a 'lost' breeding colony of black guillemots. It stretched southeast before him for 14 miles. On the Great Plain of the Koukdjuak on Bamn Island today, a traveler, crossing the rivers and wading through the ponds and braided streams that exhaust and finally defeat the predatory fox, will come on great windrows of feathers from molting geese, feathers that can be taken in handfuls and thrown up in the air to drift downward like chaff. From the cliffs of Digges Island and adjacent Cape Wolstenholme in Hudson Strait, 2 million thick-billed murres will swim away across the water, headed for their winter grounds on the Grand Banks.

Such enormous concentrations of life in the Arctic are, as I have suggested, temporary and misleading. Between these arctic oases stretch hundreds of miles of coastal cliffs, marshes, and riverine valleys where no waterfowl, no seabird, nests. And the flocks of migratory geese and ducks come and go quickly, laying their eggs, molting, and getting their young into the air in five or six weeks. What one witnesses in the great breeding colonies is a kind of paradox. For a time the snow and ice disappear, allowing life to flourish and birds both to find food and retrieve it. Protected from terrestrial predators on their island refuges and on nesting grounds deep within flooded coastal plains, birds can molt all their flight feathers at once, without fearing the fact that this form of escape will be lost to them for a few weeks. And, for a while, food is plentiful enough to more than serve their daily needs; it provides the additional energy needed for the molt, and for a buildup of fat reserves for the southward journey.

For the birds, these fleeting weeks of advantage are crucial. If the weather is fair and their timing has been good, they arrive on their winter grounds with a strange, primal air of achievement. When the snow geese land at Tule Lake in October, it is not necessary in order to appreciate them to picture precisely the line and shading of those few faraway places where every one of them was born — Egg River on Banks Island, the mouth of the Anderson River in the Northwest Territories, the Tundovaya River Valley on Wrangel Island. Merely knowing that each one began its life, took first breath, on those intemperate arctic edges and that it alights here now for the first or fifth or tenth time is enough. Their success urges one to wonder at such a life, stretched out over so many thousands of miles, and moving on every four or five weeks, always moving on. Food and light running out behind in the fall, looming ahead in the spring.

I would watch the geese lift off the lake in the morning, spiral up white into the blue California sky and head for fields of two-row barley to feed, able only to wonder what this kind of nomadic life meant, how their lives fit in the flow of time and made clearer the extent of space between ground and sky, between here and the Far North. They flew beautifully each morning in the directions they intended, movements of desire, arabesques in the long sweep south from Tundovaya Valley and Egg River. At that hour of the day their lives seemed flush with yearning.

One is not long in the field before sensing that the scale of time and distance for most animals is different from one's own. Their overall size, their methods of locomotion, the nature of the obstacles they face, the media they move through, and the length of a full life are all different. Formerly, because of the ready analogy with human migration and a tendency to think only on a human scale, biologists treated migratory behavior as a special event in the lives of animals. They stressed the great distances involved or remarkable feats of navigation. The practice today is not to differentiate so sharply between migration and other forms of animal (and plant) movement. The maple seed spiraling down toward the forest floor, the butterfly zigzagging across a summer meadow, and the arctic tern outward bound on its 12,000-mile fall journey are all after the same thing: an environment more conducive to their continued growth and survival. Further, scientists now understand animal movements in terms of navigational senses we are still unfamiliar with, such as an ability to detect an electromagnetic field or to use sound echos or differences in air pressure as guides.

In discussing large-scale migration like that of snow geese, biologists posit a 'familiar area' for each animal and then speak of its 'home range' within that area, which includes its winter and summer ranges, its breeding range, and any migratory corridors. The familiar area takes in the whole of the landscape an animal has any notion of, an understanding it gains largely through exploration of territory adjacent to its home range during adolescence. Intense adolescent exploration, as far as we know, is common to all animals. Science's speculation is that such exploring ensures the survival of a group of animals by familiarizing them with alternatives to their home ranges, which they can turn to in an emergency.

A question that arises about the utilization of a home range is: how do animals find their way to portions of the home range they have never seen? And how do they know when going there would be beneficial? The answers to these questions still elude us, but the response to them is what we call migration, and we have some idea about how animals manage those journeys. Many animals, even primitive creatures like anemones, possess a spatial memory of some sort and use it to find their way in the world. Part of this memory is apparently genetically based, and part of it is learned during travel with parents and in exploring alone. We know animals use a considerable range of senses to navigate from one place to another, to locate themselves in space, and actually to learn an environment, but which senses in which combinations are used, and precisely what information is stored – so far we can only speculate.

The vision most of us have of migration is of movements on a large scale, of birds arriving on their wintering grounds, of spawning salmon moving upstream, or of wildebeest, zebra, and gazelle trekking over the plains of East Africa. The movements of these latter animals coincide with a pattern of rainfall in the Serengeti-Mara ecosystem; and their annual, roughly circular migration in the wake of the rains reveals a marvelous and intricate network of benefits to all the organisms involved – grazers, grasses, and predators. The timing of these events – the heading of grasses in seed, the dropping of manure, the arrival of the rains, the birth of the young – seems perfectly fortuitous, a melding of needs and satisfactions that caused those who first examined the events to speak of a divine plan.

The dependable arrival of swallows at the mission of San Juan Capistrano, the appearance of gray whales off the Oregon coast in March, and the movement of animals like elk from higher to lower ranges in Wyoming in the fall are other examples of migration familiar in North America. I first went into the Arctic with no other ideas than these, somewhat outsize events to guide me. They opened my mind sufficiently, however, to a prodigious and diverse movement of life through the Arctic; they also prompted a realization of how intricate these seemingly simple natural events are. And as I watched the movement of whales and birds and caribou, I thought I discerned the ground from which some people have derived so much of their metaphorical understanding of symmetry, cadence, and harmony in the universe.

Several different kinds of migration are going on in the Arctic at the same time, not all of them keyed to the earth's annual cycle. Animals are still adjusting to the retreat of the Pleistocene glaciers, which began about 20,000 years ago. Some temperate-zone species are moving gradually but steadily northward, altering their behavior or, like the collared lemming and the arctic fox, growing heavier coats of fur as required.

Climatic fluctuations measured over a much shorter period of time – on the order of several hundred years – are responsible for cyclic shifts of some animal populations north and south during these periods. Over the last fifty years, for example, cod and several species of bird have been moving farther north up the west coast of Greenland, while populations of red fox have been establishing themselves farther north on the North American tundra.* As animals long resident in the Arctic respond to certain kinds of short-term ecological disaster, as was the case with muskoxen in the winter of 1973–74, or to violent fluctuations in their population, as with lemmings, they reinhabit, over time, former landscapes and abandon others.

To cope with annual cycles – the drop in temperature, the loss of light, the presence of snow cover, and a reduction in the amount

---

* American robins have moved as far north as Baffin Island in recent years. The Eskimos around Pond Inlet and Arctic Bay, who recognized the bird from stories white travelers told them about it, first saw them around 1942. Eskimos say the robin came that far north then because there was 'a lot of fighting in the south' at that time.

of food available – arctic animals have evolved several strategies. Lemmings move under the snow; bumblebees hibernate; and arctic foxes move out onto the sea ice. Many other animals, including caribou, walrus, whales, and birds, migrate over quite significant distances. Arctic terns, for example, fly to the Antarctic Ocean at the end of the arctic summer, an annual circuit on which they see fewer hours of darkness than probably any animal on earth. Other migratory birds that head out to sea change their ecological niche. The long-tailed jaeger, a rodent hunter on the summer tundra, becomes a pelagic scavenger on the high seas in winter.

On a scale smaller yet than these annual cycles are the migrations of animals during a season, like the movement of muskoxen; and the regular patterns of localized movement keyed to an animal's diurnal rhythms, like the habit among some wolf packs of leaving a den each evening to hunt. (Arctic animals, as mentioned earlier, maintain a diurnal pattern in spite of the presence of continuous daylight in summer.)

When one considers all these comings and goings, and that an animal like the muskox might be involved simultaneously in several of these cycles, or that when the lemming population crashes, snowy owls must fly off in the direction of an alternative food supply, and when one adds to it the movement of animals to the floe edges in spring, or the insects that rise in such stupendous numbers on the summer tundra, a vast and complex pattern of animal movement in the Arctic begins to emerge. Also to be considered are the release of fish and primitive arthropods with the melting of lake and ground ice. And the peregrinations of bears. And a final, wondrous image – the great ocean of aerial plankton, that almost separate universe of ballooning spiders and delicate larval creatures that drifts over the land in the summer.

The extent of all this movement is difficult to hold in the mind.

Deepening the complications for anyone who would try to fix this order in time is that within the rough outlines of their traditional behaviors, animals are always testing the landscape. They are always setting off in response to hints and admonitions not evident to us.

The movement of animals in the Arctic is especially compelling because the events are compressed into but a few short months. Migratory animals like the bowhead whale and the snow goose often arrive on the last breath of winter. They feed and rest, bear their young, and prepare for their southward journey in that window of light before freeze-up and the first fall snowstorms. They come north in staggering numbers, travel hundreds or even thousands of miles to be here during those few weeks when life swirls in the water and on the tundra and in the balmy air. Standing there on the ground, you can feel the land filling up, feel something physical rising in it under the influence of the light, an embrace or exaltation. Watching the animals come and go, and feeling the land swell up to meet them and then feeling it grow still at their departure, I came to think of the migrations as breath, as the land breathing. In spring a great inhalation of light and animals. The long-bated breath of summer. And an exhalation that propelled them all south in the fall.

For years scientists have been aware of different rhythms of life in the Arctic, though they are not particularly arctic rhythms. Tundra soil cores examined by fossil-pollen experts have shown that changes in the composition of arctic plant communities have occurred periodically with a change in climate. Borings in the Greenland ice cap have revealed rhythmic fluctuations in average temperature over the centuries. A careful examination of arctic refuse middens by archaeologists, paleobotanists, and paleozoologists has revealed a succession of differently equipped early human cultures, whose entries into the Arctic are also related to periods of climatic change. The animal bones found in their camps confirm parallel fluctuations in the populations of the animals they hunted.

A number of scientists feel all this information should mesh, that in some way the rhythms of human migration, climatic change, and animal population cycles should be interrelated. With a precise enough mathematics even the 'nine-year lynx-snowshoe hare cycle' and the 'seventy-year caribou cycle' should fit neatly into a basic pattern. Few have sought to rigorously integrate this material, and many don't believe the relationships even exist, except in a general way. Since the 1930s, however, the Danish scientist Christian Vibe has taken the possibility very seriously, and no other body of work has been so clearly linked with the attempt to find a basic period of arctic cycling, a tantalizing bit of information of enormous interest to biologists, historians, and arctic developers.

Climatic change – the advance and retreat of glacial ice in the Northern Hemisphere – is the hallmark of the Pleistocene, the epoch of man's emergence.[*] Vibe, keeping this in mind, and believing whatever he learned could be applied to understanding the climatic future of Europe and America, posed certain questions for himself. Why, he asked, were seals scarce at Ammassalik on the east coast of Greenland at the turn of the century, while at the same time they were plentiful along Greenland's southwest coast? Why did the caribou population of western Greenland crash suddenly at the end of both the eighteenth and nineteenth centuries? And what

---

[*] Glacial periods are relatively rare in the earth's history. Scientists have discovered only four in the last 600 million years, the last of which is stlll going on. The Holocene, as far as we know, is only an interglacial stage, a reprieve, between the retreat of the Wisconsin ice (or Würm ice in Europe) and the next glacial advance.

accounted for the periodic northward movements of Atlantic herring and cod in the North Atlantic?

Vibe scrutinized the records of the Royal Greenland Trading
Company, which took in sealskins and fox skins, narwhal ivory and
other indicators, and by comparing these records with annual
records of sea-ice movement and annual rainfall and snowfall, Vibe
thought he could discern patterns. He checked his findings, to cor-
roborate them further, by going over 232 years of fur-trading
records from the Hudson's Bay Company in Canada, and by examining records kept by wool growers in southwest Greenland.

The first pattern to emerge for Vibe was a cycle of sea-ice formation and movement that lasted about 150 years, which records
from arctic ships of exploration seemed to support. Vibe regarded
as a key insight in this early work the fact that fluctuations in the
arctic climate that were responsible for shifts of land and sea animals north and south over prolonged periods were tied to a lunar
cycle of 18.6 years (the time it takes the moon to intersect the
earth's orbit around the sun again at the same spot). Because the
length of this lunar cycle is not a whole number, the maximum and
minimum effect it has on the earth's tides (and therefore on ice formation and weather) can occur at different seasons of the year, in
successive 18.6-year periods. This led Vibe to posit a primary
period of 698 years for the Arctic's weather pattern, with second-
ary periods of 116.3 years, and what Vibe calls a basic 'true
ecological cycling period' of 11.6 years.

Depending upon your point of view, either Vibe's insights are
ingenious and his mathematics elegant, or his system is impossibly
broad and complicated and of little help in understanding arctic
change. His inquiry might be considered an entirely esoteric and
rarefied pursuit, in fact, if it were not for two things. In the Arctic
one is constantly aware of sharp oscillation. It is as familiar a

pattern of human thought and animal movement to the arctic resident as the pattern of four seasons is to a dweller in the Temperate Zone. In spite of the many manifestations of this rhythm, and the effect of sharp oscillation not only on resident animals but, probably, too, on the cultures that matured in these regions, Vibe's remains the only serious attempt at a description. Second, insofar as Vibe's theories explain oscillation in temperate-zone climate patterns or indicate harbingers of another ice age, they have a significant bearing on our developing patterns of commerce and economics, especially in the Arctic.

It is easy to say that the Arctic is characterized by sharp oscillation, just as it is to say that the airs of a temperate-zone spring are felicitous, but it is difficult to say precisely why. The basal annual rhythm of the North is winter/summer. The weeks during breakup and freeze-up are short, frequently perilous times, when strategies employed by both animals and human hunters to secure food are momentarily disrupted. The long winter and short summer constitute a temporal pattern around which life carefully arranges itself. Preparations for winter show up clearly everywhere in the land. The short-tailed weasel grows its white coat and the collared lemming its long snow claws. Tundra rodents shift from their night-active summer pattern to a day-active winter pattern, with but a few days of irregular rhythm in between. The arctic fox lines lemmings up in neat rows in its winter caches.

A second pattern complements this oscillation — long stillnesses broken by sudden movement. The river you have been traveling over by dogsled every week for eight months, and have come to think of as a solid piece of the earth, you wake one day to find a heaving jumble of ice. The spring silence is broken by pistol reports of cracking on the river, and then the sound of breaking branches and the whining pop of a falling tree as the careening blocks of ice gouge the riverbanks. A related but far eerier phenomenon occurs in the coastal ice. Suddenly in the middle of winter and without warning a huge piece of sea ice surges hundreds of feet inland, like something alive. The Eskimo call it *ivu*.* The silent arrival of caribou in an otherwise empty landscape is another example. The long wait at a seal hole for prey to surface. Waiting for a lead to close. The Eskimo have a word for this kind of long waiting, prepared for a sudden event: *quinuituq*. Deep patience.

As I moved through the Arctic I thought often about a rhythm indigenous to this land, not one imposed on it. The imposed view, however innocent, always obscures. The evidence that there *is* a different rhythm of life here seemed inescapably a part of the expression of the animals I encountered, though I cannot say precisely why. A coherent sense of the pervasiveness of such a rhythm is elusive.

The indigenous rhythm, or rhythms, of arctic life is important to discern for more than merely academic reasons. To understand why a region is different, to show an initial deference toward its mysteries, is to guard against a kind of provincialism that vitiates the imagination, that stifles the capacity to envision what is different.

Another reason to wonder which rhythms are innate, and what they might be, is related as well to the survival of the capacity to imagine beyond the familiar. We have long regarded animals as a kind of machinery, and the landscapes they move through as backdrops, as paintings. In recent years this antiquated view has begun to change. Animals are understood as mysterious, within the

---

* Eskimo descriptions of this phenomenon were not taken seriously until 1982, when archaeologists working at Utqiagvik, a prehistoric village site near Barrow, Alaska, discovered a family of five people that had been crushed to death in such an incident.

context of sophisticated Western learning that takes into account such things as biochemistry and genetics. They are changeable, not fixed, entities, predictable in their behavior only to a certain extent. The world of variables they are alert to is astonishingly complex, and their responses are sometimes highly sophisticated. The closer biologists look, the more the individual animal, like the individual human being, seems a reflection of that organization of energy that quantum mechanics predicts for the particles that compose an atom.

The animal's environment, the background against which we see it, can be rendered as something like the animal itself – partly unchartable. And to try to understand the animal apart from its background, except as an imaginative exercise, is to risk the collapse of both. To be what they are they require each other.

Spatial perception and the nature of movement, the shape and direction something takes in time, are topics that have been cogently addressed by people like Werner Heisenberg, Erwin Schrödinger, Paul Dirac, and David Bohm, all writing about subatomic phenomena. I believe that similar thoughts, potentially as beautiful in their complexity, arise with a consideration of how animals move in their landscapes – the path of a raven directly up a valley, the meander of grazing caribou, the winter movements of a single bear over the sea ice. We hardly know what these movements are in response to; we choose the dimensions of space and the durations of time we think appropriate to describe them, but we have no assurance that these are relevant. To watch a gyrfalcon and a snowy owl pass each other in the same sky is to wonder how the life of the one affects the other. To sit on a hillside and watch the slow intermingling of two herds of muskoxen feeding in a sedge meadow and to try to discern the logic of it is to grapple with uncertainty. To watch a flock of snow geese roll off a head-wind together is to wonder where one animal begins and another ends. Animals confound us not because they are deceptively simple but because they are finally inseparable from the complexities of life. It is precisely these subtleties of fact and conception that comprise particle physics, which passes for the natural philosophy of our age. Animals move more slowly than beta particles, and through a space bewildering larger than that encompassed by a cloud of electrons, but they urge us, if we allow them, toward a consideration of the same questions about the fundamental nature of life, about the relationships that bind forms of energy into recognizable patterns.

CHAPTER 18

'ALIBERTI'S RIDE'

from *This Cold Heaven* (2001)

Gretel Ehrlich

Gretel Ehrlich made her first trip to Greenland in 1993. Over the next seven years, she returned repeatedly, drawn by the landscape and by a desire to understand native culture. In the passage below, she travels by dogsled with a hunter named Aliberti from the tiny island town of Uummannaq to the even tinier town of Niaqornat.

The shit truck's chained snow tires awakened me. It had taken only a day for all of us to fill up the toilet. The door opened. Two young men slipped in, emptied the bucket, returned it, then disappeared down the narrow street. It was a good job because it paid well and they were finished with their work early, so they could go out hunting in the evening. I thought of the Buddhist monks who asked for the job of cleaning toilets in cities to help 'ground' them, bind them to what is actual during a long course of otherworldly practices. But how much grounding does a subsistence hunter need?

The household woke slowly. We dressed for frigid weather and carted loads down the steep hill to the ice where the dogs were staked out – food, sleeping bags, fuel, stoves, warm clothes, presents for friends. Our route would take us from Uummannaq to

Ukkusissat, to Illorsuit, north to Nuugaatsiaq, back to Illorsuit, then to Niaqornat, Qaarsut, and home.

The ice at the base of the town was a Coney Island of hunters, sleds, children, and six thousand dogs all yipping, howling, barking, screeching, and yapping. Children played tag between sleds while hunters harnessed their teams. One team was being fed frozen halibut. They yelped and yapped as the chunks were tossed into their mouths while the other teams looked on silently, knowing there would be no food for them. After a long winter, the dogs had spring fever: females in heat ranged freely among chained-up males, causing yowls of sexual union and longing. Everywhere I looked, dogs were fucking, getting stuck together, crouching, sitting, biting, and yapping. One male grabbed the trace line of the female he wanted, jerked it tight, then jumped on her from the rear. A dog that had been left behind sat up on his hind legs, a lone figure pawing at a world of ice and air.

Our party consisted of sixty-six dogs, six children, and seven adults. Aliberti was the hunter with whom I would travel, as his only passenger. It was his sled and those of two other hunters – Jacob and Unatoq, or 'Mr. Warm' – that we had seen coming the night before from Ikerasak. The other adults were Ann, Olejorgen, and an Inuit woman from the Children's House, Louisa.

At fifty-eight, Aliberti's face was weathered, making him look older than his years. He had the small, tight build typical of Inuit hunters and moved like a cat. A cigarette dangled from his mouth. When I laid my duffle and sleeping bag on the sled, he smiled, and the cigarette stuck to his lower lip. He was nearly toothless – just a few black stubs. Standing face to face we could look straight into each other's eyes. He slipped my parka and duffle under caribou skins and lashed them tight.

Seven cigarettes were stubbed out on the ice; we had been

waiting. Olejorgen's dogs were tangled and fighting. One female got loose and ran away through the midst of six thousand other dogs chained up on the ice or being harnessed, and a collective howl rose, echoing. The young sled drivers — Ludwig and Aliberti's son — were having troubles too: their trace lines had broken and two more dogs got loose and ran off with another team.

Aliberti looked on coolly. It is not the Inuit way to give help unless there is real danger, otherwise no lessons will be learned. He tightened the lash ropes on our sled again, blew his nose, secured his mittens under the lines — until finally he couldn't stand it any-more. Shaking his head, he hooked the trace lines to the sled. The dogs lurched forward and with one flying leap we landed side by side on the sled. He looked back at the chaos behind us and laughed. It would be some time before the others could follow.

I thought of a story told to Rasmussen by Inaluk in 1902: 'There was once an orphan boy who drifted out to sea on an ice-floe, and arrived among strange people. They took him into their service at once and used him for all their menial work. But he had a brother who was a great magician and who, when the little boy did not come back, began to look for him in soul-flights. . . .'

Now, almost one hundred years later, Aliberti had his own story. Three days before Christmas in 1959, Aliberti, then nineteen, went out to get a seal. He lived on the island of Ikerasak. A warm wind, a foehn, blew and the fjord ice began to break up. Before he knew what was happening, Aliberti was adrift with his dogs on an icy slab. He had no food, no stove to melt ice for water, no extra clothes, just his rifle — he hadn't been planning to stay out very long.

Aliberti's ride lasted five days. At night the temperature was 20 below zero. He drifted past the village of Uummannaq, then north up the coast past Niaqornat. He had gotten wet trying to jump to shore and his clothes froze stiff. There was no way to get dry or warm. It was December and completely dark, with no light at all in the sky. That week there wasn't even a moon. Up the coast he went, pushed by currents and pulled by tides. No one saw him drifting.

His parents waited. By Christmas Day he was presumed dead. Perhaps he had slipped under the ice, as so many had done before. His obituary was read on the radio. But he was alive and still drift-ing. 'I remember seeing the candles in people's houses at the villages. Christmas came and went. I could hear singing. No one could see me. I didn't think I would live.'

The currents took him north into the Illorsuit Strait along the east coast of Ubekendt Ejland – Unknown Island. He had already drifted seventy miles. 'Things got worse. When it's that cold and you have no food or water, *sila* becomes stronger than you are. My dogs died one by one and I pushed them over into the water. I just lay on my sled and waited. On the fourth day I noticed that the ice floe had gotten smaller. Then it split in half and I had to jump from the bad part to what was left of the floe. The ice didn't look like it would hold. I wondered what my family was thinking. They could-n't come look for me because there was too much ice to go out in a boat and not enough to travel by dogsled. My clothes were wet on the inside and frozen on the outside. You get pretty cold. On the fifth day something woke me. I had been drifting in my mind too, but I heard the ice bump against something. I looked up: I had come to a stop a hundred yards from the village of Illorsuit.

'For a moment I thought a miracle had happened. I could see people in their houses with candles burning. They would see me and rescue me and I would live after all. I lamented the fact that all but one of my dogs had died. I allowed myself to think about eating and drinking. I lifted up on one arm and yelled and waved. But no one came. Another day passed. I was telling time by the rising and setting of the moon. Sometimes I called out with what strength I had left, but the wind was blowing the wrong way. My last dog died.

'A villager came outside to pee and he saw me. He yelled out and I lifted an arm. Then he went back inside his house. He was gone a long time. I gave up hope. I think I fell asleep. The sound of voices jarred me awake. I didn't know if they were human. The man I'd seen on the beach and another hunter were making their way toward me in a skiff, pushing big pieces of ice aside with an oar. When they got close they looked like giants. I wasn't right in the head by then. They took me to shore.

'The hunters thought I was a ghost because my death had already been announced on the radio. My hair was coming out in handfuls and my teeth were loose. When they carried me ashore, people ran the other direction.

'The hunter took me to his parents' house. There I was fed and kept warm. They got through to my parents on the two-way radio and told them that I was alive but my mother didn't believe it. After a few days, the weather improved and the hunters took me home to Ikerasak. And as you can see, I am still alive.'

Bright sun, clear skies, a slight breeze, the temperature about zero. The ice was smooth and fast. With our light load, the sled fishtailed and the dogs' panting became the only sound we heard as we slid from the noise of town. The smoke from Aliberti's cigarette snaked back across his cheek as we glided forward. He turned and smiled. There was no need to talk. To be alive and on a dogsled in Greenland was enough and I was happy.

Far out in the middle of the fjord, the dogs slowed to a trot. My whole body worked like an eye, watching the world scroll under and over us. Aliberti and the five others headed straight north, gliding between the uninhabited islands of Abut and Saleq, then veered northwest toward the village of Ukkusissat on the thumb's tip of land that extended from under the ice cap.

Cool, alert, and relaxed, Aliberti sat sideways at the front of the sled with his legs sticking out straight. Seagulls and eider ducks flew overhead in flocks – a sign of spring. From shoreline – ice line – everything looked mathematical. We glided through its permutations. If water is time's shapeless infinity, then ice is time's body, inhabited by light and shadow, tormented by sun and cold.

A row of stranded icebergs was a giant slalom course leading out to sea. We glided by, staring at their outsize beauty. Icebergs are lessons in geometry: they give and take light at will, changing a shined, chrome side into a dull fastness, then back to a sizzling angle of vitality, with a fine, thin, razor-sharp ridge cutting winter out of the sky.

Jacob and Unatoq came up behind us on their two sleds, carrying Ann on one and Louisa and a boy from the Children's House on the other. Finally the others – Olejorgen, Ludwig, and Aliberti's son – caught up. Ann zinged by, whooping, then Louisa and the boy. They shouted something in Greenlandic I couldn't understand. The teenage girls rode with the teenage boys and they were always last. This was an Eskimo–Danish–Faroe Islander–American laughing, gossiping sled party heading north. First stop, Ukkusissat, where we would celebrate the birthday of a friend.

Between Uummannaq and the mainland the ice was rough. We bumped over small waves, their topsy-turvydom frozen in place, then stopped and waited again for the others. Olejorgen pulled up beside us and whistled his dogs to a stop. With his movie-star looks, he resembled an Eskimo pasha reclining on a bearskin rug and wearing polar bear pants. His hair had grown long and he wore dark glasses. I imagined a remake of *Doctor Zhivago*, set in Greenland rather than Russia. As he tried to settle the dogs, he promptly ran over one of them. The animal screamed in pain. We lifted the sled up and Olejorgen held the injured animal. He wasn't sure what to do next, so Aliberti told him to carry the dog on the front of the sled until we got to the village. The others showed up and we continued on.

Seagulls flew over: there must be open water somewhere. A slow-moving sled pulled by five skinny dogs passed us going the other way. The hunter looked comatose, lying flat on his back and gazing skyward, his dogs wandering. When we stopped for lunch, Jacob said that during his monthlong sled trip to Qaanaaq the previous spring he had developed stomach pains. He stopped in Upernavik and the next day he was operated on there. While the others continued north, he rested. When they returned three weeks later, Jacob drove his own dogsled home.

On the way, Jacob was lucky and got a polar bear – he was in need of new pants for the next winter. 'Not only did he get an ice bear,' Olejorgen exclaimed, 'the bear fell over dead on Jacob's sled, almost killing him!' Laughter.

Jacob quipped: 'We call this story "How I almost died twice in one springtime hunting trip."'

Rounding a bend, we saw a long arm of rock pushing out into the fjord. On its tip was Ukkusissat. As we approached, litter blew across multiple sled tracks – beer bottles and plastic bags. Ann insisted on stopping and picking up every piece, indignant for her beloved (though not native) Greenland. 'We must not be so dirty,' she exclaimed to no one in particular. The hunters smiled. Her garrulousness amused them, but she also held their respect for the fine job she did with the children.

Ukkusissat consisted of a few small houses set in stepping-stone fashion up a hill. Behind the last building a towering wall of basalt lay crumbled in ruin, as if an older village had once been sited there. Birthe ran down the hill to greet us. Fine-boned, strong-willed, and skittish as a colt, she was joyous at having company. She was the only Dane in this village of one hundred people and she drove her own dogsled. 'I just barely know how to do it,' she said apologetically. 'But it's transportation between here and my friends in Uummannaq.' After the dogs were unharnessed and fed and the duffles and sleeping bags had been unloaded, we sat on the empty sleds and basked in the evening sun.

An old man came to inspect the injured dog, who had been laid on the snow. The dog's back was broken. The man told Olejorgen: 'After you have gone, I will shoot him for you.'

The birthday celebration began at Birthe's house that evening. We cooked seal ribs, potatoes, and onions, and drank warm Tuborg beer. How quickly and effortlessly food for twelve was prepared. At midnight the sun hovered, then began to slide behind the mountains into the northern part of the sky. One by one the others went to bed. Ann and Olejorgen appropriated Birthe's bed, so she and I stayed up late, talking.

There was no night, no darkness. I trudged down to the ice. Aliberti had pitched a canvas tent over his sled, blue canvas at one end to keep the sunlight out. Inside, a Primus stove was lit to keep him warm. I unrolled my sleeping bag next to his on the sled and slept. At three in the morning gold and purple stripes of light lay across the ice. The sounds from the village subsided, but the dogs, staked out everywhere in a vast slumber party, talked for the rest of the night.

When we woke there was no sun and the dog whose back was broken was still alive. He lay unattended in the snow covered with rime frost. A fog had come in and sealed itself to the ice. The dogs sat hunched and waiting. As the fog lifted, an eerie yellow light shone through.

I helped Birthe move her dogs from behind her house to the ice. She had decided to accompany us to the next village. One by one they pulled us downhill – that's all they know how to do. After, we carried the toilet bucket from her house and poured the contents into a pipe that emptied into the fjord. City living, she said with a grin, because on hunting trips any piece of rough ice served as a bathroom.

Aliberti broke camp, harnessed the dogs, and loaded the sled. The flying *S* of his whip snapped: we were on our way to Illorsuit, the village where he was saved after drifting for five days, where Rockwell Kent lived with Salamina, where I spent a summer with Marie Louisa. Again we took off before the others were ready. All was lost behind us in fog. We drove in a white shroud, a white darkness, continually breaking through a crust of ice that had melted and refrozen.

'*Sumiippa?*' I asked. Where are we? Aliberti smiled but said nothing. We were dressed in skins: sealskin pants, sealskin anoraks with fox-fur ruffs around the hood, sealskin kamiks, and sealskin mittens with dog-hair ruffs at the wrist. His whip straightened out above the dogs' heads like a thought coming apart. Sun shone behind mist; now we traveled in a brightening cloud. '*Uatsi*,' I said. Please wait. I got off the sled to pee. When I looked down, I found that I'd unexpectedly gotten my period.

In the Arctic there is no privacy: Aliberti walked over, looked at the blood on the ice, and laughed. 'This is good! It looks like we killed a seal! They will think I am a very good hunter to find a seal in this fog. And also, they will be able to find us.'

Soon Jacob, Louisa, and the little boy pulled up and together we waited for the others. Hot tea and a bag of frozen shrimp were passed around. The boy started a game of tag. He was short for his age, as though stunted, and had come to the Children's House from a family where sexual abuse was epidemic. He ran around the circle of adults, then tagged me so hard that I fell, stood, and fell again. We were five people slipping and sliding, playing tag 700 miles from the North Pole in the middle of a frozen ocean with no land in sight. When Louisa was tagged and turned to tag the boy, he vanished into thick mist.

Another hour went by. The horizon's seamless wall of white frayed. I sat on the edge of the sled as if it were the edge of the world, with my hands over my eyes, trying to locate myself; my body was still, but my eyes tumbled around; my head was a goblet of ice. Is ice a form of indifference or is its intent to obscure? How absurd we must have seemed to the marine mammals swimming below, to the walrus with its colossal appetite and backward stroke, feasting orgiastically on shellfish, and the narwhal with its mysterious white tusk needling the ocean floor for food.

Aliberti dozed on the sled. We were not really lost, just living under the thumb of weather and it was pressing down on us hard. Good time to sleep, he said. But I kept trying to see. My eyes wandered . . . I was looking at a world that had overflowed its outlines, where everything had grown into invisibility.

Finally the others came. Birthe's dogs had gotten loose in the village and she had to start the harnessing process all over again. By tacit agreement, Aliberti took the lead once again. He was still honored in Ikerasak for having survived his five-day ordeal on the drift ice. '*Meeeeuuww, meeeeuuuw*,' he called out, and we took off, seven sleds abreast amid dogfights, tangled trace lines, and laughter. Then the dog-pant, dogtrot rhythm began again.

We drove through a flock of thousands of Arctic gulls. One

bird's foot had frozen to the ice. As we approached it struggled to escape. The other gulls, seeing an easy meal, attacked and killed him. Aliberti watched impassively as we slid by, then turned to see if I'd seen. My eyes went from the cannibalized bird to him. He flashed a look that said, yes, it's tough up here. To the north, icebergs sprouted clouds, then fog closed in again, more tightly than ever, hiding my trail of blood.

Mist constricted and freed us simultaneously. Our slip-and-slide dealings with our psyches were never more evident: we long for solitude, but as soon as we have it, we are desperate for friends. I contemplated the shape of Aliberti's head, wondering what a PET scan might reveal about his ability to draw perfect maps of this coast from memory. Plato thought that vision was 'a stream of fire or light that issues from the observing eye and coalesces with sunlight.' But there was no sun and a hard, glasslike crust slowed down the dogs.

Gliding blind, I lost my bearings, wondering what life must be like for my mother, who was going blind. 'The worst part of it is not being able to drive,' she told me. Olejorgen's sled passed us, then fell back. I blinked: a rock wall shot up in front of us spangled with ice crystals and new snow. *'Takurngaqtuq!'* I yelled. 'I feel as if I'm seeing [something icy] for the first time.'

Aliberti turned and smiled. 'It is called Apaat . . . this rock.'

The way to Illorsuit was silvered, the top sift of snow blowing across our path as if swept by a giant broom. We cut through long-tailed drifts that pointed north like arrows toward the open end of the fjord, which gave onto an entire ocean paved with ice. Where snow had blown off stranded icebergs, exposed walls had been fired by sun and refrozen into glass – all glint and glaze and broken crust like crème brûlée. The snowed-on, fog-sealed ice in front of the sled revealed only the toes of things – icebergs whose drift toward the sea had been postponed by winter.

A headland loomed topped with crosses: Illorsuit's cemetery, which doubled as the heliport. Around a bend the village appeared, the same ramshackle houses lying in the arc of a half-moon bay. Seeing and smelling other dogs excited our dogs. Our seven sleds raced each other to the edge of the village. I took a deep seat and hung on to the lash ropes: we flew through the uneven middle of a decapitated iceberg and lurched down onto flat ice. Aliberti was in the lead, but at the last moment, when we had to go around a piece of rough ice, he was beaten by Mr. Warm.

I saw a young girl weaving between sleds and dogs lying in soft snow, noses tucked under tails, others yowling while being fed, and children pulling handmade toys on a string. She walked toward me, then sat on a sled nearby and waited. *Kina una?* I asked tentatively. Who are you? She smiled. I was still puzzled. *Kina una?* I asked again. Then I knew it was Marie Louisa.

She had grown. Her black hair hung down in a long braid, her cheeks had fattened, and she was four inches taller than she had been two years ago. Then someone grabbed me from behind and spun me around: Hans. We all laughed and hugged. He was grayer and thinner and immediately launched into a litany of grievances about village politics: 'Last week they passed a bill allowing snow scooters in this district. Nothing will be the same. Now they say we need a truck in the village. All these hundreds of years we've walked and used a wheelbarrow and in winter a sled to transport our supplies. Now we will have to worry about our children and dogs getting run over.'

'Where is your sled?' I asked as he loaded my duffle onto the back of the town's one snowmobile.

He gave a disgruntled shrug. 'Last week they began selling Coca-Cola in Greenland. The helicopter brought it and it was sold out within half an hour.' He told me to get on the snow scooter.

'This is against my religion,' I said.

He laughed ruefully. 'Yes. Those are my feelings too.'

'Takuus!' I yelled to Aliberti as we sped off. See you soon. The others dispersed: Ann and Olejorgen went to the schoolteacher's house, the children and Louisa to the clinic (used for extra housing for visitors), the hunters to the house of the family who had saved Aliberti's life forty years ago.

Hans's house had not changed. The walls were pale blue and yellow, the rug was red, the clock still gave the time as noon, and the photographs from his hippie days in Christiana were still on the wall. Snow sifted through the broken skylight and left a perfect white pyramid on the floor. Because there was no word in Greenlandic for pyramid, we referred to the invading snow as 'the igloo of Egyptians.' The living room was still empty except for the foam pad – my bed – on the floor. 'I haven't moved it since you left two years ago,' Hans said.

Only one thing had changed: Arnnannguaq was not there. 'I told her she was not to come to the house when she was drinking,' Hans said. What had been a minor problem had escalated. Now she was drinking all the time. Hendrik and Marie Louisa burst in the door and jumped on the pad, burrowing under the covers. We hugged and wrestled and spoke our usual jumble of Greenlandic and English which only we understood.

In the middle of the night I found myself at the small window where I had kneeled sleepless so many times before. The view across the fjord was marked indelibly on my mind: the rock-faced mountain with two glaciers spilling out on either side like grand stairways, and the gleaming fortress of the ice cap looming above.

Dogs howled, the diesel generator chugged, and the weather worsened. Blue sky fused with white, its porcelain fracturing into frostfall.

The children woke and joined me in the living room. We watched the sun droop in the west and bounce back up to circle the northern sky. Despite the sun, the living room started to feel frosty. We looked: the heater was off and the thermometer had dropped to 16 below. The children huddled under my sleeping bag until Hans fixed the heater again.

Much later Marie Louisa awoke and was upset. *'Anaana, Anaana!'* Mother, Mother, she cried out, nuzzling my breasts like a baby. But she was eight years old. I held her tight. Things had not been good for her here.

We slept huddled together during the two hours of twilight in the middle of the night. As soon as the sky lightened again, it began to snow. Marie Louisa looked up and asked if the world was really round. I said yes, but realized that I was only repeating received information, that I hadn't actually laid my hands on the rounded fender of this planet. I asked how she thought the world was made and she said, 'Big flat pieces of ice pushed together.' She still didn't understand how we stayed attached to a sphere. I said, 'Gravity – a kind of glue.'

In the morning Hans played 'Mr. Tambourine Man' while I made pancakes for the children. Marie Louisa played the electric piano that Hans had given her for Christmas and tried to keep up with the song. Later, when the children went off to play, Hans told me his troubles with A.: 'She is drunk most of the time now; she doesn't give love when the children need it, only when she wants it. This is no good. But what can I do? Where can I go? I'm fifty years old with an unfinished education and it's too late for me to go home to Denmark and get a job. I didn't think about these things when I was young. Now the children need more education, which means I have to go somewhere else. The law isn't in my favor because we are not married, the law will want to give her the children. But I have been feeding and dressing and taking the children to school every day for years. But how can I prove that to the Greenlandic social worker in Uummannaq? Who will believe me?'

When Aliberti, Olejorgen, Ann, Jacob, Louisa, Unatoq, and the children packed up the sleds and continued north to the village of Nuugaatsiaq, I stayed behind to help Hans. A foot of new snow fell during the week, then another. Arnnannguaq came home, sober. I helped her get water. Two years earlier we had collected water from a spring behind their house. Now water was fetched from a huge red tank on the hill. 'Progress,' Hans said.

The Arctic geometries began to soften. Sky and ice turned powder blue and the glaciers on the far side of the fjord bent up into a white nothingness. All afternoon the north-facing village rested in shadow, but at night it was bathed in bright sun. Kristian Moller, who had brought me to Illorsuit on his boat two summers before, stood on the beach and looked at his dogs while Marie Louisa and I played catch on the ice with a pink ball. Later, I watched her pounding up and down the hill behind the village on short red skis. I told Hans that I would take her to live with me and go to school if he found he couldn't leave the village. She trusted me and I loved her and I would bring her home to him for the summers. He agreed. The next night she slept curled up against me. Her face shone in the midnight sun. A tremendous wind howled.

We climbed the steep mountain behind the village, kicking footholds in ice and snow. Near the top we stopped to rest. From above I could see that the way was swept clean. The grooves the glacier had made on the rock were free of snow. Across the fjord two glaciers flanked an immense rock wall, their gashed roofs carrying debris like dark hats to the sea. Above the crumbling snout and the stretched *seracs*, the castellated masses of the glacier, the ice mound was aswirl in blowing snow.

We descended, following a track made by a rolling stone that led us under the thin spray of a frozen waterfall where, in summer, we had bathed daily, then came down to the shadowed crescent where the houses were. The beach was all gravel laced with ice. The lines made fast to skiffs went slack and taut, slapping the open water and leaving marks that looked like arrows pointing toward another season.

Our heels had pushed down through snow, then scree. We jumped over the boggy grass around a spring and landed on the beach where chunks of ice caught on pebbles. In the summer, Marie Louisa liked to take off her clothes and swim in the frigid Arctic water. Now it was a white floor on which she danced, tossing the pink ball, then skate-skied as fast as she could away from where I was standing.

The fjord is six miles wide but looked narrower. The brown wall we had descended was a soft amphitheater into which the sounds of collapsing icebergs would soon be gathered. Behind us the village lay in shadow. Out on the ice Marie Louisa grew smaller and smaller. Come back to me, I wanted to yell, but did not. I suddenly sensed how forbidding solitude could be here, how effortlessly death could occur – just a slip through the ice. Then I did yell, and Marie Louisa turned laughing, then went farther until she was no bigger than an ant. Finally she skied toward me.

The next day Olejorgen, Ann, and the Uummannaq bunch returned in snow that was so deep, it came up to the middle of the dogs' chests. They could barely move; the hunters had to walk in front to break trail. While they rested for a few days, the wind began to blow. Snow stuck to brown rock behind the long string of houses. The light shifted and the sky came apart as frostfall, glitter from the Land of Day.

The last night the children climbed into my sleeping bag with me – a slumber party, I said – but they didn't understand. Framed in the window was a pyramid-shaped iceberg. An eerie twilight filled the room. Toward morning, a ring circled the sun, which meant bad weather.

The sleds were packed. As Aliberti took off in the lead, Marie Louisa ran after us calling '*Anaana.*' The sky cleared and it was deeply cold. We pulled our sealskin anoraks on. From the numbness beginning in my feet, I knew it must be zero.

On our seven-sled procession out of Illorsuit, sharp bits of ice flew in our faces. We bowed our heads in the face of Sila as the dogs' fur grew thick with snow. 'Sometimes spring feels colder than winter,' Aliberti said, pulling his hood up tight around his face. We were dressed head-to-toe in sealskin pants and anoraks with fox-fur ruffs. 'We eat the inside and wear the outside,' Olejorgen said, passing us as we left the village. Marie Louisa stood in the ice storm watching. I wanted to take her with me right then, but she was still in school. Hans said he would call me in Uummannaq. I knelt backwards on the sled, waving until she was out of sight.

Where pieces of ice stuck up like gravestones, snow had drifted in long inverted V's and the wind broke these apart into scudding curds that slid on ice. The rest of the ice was clear. Beneath us a tormented ocean heaved, while continually pushing up against the lid of ice, the topside was smooth and mirrorlike, reflecting only calm. The poet Muso Soseki wrote 'No clarity can flatten torment, no fragment can undo clarity. . . .'

Aliberti cracked the whip in a circular underhand motion and the dogs ran. A cloud bank grayed the horizon and sun lit the place where the fjord gave way to the whole of Baffin Bay. We veered southwest toward the village of Niaqornat. Wind howled out of the west and blew from distant headlands all the way across the frozen sea. When we passed behind an iceberg, we were shielded from wind, but the snow grew suddenly deeper where it had drifted, almost bringing the dogs to a standstill. Between stranded floes, the ice was blown clear. The dogs speeded up and the sled fishtailed on what looked like a thousand-mile-long mirror.

Halfway down the flank of Unknown Island, the weather worsened: a ground blizzard stirred. Bits of ice, like tiny continents, blasted our eyes. Aliberti motioned to me to lie down behind him on the sled. He laid his right hand on my hip and I draped my left arm over his shoulder. The sled tipped and bumped: we held each other on. Wind-driven ice tore at the dogs. Their feet and legs were bleeding and their muzzles were encrusted. The fog lifted but still we couldn't see. I looked down at my body and Aliberti's. Dressed like seals we slid over seals: thousands of pinnipeds, with only a thin sheaf of ice separating us. If they could see us, would they think we were seals?

Ice flew. We slid closer together and pulled our hoods down almost over our eyes. Once in a while I saw one of the other sleds in the distance, then it disappeared. Where the ice under us was smooth, we could almost doze. Then we hit a rough patch and had to hold on. Ice cut us; snow blinded us. So much in the Arctic attempts to obstruct vision: fog, snow, darkness, ice. But each element has its built-in clarity, an opaque shine. Another ancient theory of vision went like this: 'An eye obviously has fire within, for when one is struck, this fire flashes out.'

We bumped along lying close. Seen another way, we were fake seals, like decoys, trying to attract the seals under the ice, as we made gestures of intimacy, my feet in his hands, his back against my chest, my hand on his sealskin shoulder: seal love with no thought of possession. All I knew was that the seal body in front of me was blessedly blocking the wind.

We traveled for eight hours without talk, chastely intimate in a bond of blood, snow, and fur. Yet I knew that what I was seeing was transient: glaciers, human love, sea ice, dogs, humans, and my own perishable body and his – Aliberti's. Too often we confuse what is happening in the moment with notions of permanence. The intimacy would not last.

My feet hurt with the cold. Even on a simple trip such as this one, things could go wrong. Jorgen Brönlund, who had traveled with Rasmussen up this strait, wrote in his diary of the 1908 Denmark Expedition: 'Perished on 79th Latitude North after attempt home – journey round the inland ice, in November I came here in a waning moon and could not continue because of frost-bitten feet and the darkness. Hagen died on 15 November and Mylius about 10 days later.'

A few hours later we came to a hut. Two sleds from our party had reached it before us. Aliberti stopped the dogs. We stood up and looked at each other: we were both blasted white with snow. I stumbled when I walked: my feet were completely numb, but I said nothing since I hadn't brought an extra pair of kamiks. Inside, tea and coffee were being brewed. I passed around nuts, raisins, and figs from California. When Aliberti saw me wriggling my toes, he quietly removed my boots and socks and began massaging my toes.

Years ago in a Wyoming winter, two of my toes were frostbitten; a neighbor who had lived through seventy winters helped thaw them out. Now they were white and painful again. Aliberti held them between his knees while he drank coffee. Nothing was said. Then he signaled to one of the young boys and said something in Greenlandic. A moment later he was slipping a different pair of boots on my feet.

It was time to go. Aliberti motioned to me and I followed. We were two seals who had sprouted legs. Untangling the traces, he hooked the dogs in and the lines pulled tight. We flew off the lip of a cornice and slammed down onto the ice, hooked together on the sled. My feet were warm again as we clattered, bumped, tipped, and shuddered across the frozen sea toward the village of Niaqornat.

Sunday morning. Complacencies of the anorak and the doubletime contrapuntal panting of dogs. Nothing moved but my eyes. All beauty stayed behind only to give way to more — not the green freedom of the cockatoo, but the liberation of the diamondlike ice and Arctic sun that, after ten days of traveling, no longer went down, but only lingered at the eastern and western extremities of the sky, enticing us forward.

When the dogs' paws bled because they were trotting through glass, we stopped to put sealskin booties on their feet. A northwest wind poured across the fjord like cold water. Earlier, the Greenlandic radio played Marilyn Monroe singing 'Diamonds Are a Girl's Best Friend.' We drove over wind-drifted humps of ice blown free of snow, a rocky road paved with shining, beveled diamonds, then stopped to hack off a piece of young ice to be melted for drinking water. Its faceted interior was a blue wilderness. At its base, droplets of dog blood stained the snow.

Snowy polka dots dappled the sled track in front of us. They looked like eyes. Who was watching? Could Sila see? Fog was snow-flecked. Was it possible to draw eyeballs on chaos?

When the storm cleared two ravens flew in front of the sled, one on top of the other. Aliberti pointed at the double-decker birds and made a quick gesture to indicate 'fucking.' He laughed and his black teeth showed. A dog got tangled in the loose trace lines. Aliberti jumped off the moving sled, ran alongside, plunged into the middle of the dogs, snapped a line, tied a knot in another, jumped back out, and leaped back on.

We traveled close to the brown flank of Ubekendt Ejland. The island was brown, copper, and slate – all mudstones piled vertically and opening out at the bottom in fluted vaginas cut in half by ice. Ahead the way was silvered, the top sift of snow blowing across our path and sweeping it clean, then refilling it again.

Where Illorsuit Strait flooded into Baffin Bay, a sweep of ice filled my eye, stopped by the hammered silver at the horizon. We turned and headed into Uummannaq Fjord. I dozed until Aliberti shook me awake to show me an eider duck flying by. Then we lay on the sled as we had become accustomed to doing, hooked together: we were two seals moving over a world of seals with only a thin sliver of ice between us. I felt the weight of his hand on my thigh; my hand rested on his shoulder. Palisades of rock strobed by. We slipped across sea ice that had no end.

CHAPTER 19

'UNEXPECTED POISONS'

from *Silent Snow* (2005)

Marla Cone

In 1996, Marla Cone, an environmental reporter for the Los Angeles Times, *was researching a series of articles on chemicals that suppress the immune system when she learned that some of the most heavily exposed populations on earth live in the remotest regions. This realization became the impetus for her book* Silent Snow, *which documents how the Arctic and its people are disproportionately burdened with toxins like DDT and PCBs.*

Back in the early 1970s, Tom Smith knew more about seals than any white man in Holman, a treeless expanse of frozen tundra that is one of the northernmost outposts in all of Canada. He knew when the seals had pups, how long they lactated, how big they grew, what they ate. Most of what he learned as a field scientist he gathered with the help of Inuit hunters, who camped on the sea ice of Canada's Northwest Territories every winter, enduring twenty-below Fahrenheit temperatures as they waited for ringed seals to pop through their breathing holes. The few hundred people of Holman, who hunted seals for food, skins, and oil, still lived like their ancestors did and had little contact with the rest of the world.

Sometimes Smith would persuade the hunters to share their prey with him, and he used the blubber to explore whether Arctic seals were healthy and well-nourished.

One day Smith read a piece in an obscure scientific journal written by a chemist in Nova Scotia who had tested harp seals in the waters off Québec's urbanized coast. The chemist, Richard Addison, had discovered toxic pesticides and industrial compounds in the urban seals' blubber. It was 1973, an era of extraordinary pollution, when DDT, PCBs, and other compounds were building up in animals throughout North America and Europe. Many birds – eagles, robins, pelicans – were vanishing as the chemicals destroyed their eggs. More curious than concerned about his seals, Smith thought that the specimens he had been collecting in Holman could be a treasure trove for a chemist since no one had ever tested the seals before. So he called Addison and asked: Would you like some Arctic blubber?

Addison had never been to Holman. In fact, he had never been to the Arctic at all. A few years earlier, in 1969, a Scottish fisheries scientist, Alan Holden, had found residue of DDT and PCBs in a few Arctic seals from Norway's northern coast and Canada's Baffin Island. The amounts were minute, almost undetectable, and Holden had declared them 'substantially free of contamination in all but the "background" sense.' With the Holman seals inhabiting such remote waters of the Beaufort Sea, Addison thought it was likely that they, too, would essentially be 'blanks,' carrying no toxic substances or mere traces. Nevertheless, on a whim, Addison told Smith: Sure, send them and I'll take a look.

Soon afterward, blubber from about forty Arctic seals arrived at Addison's lab in Dartmouth, Nova Scotia, wrapped in foil and still frozen. It offered the first tangible clue to toxic detectives that chemicals were invading the far North.

Addison knew a lot about animal fat. Growing up Belfast, Northern Ireland, he had gotten his doctorate in agriculture, specifically studying the fat intake of poultry. He was most interested in applying chemistry to the real world, and when he was offered a job in Halifax, Canada, working in the 'lipids group' for the government's fisheries research board, he accepted. He knew nothing about fish but he thought it would be a chance to help Canada figure out some commercial uses for blubber and fish oil. He started work there in 1966 – when the environmental age was in its infancy. Chemical crises were just beginning to unfold around the world. PCBs were being detected in Swedish fish and Great Lakes birds. DDT was building up in California seabirds. As a chemist working with fish, Addison soon found himself completely drawn into Canada's emerging environmental problems. In January 1969, a large detergent factory had opened along the shore of Newfoundland, and within two months, local fishermen noticed thousands of dead herring. Divers were sent down and reported that everything in the harbor was dead. It was an ecological and economic disaster – the first pollution event in Canada attracting national attention. The government directed Addison to investigate. It was a time when environmental chemistry didn't even exist, when environmental science of all types was in its infancy and there were few laws governing industry's handling of chemicals. Addison saw huge amounts of effluent flowing from the plant, a brew of unknown chemicals. Developing new detection techniques for seawater, he identified the culprit in the fish kill – phosphorus from detergents. The plant was shut down and the harbor floor dredged and paved over.

After that crisis, Canada decided to open up a pollution lab in

Dartmouth, and Addison, hooked by the new science, took a job there in 1971, with the goal of developing ways to measure the new 'bad boys' of pollution, organochlorines – chlorinated chemicals such as DDT and PCBs that had just begun showing up in wildlife. Addison knew he needed to push the limits of old-fashioned detectors in searching the environment for these chlorinated compounds, but he wasn't sure which medium to measure. Most scientists had been sampling water. He could have chosen fish or plankton but he decided on something he knew – fat. He needed large reservoirs of it for the sampling. What could be better than a plump seal with its thick layer of blubber? Canada certainly had lots of seals, and they were fairly easy to catch. He set out to turn seals into a sentinel species, an environmental monitor for the health of the whole oceanic ecosystem. He started in the foul waters of the Gulf of St. Lawrence off Québec.

Science is often serendipity, and in this case, Addison recalls, 'the Arctic connection was purely accidental.' He never would have thought to sample Arctic animals if Tom Smith hadn't seen his report and happened to pick up the phone. Addison was intrigued but not alarmed by what he detected in the blubber Smith sent: The levels of DDT and PCBs seemed pretty benign, an order of magnitude lower than animals in urban environments such as the Great Lakes. In 1974, Addison published a concise, three-page report documenting that the males were more than twice as contaminated as the females, a sign that the mothers were offloading the chemicals to their pups in their milk. A year later, two Canadian scientists reported PCBs in another Arctic species, polar bears.

At their labs in Scotland and Canada, Holden and Addison suspected that the chemicals they found in the Arctic were coming from distant, urban lands. How else could pesticides and PCBs be turning up in northern latitudes, and even in Antarctica? And what else could explain why DDT was decreasing rapidly in urban seals but not in Arctic ones? As early as 1969, Holden sounded a warning, the first of many to come: 'One further aspect . . . should be emphasized,' he wrote at the conclusion of a paper written for a meeting of European marine scientists. 'The global distribution of the organochlorine contaminants in the marine environment has been demonstrated. These contaminants, particularly the PCBs, are chemically very stable and presumably other substances of similar stability will also be globally distributed.' This contamination, Holden wrote, 'could be potentially damaging' to Arctic seals and other animals, just as it has been to urban birds.

It was a prophetic warning – that large volumes of chemicals were spreading globally – but no one in the scientific community or the public heeded it at the time. The early discoveries about one of the most isolated places on Earth were promptly forgotten. No one bothered to follow up on them for nearly a decade. More pressing environmental crises were mounting in cities around the world in the 1970s. In the United States, oil gushed from rigs, rivers caught fire, skies were blackened by soot and smog, songbirds dropped dead, and many species were on the verge of extinction. The Great Lakes and Europe's Baltic and North seas were far more contaminated than the Arctic Ocean. Scientists were busy testing for chemicals in cow's milk and beef and chicken and butter and eggs and fish. Why should anyone care about a few seals or bears near the North Pole? It didn't dawn on them that there was another creature precariously perched at the very top of the food chain, eating marine mammals and passing the chemicals to its young. No one gave a second thought to the Arctic's human hunters.

Eric Dewailly was a teenager about to graduate from high school in northern France when he visited Africa's poverty-stricken Ivory

Coast. His father was a doctor, a gastroenterologist, but Dewailly had no interest whatsoever in medicine. Instead, he was fascinated by the forces that made life in isolated Third World places so difficult, and he expected to become a sociologist. By chance, while there, he met a physician handling infectious diseases and visited a clinic, watching the doctor take preventive steps that actually saved people's lives – administering vaccines, cleaning up sewage, finding clean drinking water. He was so impressed that he decided to enroll in medical school, and he knew immediately that protecting public health was his calling.

Dewailly thought tropical medicine would be his specialty, but instead, because of an exchange program between France and the French-speaking Canadian province of Québec, he wound up in the opposite hemisphere. When he was asked in 1983 to return to Québec City to start an environmental health program at Laval University, he jumped at the chance. At the time, chemicals were being discovered in the breast milk of women in the United States and Europe, but little was known about Canada. The Québec provincial government asked Dewailly to survey women and, in 1986, he chose women giving birth at twenty-two hospitals, mostly from around Montreal, which he assumed would have the worst contaminant levels.

As his project began, he happened to meet Johanne Gagnon, a midwife from East Hudson Bay, at a public health meeting in June of 1986. Gagnon asked him if he would like to include women in Nunavik, the Arctic region of Québec, home to about eight thousand Inuit. At first, he had little interest. Too many logistical nightmares. And the milk of women so far from industries would most certainly be pristine. Nevertheless, he agreed, thinking a few samples might be useful as blanks so he could compare an unexposed population to an urban one.

About a year later, in the fall of 1987, the first batch of samples from Nunavik – glass vials holding a half-cup of frozen milk from each of twenty-four women – arrived via air mail at the laboratory in Québec City. Lab technician Evelyne Pelletier removed a sample from a walk-in refrigerator and began the daylong preparations to analyze it. She first extracted the chemicals by adding a solvent compound to the breast milk and shaking it, then mixing in an acid to destroy the fat so it wouldn't plug up the instruments. She poured the organochlorine mixture into a narrow glass column, removed the impurities, and spun it in a centrifuge so that the liquids evaporated and only the highly concentrated chemicals were left. The next day, using a gas chromatograph, Pelletier screened the extract for twenty-two chemicals – ten insecticides and twelve PCB compounds. She stood at the chart recorder as the machine spit out reams of data, one chemical at a time. Within minutes, Pelletier knew something was wrong. The concentrations of chemicals were off the charts – literally. In a normal test, technicians find individual, needlelike peaks, like those on an electrocardiogram. Instead, the peaks had overloaded the lab's equipment, running off the page. Pelletier showed the charts to the lab director, Jean-Philippe Weber. He had never seen his lab's equipment overloaded by a sample. The concentrations were about thirty times higher than anything he had ever seen before. When he saw that the samples were the milk of Arctic women, making the results even more improbable, he called Dewailly. 'We have a problem here,' he said. Something was wrong with the Arctic milk. He thought it might have been tainted in transit with some type of solvent.

They decided to test the sample again, diluting it this time to get a more accurate reading, and then tried another batch of Arctic milk, and another. 'We knew then that this was not accidental contamination,' Weber said. The chemicals were real. They were the

same contaminants found in the milk of women in the south –
PCBs and pesticides – but the milk of the Arctic mothers had up to
ten times more than that of the mothers in Canada's biggest cities.

To Dewailly, who grew up near the North Sea, in one of
Europe's most polluted regions, it belied all logic – until he began
to search ecological journals and unearth data about PCBs and
DDT, including Addison's long-forgotten 1974 report about seals.
It became clear that the seals of Holman had been an unrecognized
omen. Dewailly knew that the Inuit ate marine mammals but, like
most doctors, he had no idea that toxic substances were building up
in Arctic animals, as the data were not published in the medical
journals he read, only in ecological journals he had never even
heard of. Dewailly contacted the World Health Organization in
Geneva, where an expert in chemical safety told him that the PCB
levels were the highest he had ever seen. Those women, the expert
said, should stop breast-feeding their babies – immediately.

Dewailly hung up the phone, his mind reeling. He knew that no
food is more nutritious than mother's milk and that Nunavik is so
remote that mothers had nothing else to feed their infants. As a
doctor, he couldn't, in good conscience, tell them to stop breast-
feeding. But he couldn't hide the problem either. 'Breast milk is
supposed to be a gift,' Dewailly says. 'It isn't supposed to be a
poison.' At the same time, elsewhere in Canada, in a small Inuit
community on Baffin Island, other medical researchers were finding similar levels of contamination in breast milk there. The news
about Nunavik and Baffin Island spread to the highest levels of
government in Canada in 1988, frightening and angering Inuit lead-
ers and triggering an international investigation into the health of
all Arctic inhabitants.

Dewailly, teaming with a doctor in Greenland, soon discovered
that the bodies of some Inuit there carried such extraordinary loads

of chemicals that their bodies and breast milk could be classified as hazardous waste. Over the next decade and a half, Dewailly led a team investigating the effects on the babies of Nunavik. He discovered that the Inuit's traditional diet of seal meat, beluga blubber, and walrus is part tonic, part poison: Rich in nutritious fatty acids, the foods protect the Inuit from cancer and heart disease but the research suggests that they also make babies more susceptible to infectious diseases and damage their developing brains. Nevertheless, Dewailly still firmly believes that the Inuit should keep nursing their babies and eating their traditional foods. Even today, almost two decades later, Canada remains embroiled in a debate over how to protect the health of its aboriginal people from the extreme levels of contaminants.

At about the time Dewailly began testing breast milk in Nunavik, Pál Weihe, across the Atlantic, was wondering about the childen of his own homeland. The son of a harbormaster, Weihe was born in the tiny seafaring village of Sørvágur in the Faroe Islands, a Danish territory in the middle of the North Atlantic, south of the Arctic Circle. In 1969, when he graduated high school, he left for Copenhagen to become a doctor – a surgeon, he thought. But upon studying occupational medicine, he learned about the dangers of chemicals and found this field more intriguing than his surgical studies. Surgery carries few surprises, he decided, but determining the risks of chemical exposure was so full of uncertainty, so mysterious, yet so vital to public health. In 1985, soon after his second child was born, Weihe heard about high levels of mercury in whales of the North Atlantic. The Faroese people are Nordic, not Inuit, but one thing separates them from the rest of their Danish compatriots: They eat pilot whales, in a tradition dating back centuries, perhaps to the days of the Vikings. Sometimes called 'black torpedoes,' pilot whales migrate long distances along the shores of the Atlantic, accumulating excessive levels of mercury from a variety of sources, including emissions spewed by coal-burning power plants thousands of miles from the Faroe Islands. The evidence that mercury is a neurotoxin that scrambles the brain dates back at least two centuries. 'Mad as a hatter,' a phrase made famous in *Alice in Wonderland*, originated from the tremors, confused speech, and hallucinations of nineteenth-century hatters poisoned by mercury used to cure felt. Yet it wasn't until the 1950s when the dangers to an infant's developing brain became apparent. At Japan's Minamata Bay, where a chemical factory dumped tons of mercury, thousands of people died or suffered various degrees of brain damage from eating fish, and an unexpected impact surfaced with the next generation: Thousands of children were born with mental retardation, deformed limbs, and other severe problems. Iraqi children suffered a similar fate in the 1970s when grain was contaminated with mercury.

Weihe knew Faroese babies were not exposed to enough mercury to cause retardation as in Minamata or Iraq. Nevertheless, he wondered if there were more subtle neurological effects at the lower exposures of his fellow islanders. Weihe approached Philippe Grandjean, a Danish environmental epidemiologist known at the time for his studies of another heavy metal, lead, which damages the brains of babies and children. Weihe told him about the pilot whales. Grandjean's response reinforced his concerns. 'I'm afraid mercury could very well be like lead,' Grandjean said.

Weihe returned to the Faroes as medical director at its hospital system and began to collect blood samples from adults. Sure enough, their bodies contained large amounts of mercury. Weihe and Grandjean mapped out an ambitious plan: Even though they knew it would mean a lifetime of work, they decided to assemble a group of subjects, called a cohort, and follow them from birth. Their first grant proposal was denied but the Danish government gave them $15,000 in support, enough to get started. They asked pregnant women throughout the Faroe Islands to participate. Very few said no. They wound up recruiting 1,023 pregnant women – 80 percent of the women who gave birth on the islands in 1986 and 1987. Their umbilical cord blood was stored for mercury analysis.

When the babies were born, Weihe and Grandjean saw no indication of any immediate damage to the infants. But they didn't expect to. Maturation of the brain is what's at stake with lower levels of mercury exposure. Weihe and Grandjean decided to test the children when they reached seven years, the age school begins in the Faroe Islands. In the spring of 1993, the children underwent an extensive series of psychological and neurological tests designed to see whether the mercury impaired any of their mental skills. The results: a measurable delay in transmission of signals from the ears of the most highly exposed children to their brains, a subtle slowing of a key neurological function. It was the 'eureka' moment, Grandjean recalls. Other tests on the children found impaired vocabulary, memory, and attention span at what had previously been considered a low and safe level of mercury in pregnant women. Grandjean and Weihe wrote up their first findings in 1994 but the scientific paper came back three times from the publisher for more review because the findings were so worrisome for seafood eaters around the world. The first results were finally published in 1997. Years later, in 2004, results of tests on the children when they reached age fourteen were published, suggesting that at least some of the neurological impacts of mercury are long-lasting, perhaps permanent.

After having tested nearly 2,000 Faroese children, Weihe now is convinced that the effects are real. As a scientist, he finds the research, which has had international repercussions for setting health standards, exhilarating, but as a doctor with strong ties to the people of his homeland, he is dismayed. Unlike the Inuit of Canada and Greenland, women in the Faroe Islands are now advised, based on Weihe's recommendations as head doctor of the hospital system, to stop eating the whale meat and blubber that have been important to their culture for centuries. It doesn't make Weihe, now fifty-five years old, the most popular person in the islands. But almost 2,000 mothers have come to trust Weihe, the 'mercury doctor,' with the well-being of their children, returning year after year to his small clinic in a residential neighborhood of Tórsham to undergo the neurological tests.

'My first assumption, back in 1985, was that we would not find any effects, that we have adapted to our diet over hundreds of years,' Weihe says. Now he knows he was wrong.

Jim Estes was trying to solve a mystery of his own on another string of sub-Arctic islands half a world away, between the North Pacific and the Bering Sea. A marine biologist at the U.S. Geological Survey (USGS) in Santa Cruz, California, Estes for years had devoted his career to studying sea otters inhabiting the ocean off central California, trying to figure out why they had such a high death rate. Could pollutants like DDT and PCBs be to blame? After all, everyone knew California's waters were contaminated. For the sake of comparison, in the summers of 1991 and 1992, he traveled to the place where everyone assumed sea otters were clean, healthy, and thriving: Alaska's Aleutian Islands. He returned to Santa Cruz with ice chests containing samples of blood and fat from otters on Adak Island, and asked Walter Jarman, a pollutants expert then at the University of Utah, to take a look at their chemical content. The day the lab results came back, Jarman scanned the columns of numbers. No way, he thought. The Aleutian otters were supposed to be the uncontaminated ones, but he had never seen PCB numbers so high. How could otters inhabiting these remote Alaskan islands contain twice as much of these industrial compounds as otters off urban California? They carried 309 parts per billion of total PCBs – thirty-eight times more than otters in southeast Alaska. At the same time, another USGS scientist, Robert Anthony of Oregon, was finding surprisingly high concentrations of DDT and mercury in the eggs of bald eagles nesting in western parts of the Aleutians. Most baffling of all, neither the otters nor the eagles ever migrated. They were somehow picking up the chemicals without ever leaving the islands.

Within a few years, by 1997, Estes had an even bigger mystery on his hands. The ecosystem of the Aleutians had collapsed. Tens of thousands of the Aleutians' otters disappeared within a matter of years, bringing them perilously close to extinction. There were no bodies to dissect, no clues to decipher. The otters weren't starving. They weren't sick. They simply vanished from the Aleutians without a trace, along with other sea mammals, particularly seals and sea lions, that had begun their descent in the 1980s. Estes believes that contaminants are not the main culprit, although they may play some minor role. Instead, he and his team have collected clues suggesting that various other human impacts, dating all the way back to commercial whaling a half-century ago, have triggered a series of events that upset the region's ecological equilibrium, upending its balance of predator and prey.

Piece by piece, Estes and other scientists think they are cobbling together this intricate puzzle, although the answers are more disturbing than satisfying, more elusive than conclusive. Estes predicts that the Aleutians' otters, in all likelihood, will be extinct in ten years, and their loss will reverberate throughout this entire ecosystem. It seems the ocean's chain of life is actually a fragile silk web. If you remove a strand, the whole thing unravels. And it may never be whole again.

In the late 1980s, scientists worried that the effects of contaminants in the Arctic were too subtle to see in its wildlife but that, slowly, over time, its populations could be decimated. They realized that they needed to probe the bodies of animals for minute biochemical changes. By the 1990s, wildlife researchers, using new techniques honed in part by AIDS researchers, had succeeded: They developed technology to look at specific parameters – such as immune cells, antibodies, or testosterone levels – and see if they changed with concentrations of toxic chemicals in the bodies of animals. By searching for such connections, they could finally answer the question: Were chemicals harming Arctic wildlife in ways impossible to detect with the naked eye?

The answer came on Svalbard, a Norwegian archipelago where Canadian Andrew Derocher was pursuing his dream of studying animals in remote, pristine lands. Coming of age in the heyday of the environmental movement in the early 1970s, Derocher was the only one in his family interested in the outdoors. He was raised along the lush banks of British Columbia's Fraser River, where he collected bird eggs and garter snakes and fished for salmon fry, trying to keep them alive in jars. After high school, he took a job as a seasonal game warden in British Columbia's provincial parks, spending his days fly-fishing for trout as bears ambled to the banks of the river. Then he studied wildlife ecology, focusing on large mammals, particularly bears. His father, a telephone repairman who worked his way up to upper management of a telephone company, was skeptical of his son's chosen career. His other son was a doctor and his daughter was a nurse, while his middle child was 'mucking around with bears.' When he took a research job at the Norwegian Polar Institute in 1996, Derocher thought he had found polar paradise. His longtime dream as a biologist was to study polar bears in their purest form, to find a population protected from human contact. Hunting of Svalbard's bears dates back to the sixteenth century – several hundred were trapped and shot for their fur each year – but since 1973, the archipelago has been a revered national refuge where hunting is banned. When Derocher arrived a quarter-century later, the population should have been fully recovered.

It wasn't long before he knew something was wrong. 'Things just don't appear right,' Derocher told his colleagues. It was as if these bears were still being hunted. Why weren't there more bears? Where were the older ones? Why were there so few females over the age of fifteen bearing cubs? Were they dying? Were they infertile? 'Within the first year, it became pretty darned clear that I wasn't working with an unperturbed population,' he says. In his second season on Svalbard, Derocher checked the sex of one bear as he routinely did, and found both a vagina and a penis-like knob. 'What the hell is this?' he thought. He had examined more polar bears than just about anyone on Earth, yet he had never seen that before. Then he started finding more – three or four out of every one hundred examined. Derocher immediately suspected that chemicals were to blame.

By then, it was indisputable that Svalbard's bears had extraordinarily high concentrations of PCBs. In living animals, worse doses had been found only a handful of times: in Pacific Northwest orcas, European seals, and St. Lawrence River belugas. A few years later, in 2004, Derocher and Norwegian scientists published some groundbreaking findings, documenting an array of effects in Svalbard's polar bears they linked to the PCBs. Included are altered sex hormones – reductions in testosterone, increases in progesterone – as well as depleted thyroid hormones, which regulate brain development of a fetus. The bears also suffer suppressed immune cells and antibodies; altered cortisol, which is important for managing stress and crucial body functions; lower retinol (vitamin A), which controls growth; and even osteoporosis. Such biochemical changes could impair the bears' ability to fight off disease and give birth to healthy cubs. Polar bear scientists theorize that the chemicals are culling older bears and weakening or killing cubs, perhaps leaving a missing generation of mother bears. Only 11 percent of Svalbard's bears with cubs are over fifteen years old, compared with 48 percent in Canada. When it comes to the most dramatic discovery – the pseudohermaphroditic polar bears with female and partial male genitalia – some scientists now suspect that they are natural occurrences, unrelated to the contaminants. Derocher and others, however, say that contaminants are a more plausible explanation. Essentially, no one really knows.

Nevertheless, Derocher is now virtually certain that there is some connection between the low numbers of bears in Svalbard and the toxic chemicals. 'Could you realistically put two hundred to five hundred foreign compounds into an organism and expect them to have absolutely no effect?' he says. 'I would be happier if I could find no evidence of pollution affecting polar bears, but so far, the data suggest otherwise.'

Today, more than thirty years after the first traces of DDT were found in the Canadian seals, the evidence is overwhelming that toxic substances have spread throughout the Arctic, harming animals and people of the far North. An international body of scientists called the Arctic Monitoring and Assessment Programme (AMAP) concluded in a 2002 report that the contamination raises 'fundamental questions of cultural survival, for it threatens to drive a wedge of fear between people and the land that sustains them.'

Several generations have passed since chemicals first hitched a ride to the Arctic around World War II. The hunters who ate the seals sampled by Tom Smith are now likely to be grandparents, and the infants who drank the breast milk sent to Eric Dewailly's laboratory in Québec are teenagers, about to bestow on their children the chemical load amassing in their bodies from their consumption of marine life. Yet little has changed to protect the next generation of Arctic children.

After a half-century of research, scientists now ponder why it took them so long to make the connection between the Inuit and their prey, and to realize that toxic chemicals can wreak subtle damage on animals and people. Arriving in the 1940s and discovered in the early 1970s, Arctic contamination was ignored until the late 1980s, and by then it was too late. It had reached extraordinary levels throughout the circumpolar north. 'We knew that there were contaminants of concern in the Arctic as early as the 1970s. Why it took twenty years for the other shoe to drop is a puzzle,' says Rob Macdonald of Canada's Institute of Ocean Sciences. 'There are many we could fault – maybe scientists, maybe politicians, maybe society. We could point fingers in lots of directions. But I think it's probably more instructive to say that sometimes we don't pay attention to things that we should, that we don't connect things well.'

Making matters worse, contaminants aren't the only environmental threat to the Arctic. It faces a triple whammy of human influences – contaminants, climate change, and commercial development – that the United Nations Environment Programme says is likely to inflict drastic changes on its natural resources and way of life this century. Seemingly hearty, the Arctic is, in fact, fragile.

What does this portend for the health of the world's children and animals, particularly in the Arctic, with its extraordinary exposure and vulnerability to contaminants? Unfortunately, no one really knows yet. The seeds of the next generation have already been planted in the Arctic, but the answers could still be generations away. The circumpolar north has been transformed into an immense living laboratory, where scientists are gradually unraveling the fate of contaminants on Earth and their effects on all its inhabitants, from pole to pole. Someone once said that ecology isn't rocket science—it's much harder. Although scientists have made great progress, most answers elude them.

Tom Smith still prowls the Arctic, evaluating the health of its seals. Richard Addison retired after a career directing a team of Canadian scientists known for breaking new ground in studying contaminants in seals and whales. [. . .] Andrew Derocher left Svalbard and returned to Canada to continue his dangerous field-work, warning that polar bears, jeopardized by melting ice as well as PCBs, might not survive this century. Pál Weihe and Philippe Grandjean are still testing the youngsters of the Faroe Islands – those born when the experiments began are now teenagers – and it endures as one of the longest-lasting human experiments ever conducted. They, along with Eric Dewailly, are now among the world's leading experts on the human health effects of exposure to industrial poisons and pesticides, and their findings guide world regulators in determining how much tainted fish and other seafood is safe to eat. Recognizing a global need for analyzing contaminated foods, Dewailly hopes to soon take his show on the road, developing a mobile laboratory to explore the symbiotic relationship between the oceans and human health and seek a balance between the benefits and risks of seafood around the world.

As with most environmental crises, there are no quick and easy solutions to the Arctic's dilemma. Even if the flow of all pesticides, PCBs, and other compounds is halted by every nation today, the tons already in the Arctic cannot be swept away or cleaned up. They are too ubiquitous, too persistent, too deeply embedded in the biota. Old PCBs, DDT, and other chemicals will remain there as long as it takes for nature to cleanse itself. And perhaps the most ominous discovery of all is that new chemicals are continually joining them.

CHAPTER 20

'SHISHMAREF, ALASKA'

from *Field Notes from a Catastrophe* (2006)

Elizabeth Kolbert

In the spring of 2004, I travelled to Greenland, Iceland, and northern Alaska to observe the effects of global warming. The passage below discusses the retreat of the Arctic sea ice and the thawing of permafrost.

The Alaskan village of Shishmaref sits on an island known as Sarichef, five miles off the coast of the Seward Peninsula. Sarichef is a small island – no more than a quarter of a mile across and two and a half miles long – and Shishmaref is basically the only thing on it. To the north is the Chukchi Sea, and in every other direction lies the Bering Land Bridge National Preserve, which probably ranks as one of the least visited national parks in the country. During the last ice age, the land bridge – exposed by a drop in sea levels of more than three hundred feet – grew to be nearly a thousand miles wide. The preserve occupies that part of it which, after more than ten thousand years of warmth, still remains above water.

Shishmaref (population 591) is an Inupiat village, and it has been inhabited, at least on a seasonal basis, for several centuries. As in many native villages in Alaska, life there combines – often disconcertingly – the very ancient and the totally modern. Almost everyone in Shishmaref still lives off subsistence hunting, primarily for bearded seals but also for walrus, moose, rabbits, and migrating birds. When I visited the village one day in April, the spring thaw was under way, and the seal-hunting season was about to begin. (Wandering around, I almost tripped over the remnants of the previous year's catch emerging from storage under the snow.) At noon, the village's transportation planner, Tony Weyiouanna, invited me to his house for lunch. In the living room, an enormous television set tuned to the local public-access station was playing a rock soundtrack. Messages like 'Happy Birthday to the following elders . . .' kept scrolling across the screen.

Traditionally, the men in Shishmaref hunted for seals by driving out over the sea ice with dogsleds or, more recently, on snowmobiles. After they hauled the seals back to the village, the women would skin and cure them, a process that takes several weeks. In the early 1990s, the hunters began to notice that the sea ice was changing. (Although the claim that the Eskimos have hundreds of words for snow is an exaggeration, the Inupiat make distinctions among many different types of ice, including *sikuliaq*, 'young ice,' *sarri*, 'pack ice,' and *tuvaq*, 'landlocked ice.') The ice was starting to form later in the fall, and also to break up earlier in the spring. Once, it had been possible to drive out twenty miles; now, by the time the seals arrived, the ice was mushy half that distance from shore. Weyiouanna described it as having the consistency of a 'slush puppy.' When you encounter it, he said, 'your hair starts sticking up. Your eyes are wide open. You can't even blink.' It became too dangerous to hunt using snowmobiles, and the men switched to boats.

Soon, the changes in the sea ice brought other problems. At its highest point, Shishmaref is only twenty-two feet above sea level, and the houses, most of which were built by the U.S. government, are small, boxy, and not particularly sturdy-looking. When the Chukchi Sea froze early, the layer of ice protected the village, the way a tarp prevents a swimming pool from getting roiled by the wind. When the sea started to freeze later, Shishmaref became more vulnerable to storm surges. A storm in October 1997 scoured away a hundred-and-twenty-five-foot-wide strip from the town's northern edge; several houses were destroyed, and more than a dozen had to be relocated. During another storm, in October 2001, the village was threatened by twelve-foot waves. In the summer of 2002, residents of Shishmaref voted, a hundred and sixty-one to twenty, to move the entire village to the mainland. In 2004, the U.S. Army Corps of Engineers completed a survey of possible sites. Most of the spots that are being considered for a new village are in areas nearly as remote as Sarichef with no roads or nearby cities or even settlements. It is estimated that a full relocation would cost the U.S. government $180 million.

People I spoke to in Shishmaref expressed divided emotions about the proposed move. Some worried that, by leaving the tiny island, they would give up their connection to the sea and become lost. 'It makes me feel lonely,' one woman said. Others seemed excited by the prospect of gaining certain conveniences, like running water, that Shishmaref lacks. Everyone seemed to agree, though, that the village's situation, already dire, was only going to get worse.

Morris Kiyutelluk, who is sixty-five, has lived in Shishmaref almost all his life. (His last name, he told me, means 'without a wooden spoon.') I spoke to him while I was hanging around the basement of the village church, which also serves as the unofficial headquarters for a group called the Shishmaref Erosion and

Relocation Coalition. 'The first time I heard about global warming, I thought, I don't believe those Japanese,' Kiyutelluk told me. 'Well, they had some good scientists, and it's become true.'

✳

The National Academy of Sciences undertook its first major study of global warming in 1979. At that point, climate modeling was still in its infancy, and only a few groups, one led by Syukuro Manabe at the National Oceanic and Atmospheric Administration and another by James Hansen at NASA's Goddard Institute for Space Studies, had considered in any detail the effects of adding carbon dioxide to the atmosphere. Still, the results of their work were alarming enough that President Jimmy Carter called on the academy to investigate. A nine–member panel was appointed. It was led by the distinguished meteorologist Jule Charney, of MIT, who, in the 1940s, had been the first meteorologist to demonstrate that numerical weather forecasting was feasible.

The Ad Hoc Study Group on Carbon Dioxide and Climate, or the Charney panel, as it became known, met for five days at the National Academy of Sciences' summer study center, in Woods Hole, Massachusetts. Its conclusions were unequivocal. Panel members had looked for flaws in the modelers' work but had been unable to find any. 'If carbon dioxide continues to increase, the study group finds no reason to doubt that climate changes will result and no reason to believe that these changes will be negligible,' the scientists wrote. For a doubling of CO_2 from preindustrial levels, they put the likely global temperature rise at between two and a half and eight degrees Fahrenheit. The panel members weren't sure how long it would take for changes already set in motion to become manifest, mainly because the climate system has a built-in time delay. The effect of adding CO_2 to the atmosphere is to throw the earth out of 'energy balance.' In order for balance to be restored – as, according to the laws of physics, it eventually must be – the entire planet has to heat up, including the oceans, a process, the Charney panel noted, that could take 'several decades.' Thus, what might seem like the most conservative approach – waiting for evidence of warming to make sure the models were accurate – actually amounted to the riskiest possible strategy: 'We may not be given a warning until the CO_2 loading is such that an appreciable climate change is inevitable.'

It is now more than twenty-five years since the Charney panel issued its report, and, in that period, Americans have been alerted to the dangers of global warming so many times that reproducing even a small fraction of these warnings would fill several volumes; indeed, entire books have been written just on the history of efforts to draw attention to the problem. (Since the Charney report, the National Academy of Sciences alone has produced nearly two hundred more studies on the subject, including, to name just a few, 'Radiative Forcing of Climate Change,' 'Understanding Climate Change Feedbacks,' and 'Policy Implications of Greenhouse Warming.') During this same period, worldwide carbon-dioxide emissions have continued to increase, from five billion to seven billion metric tons a year, and the earth's temperature, much as predicted by Manabe's and Hansen's models, has steadily risen. The year 1990 was the warmest year on record until 1991, which was equally hot. Almost every subsequent year has been warmer still. As of this writing, 1998 ranks as the hottest year since the instrumental temperature record began, but it is closely followed by 2002 and 2003, which are tied for second; 2001, which is third; and 2004, which is fourth. Since climate is innately changeable, it's difficult to say when, exactly, in this sequence natural variation could be ruled out as the sole cause. The American Geophysical Union, one of the nation's largest and most respected scientific organizations, decided in 2003 that the matter had been settled. At the group's annual meeting that year, it issued a consensus statement declaring, 'Natural influences cannot explain the rapid increase in global near-surface temperatures.' As best as can be determined, the world is now warmer than it has been at any point in the last two millennia, and, if current trends continue, by the end of the century it will likely be hotter than at any point in the last two million years.

In the same way that global warming has gradually ceased to be merely a theory, so, too, its impacts are no longer just hypothetical. Nearly every major glacier in the world is shrinking; those in Glacier National Park are retreating so quickly it has been estimated that they will vanish entirely by 2030. The oceans are becoming not just warmer but more acidic; the difference between daytime and nighttime temperatures is diminishing; animals are shifting their ranges poleward; and plants are blooming days, and in some cases weeks, earlier than they used to. These are the warning signs that the Charney panel cautioned against waiting for, and while in many parts of the globe they are still subtle enough to be overlooked, in others they can no longer be ignored. As it happens, the most dramatic changes are occurring in those places, like Shishmaref, where the fewest people tend to live. This disproportionate effect of global warming in the far north was also predicted by early climate models, which forecast, in column after column of FORTRAN-generated figures, what today can be measured and observed directly: the Arctic is melting.

Most of the land in the Arctic, and nearly a quarter of all the land in the Northern Hemisphere – some five and a half billion acres – is underlaid by zones of permafrost. A few months after I visited Shishmaref, I went back to Alaska to take a trip through the interior of the state with Vladimir Romanovsky, a geophysicist and permafrost expert. I flew into Fairbanks – Romanovsky teaches at the University of Alaska, which has its main campus there – and when I arrived, the whole city was enveloped in a dense haze that looked like fog but smelled like burning rubber. People kept telling me that I was lucky I hadn't come a couple of weeks earlier, when it had been much worse. 'Even the dogs were wearing masks,' one woman I met said. I must have smiled. 'I am not joking,' she told me.

Fairbanks, Alaska's second-largest city, is surrounded on all sides by forest, and virtually every summer lightning sets off fires in these forests, which fill the air with smoke for a few days or, in bad years, weeks. In the summer of 2004, the fires started early, in June, and were still burning two and a half months later; by the time of my visit, in late August, a record 6.3 million acres – an area roughly the size of New Hampshire—had been incinerated. The severity of the fires was clearly linked to the weather, which had been exceptionally hot and dry; the average summertime temperature in Fairbanks was the highest on record, and the amount of rainfall was the third lowest.

On my second day in Fairbanks, Romanovsky picked me up at my hotel for an underground tour of the city. Like most permafrost experts, he is from Russia. (The Soviets more or less invented the study of permafrost when they decided to build their gulags in Siberia.) A broad man with shaggy brown hair and a square jaw, Romanovsky as a student had had to choose between playing professional hockey and becoming a geophysicist. He had opted for the latter, he told me, because 'I was little bit better scientist than hockey player.' He went on to earn two master's degrees and two Ph.D.s. Romanovsky came to get me at ten A.M.; owing to all the smoke, it looked like dawn.

Any piece of ground that has remained frozen for at least two years is, by definition, permafrost. In some places, like eastern Siberia, permafrost runs nearly a mile deep; in Alaska, it varies from a couple of hundred feet to a couple of thousand feet deep. Fairbanks, which is just below the Arctic Circle, is situated in a region of discontinuous permafrost, meaning that the city is pocked with regions of frozen ground. One of the first stops on Romanovsky's tour was a hole that had opened up in a patch of permafrost not far from his house. It was about six feet wide and five feet deep. Nearby were the outlines of other, even bigger holes, which, Romanovsky told me, had been filled with gravel by the local public-works department. The holes, known as thermokarsts, had appeared suddenly when the permafrost gave way, like a rotting floorboard. (The technical term for thawed permafrost is 'talik,' from a Russian word meaning 'not frozen.') Across the road, Romanovsky pointed out a long trench running into the woods. The trench, he explained, had been formed when a wedge of underground ice had melted. The spruce trees that had been growing next to it, or perhaps on top of it, were now listing at odd angles, as if in a gale. Locally, such trees are called 'drunken.' A few of the spruces had fallen over. 'These are very drunk,' Romanovsky said.

In Alaska, the ground is riddled with ice wedges that were created during the last glaciation, when the cold earth cracked and the cracks filled with water. The wedges, which can be dozens or even hundreds of feet deep, tended to form in networks, so when they melt, they leave behind connecting diamond- or hexagon-shaped depressions. A few blocks beyond the drunken forest, we came to a house where the front yard showed clear signs of ice-wedge melt-off. The owner, trying to make the best of things, had turned the yard into a miniature-golf course. Around the corner, Romanovsky pointed out a house—no longer occupied – that basically had split in two; the main part was leaning to the right and the garage toward the left. The house had been built in the sixties or early seventies; it had survived until almost a decade ago, when the permafrost under it started to degrade. Romanovsky's mother-in-law used to own two houses on the same block. He had urged her to sell them both. He pointed out one, now under new ownership; its roof had developed an ominous-looking ripple. (When Romanovsky went to buy his own house, he looked only in permafrost-free areas.)

'Ten years ago, nobody cared about permafrost,' he told me. 'Now everybody wants to know.' Measurements that Romanovsky and his colleagues at the University of Alaska have made around Fairbanks show that the temperature of the permafrost in many places has risen to the point where it is now less than one degree below freezing. In places where the permafrost has been disturbed, by roads or houses or lawns, much of it is already thawing. Romanovsky has also been monitoring the permafrost on the North Slope and has found that there, too, are regions where the permafrost is very nearly thirty-two degrees Fahrenheit. While thermokarsts in the roadbeds and talik under the basement are the sort of problems that really only affect the people right near – or above – them, warming permafrost is significant in ways that go far beyond local real estate losses. For one thing, permafrost represents a unique record of long-term temperature trends. For another, it acts, in effect, as a repository for greenhouse gases. As the climate warms, there is a good chance that these gases will be released into the atmosphere, further contributing to global warming. Although the age of permafrost is difficult to determine, Romanovsky estimates that most of it in Alaska probably dates back to the beginning of the last glacial cycle. This means that if it thaws, it will be doing so for the first time in more than a hundred and twenty thousand years. 'It's really a very interesting time,' Romanovsky told me.

❋

The next morning, Romanovsky picked me up at seven. We were going to drive from Fairbanks nearly five hundred miles north to the town of Deadhorse, on Prudhoe Bay. Romanovsky makes the trip at least once a year, to collect data from the many electronic monitoring stations he has set up. Since the way was largely unpaved, he had rented a truck for the occasion. Its windshield was cracked in several places. When I suggested this could be a problem, Romanovsky assured me that it was 'typical Alaska.' For provisions, he had brought along an oversize bag of Tostitos.

The road that we traveled along – the Dalton Highway – had been built for Alaskan oil, and the pipeline followed it, sometimes to the left, sometimes to the right. (Because of the permafrost, the pipeline runs mostly aboveground, on pilings that contain ammonia, which acts as a refrigerant.) Trucks kept passing us, some with severed caribou heads strapped to their roofs, others belonging to the Alyeska Pipeline Service Company. The Alyeska trucks were painted with the disconcerting motto 'Nobody Gets Hurt.' About two hours outside Fairbanks, we started to pass through tracts of forest that had recently burned, then tracts that were still smoldering, and, finally, tracts that were still, intermittently, in flames. The scene was part Dante, part *Apocalypse Now*. We crawled along through the smoke. After another few hours, we reached Coldfoot, named, supposedly, for some gold prospectors who arrived at the spot in 1900, then got 'cold feet' and turned around. We stopped to have lunch at a truck stop, which made up pretty much the entire town. Just beyond Coldfoot, we passed the tree line. An evergreen was marked with a plaque that read 'Farthest North Spruce Tree on the Alaska Pipeline: Do Not Cut.' Predictably, someone had taken a knife to it. A deep gouge around the trunk was bound with duct tape. 'I think it will die,' Romanovsky told me.

Finally, at around five P.M., we reached the turnoff for the first monitoring station. By now we were traveling along the edge of the Brooks Range and the mountains were purple in the afternoon light. Because one of Romanovsky's colleagues had nursed dreams – never realized – of traveling to the station by plane, it was situated near a small airstrip, on the far side of a quickly flowing river. We pulled on rubber boots and forded the river, which, owing to the lack of rain, was running low. The site consisted of a few posts sunk into the tundra, a solar panel, a two-hundred-foot-deep borehole with heavy-gauge wire sticking out of it, and a white container, resembling an ice chest, that held computer equipment. The solar panel, which the previous summer had been mounted a few feet off the ground, was now resting on the scrub. At first, Romanovsky speculated that this was a result of vandalism, but after inspecting things more closely, he decided that it was the work of a bear. While he hooked up a laptop computer to one of the monitors inside the white container, my job was to keep an eye out for wildlife.

For the same reason that it is sweaty in a coal mine – heat flux from the center of the earth – permafrost gets warmer the farther down you go. Under equilibrium conditions – which is to say, when the climate is stable—the very warmest temperatures in a borehole will be found at the bottom and temperatures will decrease steadily as you go higher. In these circumstances, the lowest temperature will be found at the permafrost's surface, so that, plotted on a graph, the results will be a tilted line. In recent decades, though, the temperature profile of Alaska's permafrost has drooped. Now, instead of a straight line, what you get is shaped more like a sickle. The permafrost is still warmest at the very bottom, but instead of being coldest at the top, it is coldest somewhere in the middle, and warmer again toward the surface. This is a sign – and an unambiguous one—that the climate is heating up.

'It's very difficult to look at trends in air temperature, because it's so variable,' Romanovsky explained after we were back in the truck, bouncing along toward Deadhorse. It turned out that he had brought the Tostitos to stave off not hunger but fatigue—the crunching, he said, kept him awake—and by now the enormous bag was more than half empty. 'So one year you have around Fairbanks a mean annual temperature of zero' – thirty-two degrees Fahrenheit – 'and you say, "Oh yeah, it's warming," and other years you have mean annual temperature of minus six' – twenty-one degrees Fahrenheit – 'and everybody says, "Where? Where is your global warming?" In the air temperature, the signal is very small compared to noise. What permafrost does is it works as low-pass filter. That's why we can see trends much easier in permafrost temperatures than we can see them in atmosphere.' In most parts of Alaska, the permafrost has warmed by three degrees since the early 1980s. In some parts of the state, it has warmed by nearly six degrees.

When you walk around in the Arctic, you are stepping not on permafrost but on something called the 'active layer.' The active layer, which can be anywhere from a few inches to a few feet deep, freezes in the winter but thaws over the summer, and it is what supports the growth of plants – large spruce trees in places where conditions are favorable enough and, where they aren't, shrubs and, finally, just lichen. Life in the active layer proceeds much as it does in more temperate regions, with one critical difference. Temperatures are so low that when trees and grasses die they do not fully decompose. New plants grow on top of the half-rotted old ones, and when these plants die the same thing happens all over again. Eventually, through a process known as cryoturbation, organic matter is pushed down beneath the active layer into the permafrost, where it can sit for thousands of years in a botanical version of suspended animation. (In Fairbanks, grass that is still green has been found in permafrost dating back to the middle of the last ice age.) This is the reason that permafrost, much like a peat bog or, for that matter, a coal deposit, acts as a storage unit for accumulated carbon.

One of the risks of rising temperatures is that the storage process can start to run in reverse. Under the right conditions, organic material that has been frozen for millennia will begin to break down, giving off carbon dioxide or methane, which is an even more powerful (though more short-lived) greenhouse gas. In parts of the Arctic, this process is already under way. Researchers in Sweden, for example, have been measuring the methane output of a bog known as the Stordalen mire, near the town of Abisko, nine hundred miles north of Stockholm, for almost thirty-five years. As the permafrost in the area has warmed, methane releases have increased, in some spots by as much as 60 percent. Thawing permafrost could make the active layer more hospitable to plants, which are a sink for carbon. Even this, though, wouldn't be enough to offset the release of greenhouse gases. No one knows exactly how much carbon is stored in the world's permafrost, but estimates run as high as 450 billion metric tons.

'It's like ready-use mix — just a little heat, and it will start cooking,' Romanovsky told me. It was the day after we had arrived in Deadhorse, and we were driving through a steady drizzle out to another monitoring site. 'I think it's just a time bomb, just waiting for a little warmer conditions.' Romanovsky was wearing a rain suit over his canvas work clothes. I put on a rain suit that he had brought along for me. He pulled a tarp out of the back of the truck.

Whenever he has had funding, Romanovsky has added new monitoring sites to his network. There are now sixty of them, and while we were on the North Slope he spent all day and also part of the night — it stayed light until nearly eleven — rushing from one to the next. At each site, the routine was more or less the same. First, Romanovsky would hook up his computer to the data logger, which had been recording permafrost temperatures on an hourly basis since the previous summer. When it was raining, Romanovsky would perform this first step hunched under the tarp. Then he would take out a metal probe shaped like a 'T' and poke it into the ground at regular intervals, measuring the depth of the active layer. The probe was a meter long, which, it turned out, was no longer quite long enough. The summer had been so warm that almost everywhere the active layer had grown deeper, in some spots by just a few centimeters, in other spots by more than that. In places where the active layer was particularly deep, Romanovsky had had to work out a new way of measuring it using the probe and a wooden ruler. (I helped out by recording the results of this exercise in his waterproof field notebook.) Eventually, he explained, the heat that had gone into increasing the depth of the active layer would work its way downward, bringing the permafrost that much closer to the thawing point. 'Come back next year,' he advised me.

On the last day I spent on the North Slope, a friend of Romanovsky's, Nicolai Panikov, a microbiologist at the Stevens

Institute of Technology, in New Jersey, arrived. He was planning on collecting cold-loving microorganisms known as psychrophiles, which he would take back to New Jersey to study. Panikov's goal was to determine whether the organisms could have functioned in the sort of conditions that, it is believed, were once found on Mars. He told me that he was quite convinced that Martian life existed – or, at least, had existed. Romanovsky expressed his opinion on this by rolling his eyes; nevertheless, he had agreed to help Panikov dig up some permafrost.

That same day, I flew with Romanovsky by helicopter to a small island in the Arctic Ocean, where he had set up yet another monitoring site. The island, just north of the seventieth parallel, was a bleak expanse of mud dotted with little clumps of yellowing vegetation. It was filled with ice wedges that were starting to melt, creating a network of polygonal depressions. The weather was cold and wet, so while Romanovsky hunched under his tarp I stayed in the helicopter and chatted with the pilot. He had lived in Alaska since 1967. 'It's definitely gotten warmer since I've been here,' he told me. 'I have really noticed that.'

When Romanovsky emerged, we took a walk around the island. Apparently, in the spring it had been a nesting site for birds, because everywhere we went there were bits of eggshell and piles of droppings. The island was only about ten feet above sea level, and at the edges it dropped off sharply into the water. Romanovsky pointed out a spot along the shore where the previous summer a series of ice wedges had been exposed. They had since melted, and the ground behind them had given way in a cascade of black mud. In a few years, he said, he expected more ice wedges would be exposed, and then these would melt, causing further erosion. Although the process was different in its mechanics from what was going on in Shishmaref, it had much the same cause and, according to

Romanovsky, was likely to have the same result. 'Another disappearing island,' he said, gesturing toward some freshly exposed bluffs. 'It's moving very, very fast.'

On September 18, 1997, the *Des Groseilliers*, a three-hundred-and-eighteen-foot-long icebreaker with a bright-red hull, set out from the town of Tuktoyaktuk, on the Beaufort Sea, and headed north under overcast skies. Normally, the *Des Groseilliers*, which is based in Québec City, is used by the Canadian Coast Guard, but for this particular journey it was carrying a group of American geophysicists, who were planning to jam it into an ice floe. The scientists were hoping to conduct a series of experiments as they and the ship and the ice floe all drifted, as one, around the Arctic Ocean. The expedition had taken several years to prepare for, and during the planning phase its organizers had carefully consulted the findings of a previous Arctic expedition, which had taken place back in 1975. The researchers aboard the *Des Groseilliers* were aware that the Arctic sea ice was retreating; that was, in fact, precisely the phenomenon they were hoping to study. Still, they were caught off guard. Based on the data from the 1975 expedition, they had decided to look for a floe averaging nine feet thick. When they reached the area where they planned to overwinter – at seventy-five degrees north latitude—not only were there no floes nine feet thick, there were barely any that reached six feet. One of the scientists on board recalled the reaction on the *Des Groseilliers* this way: 'It was like "Here we are, all dressed up and nowhere to go." We imagined calling the sponsors at the National Science Foundation and saying, "Well, you know, we can't find any ice."'

Sea ice in the Arctic comes in two varieties. There is seasonal ice, which forms in the winter and then melts in the summer, and perennial ice, which persists year-round. To the untrained eye, all of it looks pretty much the same, but by licking it you can get a good idea of how long a particular piece has been floating around. When ice begins to form in seawater, it forces out the salt, which has no place in the crystal structure. As the ice thickens, the rejected salt collects in tiny pockets of brine too highly concentrated to freeze. If you suck on a piece of first-year ice, it will taste salty. Eventually, if the ice stays frozen long enough, these pockets of brine drain out through fine, veinlike channels, and the ice becomes fresher. Multiyear ice is so fresh that if you melt it, you can drink it.

The most precise measurements of Arctic sea ice have been made by NASA, using satellites equipped with microwave sensors. In 1979, the satellite data show, perennial sea ice covered 1.7 billion acres, or an area nearly the size of the continental United States. The ice's extent varies from year to year, but since then the overall trend has been strongly downward. The losses have been particularly great in the Beaufort and Chukchi Seas, and also considerable in the Siberian and Laptev Seas. During this same period, an atmospheric circulation pattern known as the Arctic Oscillation has mostly been in what climatologists call a 'positive' mode. The positive Arctic Oscillation is marked by low pressure over the Arctic Ocean, and it tends to produce strong winds and higher temperatures in the far north. No one really knows whether the recent behavior of the Arctic Oscilliation is independent of global warming or a product of it. By now, though, the perennial sea ice has shrunk by roughly 250 million acres, an area the size of New York, Georgia, and Texas combined. According to mathematical models, even the extended period of a positive Arctic Oscillation can account for only part of this loss.

At the time the *Des Groseilliers* set off, little information on trends in sea-ice depth was available. A few years later, a limited amount of data on this topic – gathered, for rather different purposes, by nuclear submarines – was declassified. It showed that between the 1960s and the 1990s, sea-ice depth in a large section of the Arctic Ocean declined by nearly 40 percent.

Eventually, the researchers on board the *Des Groseilliers* decided that they would just have to settle for the best ice floe they could find. They picked one that stretched over some thirty square miles. In some spots it was six feet thick, in some spots just three. Tents were set up on the floe to house experiments, and a safety protocol was established: anyone venturing out onto the ice had to travel with a buddy and a radio. (Many also carried a gun, in case of polar-bear problems.) Some of the scientists speculated that, since the ice was abnormally thin, it would grow thicker during the expedition. Just the opposite turned out to be the case. The *Des Groseilliers* spent twelve months frozen into the floe, and, during that time, it drifted some three hundred miles north. Nevertheless, at the end of the year, the average thickness of the ice had declined, in some spots by as much as a third. By August 1998, so many of the scientists had fallen through that a new requirement was added to the protocol: anyone who set foot off the ship had to wear a life jacket.

Donald Perovich has studied sea ice for thirty years, and on a rainy day not long after I got back from Deadhorse, I went to visit him at his office in Hanover, New Hampshire. Perovich works for the Cold Regions Research and Engineering Laboratory, or CRREL (pronounced 'crell'). CRREL is a division of the U.S. Army that was established in 1961 in anticipation of a very cold war. (The assumption was that if the Soviets invaded, they would probably do so from the north.) He is a tall man with black hair, very black eyebrows, and an earnest manner. His office is decorated with photographs from the *Des Groseilliers* expedition, for which he served as the lead scientist; there are shots of the ship, the tents, and, if you look closely enough, the bears. One grainy-looking photo shows someone dressed up as Santa Claus, celebrating Christmas in the darkness out on the ice. 'The most fun you could ever have' was how Perovich described the expedition to me.

Perovich's particular area of expertise, in the words of his CRREL biography, is 'the interaction of solar radiation with sea ice.' During the *Des Groseilliers* expedition, Perovich spent most of his time monitoring conditions on the floe using a device known as a spectroradiometer. Facing toward the sun, a spectroradiometer measures incident light, and facing toward earth, it measures reflected light. By dividing the latter by the former, you get a quantity known as albedo. (The term comes from the Latin word for 'whiteness.') During April and May, when conditions on the floe were relatively stable, Perovich took measurements with his spectroradiometer once a week, and during June, July, and August, when they were changing more rapidly, he took measurements every other day. The arrangement allowed him to plot exactly how the albedo varied as the snow on top of the ice turned to slush, and then the slush became puddles, and, finally, some of the puddles melted through to the water below.

An ideal white surface, which reflected all the light that shone on it, would have an albedo of one, and an ideal black surface, which absorbed all the light, would have an albedo of zero. The albedo of the earth, in aggregate, is 0.3, meaning that a little less than a third of the sunlight that strikes it is reflected back out. Anything that changes the earth's albedo changes how much energy the planet absorbs, with potentially dramatic consequences. 'I like it because it deals with simple concepts, but it's important,' Perovich told me.

At one point, Perovich asked me to imagine that we were looking down at the earth from a spaceship hovering above the North Pole. 'It's springtime, and the ice is covered with snow, and it's really bright and white,' he said. 'It reflects over 80 percent of the incident sunlight. The albedo's around 0.8, 0.9. Now, let's suppose that we melt that ice away and we're left with the ocean. The albedo of the ocean is less than 0.1; it's like 0.07.

'Not only is the albedo of the snow-covered ice high; it's the highest of anything we find on earth,' he went on. 'And not only is the albedo of water low; it's pretty much as low as anything you can find on earth. So what you're doing is you're replacing the best reflector with the worst reflector.' The more open water that's exposed, the more solar energy goes into heating the ocean. The result is a positive feedback, similar to the one between thawing permafrost and carbon releases, only more direct. This so-called ice-albedo feedback is believed to be a major reason that the Arctic is warming so rapidly.

'As we melt that ice back, we can put more heat into the system, which means we can melt the ice back even more, which means we can put more heat into it, and, you see, it just kind of builds on itself,' Perovich said. 'It takes a small nudge to the climate system and amplifies it into a big change.'

APPENDIX

A BRIEF CHRONOLOGY OF ARCTIC EXPLORATION

3rd Century B.C.	Pytheas, a Greek merchant and explorer from Massilia, now Marseille, writes of visiting an island a six days' sail from Great Britain, which he refers to as Thule. Many candidates have been proposed for Thule, including Iceland, Greenland, and the Faroe Islands. It has also been speculated that Pytheas chronicled a fictional journey
985 A.D.	Having been evicted from Iceland, Eric the Red arrives in Greenland, accompanied by nearly seven hundred followers. They establish two settlements, the Eastern Settlement, which is actually in the south, and the Western Settlement, which is to the north
1576–78	Martin Frobisher, a British sailor, makes three voyages in search of the Northwest Passage. On the second, he finds what he thinks is gold, and carries 1,500 tons back to Britain, at which point he is informed that it is iron pyrite. He gets as far as Frobisher Bay, an inlet of the Labrador Sea
1610	Henry Hudson and the crew of the *Discovery* reach what is now Hudson Bay. That winter, the ship gets iced in in James Bay. The following spring, Hudson's crew mutinies and sets him adrift in a small boat. He is never heard from again

1831   James Clark Ross locates the North Magnetic Pole on
                the west coast of Boothia Peninsula

1845   Sir John Franklin and a crew of more than a hundred
                and twenty set off in search of the Northwest Passage
                on two ships, the *Terror* and the *Erebus*. The ships
                are last sighted by Europeans in Melville Bay. After
                two years with no word from the expedition, several
                rescue ships are dispatched. (More men would be
                lost looking for members of the Franklin expedition
                than set out on it to begin with.) No survivors are
                ever found

1853   Elisha Kent Kane sets off on an American expedition
                in search of Franklin and his crew

1854   In the course of searching for survivors of the
                Franklin expedition, the British explorer Robert
                McClure and the crew of the *Investigator* become the
                first Europeans to traverse the Northwest Passage, in
                part by boat and in part by sled. Upon returning to
                England, McClure is knighted

1871   Charles Hall, an American businessman-turned-
                explorer in search of the North Pole, dies under
                mysterious circumstances

1882–83   First International Polar Year

1888   The Norwegian explorer Fridtjof Nansen completes
                the first crossing of Greenland

1895   Fridtjof Nansen reaches 86° 14´ N, the highest lati-
                tude then attained

1897   Jack London joins the Klondike Gold Rush. The
                Swedish explorer Salomon August Andrée attempts
                a balloon flight over the North Pole; he and his two
                companions perish

1906   The Norwegian explorer Roald Amundsen com-
                pletes the first expedition to successfully traverse the
                Northwest Passage by ship. The route he travels is
                not commercially viable

1909	The American explorer Robert Peary claims to have reached the North Pole
1924	Knud Rasmussen completes the Fifth Thule Expedition, a 20,000 mile trek, via dogsled, from Greenland to Siberia
1926	The American aviator Richard Byrd claims to have flown over the North Pole; this claim is later cast into doubt
1932–33	Second International Polar Year
1955	Halldór Laxness is awarded the Nobel Prize for Literature
1957–58	Third International Polar Year
1958	The USS *Nautilus*, the world's first operational nuclear submarine, makes a transit underneath the geographic North Pole. She surfaces northeast of Greenland
1959	The US Army constructs Camp Century, a research station built below the surface of the Greenland ice sheet. The camp is powered by a portable nuclear reactor
1993	The first full-length core of the Greenland ice is completed. The core is ten thousand feet long, and contains climatological data going back more than a hundred thousand years
2004	The Arctic Climate Impact Assessment concludes that 'climate change presents a major and growing challenge to the Arctic and the world as a whole'
2005	Arctic sea ice extent reaches a record low
2006	Studies predict that the Arctic Ocean could be ice-free in summer by 2040
2007–09	Fourth International Polar Year